HOME

A Life in Pursuit of the Right to Adequate Housing for Everyone, Everywhere

Foreword: Kevin Bell

Edited by Sid Vadasseri, Jen Marshall

Cover Art by Craig Brown

FIRST EDITION

ISBN: 978-1-64456-899-6 [Hardcover]
ISBN: 978-1-64456-900-9 [Paperback]
ISBN: 978-1-64456-901-6 [Kindle]
ISBN: 978-1-64456-902-3 [ePub]
ISBN: 978-1-64456-903-0 [Audiobook]

Library of Congress Control Number: 2026906886

INDIES UNITED PUBLISHING HOUSE, LLC
P.O. BOX 3071
QUINCY, IL 62305-3071
INDIESUNITED.NET

Cover: Zona Norte, Santo Domingo (Dominican Republic), 1994.
©Scott Leckie

"Scott journeys from the slums of a hundred cities to presidential palaces, bearing witness to the horrors of forced eviction, conflict and climate displacement alongside the birth of new countries and the hard fought achievements of housing rights activists and the UN human rights community. His story is a powerful testament to a life well-spent in search of justice, dignity and peace. It proves that even in our darkest times, when international solidarity and the rule of law falter, the power of our shared humanity and a common future can prevail."

Aromar Revi
Vice Chancellor, IIHS University
Bengaluru, India

"Leckie's boundless enthusiasm and love of humanity shines through —at the same time he breathes life into the abstract idea of a human right to housing."

Andrew Clapham
Professor of International Law, Geneva Graduate Institute
Author, *War*

Scott Leckie is the real deal—a combination of fierce advocate for justice for the most oppressed in our society and a laid back late-model hippie. In between his work to single-handedly build out the international structure to protect housing rights, and protect millions of people from eviction, he drops tales of his amazing adventures finding Deadheads, building networks and sparking joy. We're lucky that Scott came along and accomplished so much in what he accurately describes as that little window of time when the governments of the world could be pushed toward justice using the often-obscure goings on in Geneva. I hope this book helps inspire the next generation of human rights activists to push even further.

Cindy Cohn
Executive Director, Electronic Frontier Foundation
San Francisco, United States

"Scott Leckie's new book - part memoir, part indictment of the global community's failure to house the poorest on the planet should be titled: 'Renegade: One Man's Quest to House the World.' And I told him so. But, just as his long and storied career unfolds within the pages of this book, so does a sense of quiet modesty that finds its way even into the title. HOME takes us on a multi-decade, Panglossian journey on an attempt to alter the very nature of how we view the un-housed in the 21st Century. And though the larger effort on a global scale has thus far failed, there are enough concrete victories illustrated over the course of Leckie's career to give us hope for a better world. Read at risk of being inspired and simultaneously ashamed that we haven't yet done enough for those seeking secure housing on this one planet of ours."

Skye Fitzgerald
Filmmaker, 2x Academy® Award nominee
Portland, Oregon

"Scott Leckie's work has continually inspired countless advocates dedicated to advancing housing, land, and property rights. The strength and clarity that define his scholarship do not arise from academic rigor and professional expertise alone; they are forged through sustained engagement with those who have lost their "home"—and with it, their sense of belonging and dignity. Only those who truly meet the gaze of people in such pain—who look beyond loss to the human right at stake —can summon the conviction required to inspire others to believe in that right as well. This book stands as another cornerstone in that enduring effort, reaffirming that the right to housing is a fundamental pillar of human dignity and justice. Thank you for inspiring me!!"

Rana Arnouk Mitri
Human Rights Lawyer
Beirut, Lebanon

"The book HOME: A Life in Pursuit of the Human Right to Adequate Housing for Everyone, Everywhere by Scott Leckie is an inspiring reflection on the global struggle for housing justice. As a long-standing friend of our works in Bangladesh, Scott has consistently stood beside climate displaced people and vulnerable communities.

This book beautifully captures his dedication and reminds us that safe and dignified housing is a basic human right for all. We deeply appreciate his continued solidarity and advocacy. This work will motivate many people and organizations to keep working for housing rights and climate justice."

Dr. Md. Arifur Rahman
Founder and Chief Executive, Yong Power in Social Action (YPSA),
Chittagong, Bangladesh

"Scott Leckie has spent five decades in the world's most difficult places—slums and war zones, climate disasters and occupied territories—fighting for one deceptively simple idea: that everyone deserves a home. HOME is his story of that pursuit, told with the humor, candor, and hard-won wisdom of someone who learned that changing the world requires audacity and persistence."

Reed Brody
Author, *To Catch a Dictator*
Barcelona, Spain

"This intriguing tome reminded me of Scott's comprehensive understanding of the United Nations and its purpose. Scott guided my delegation from the jungle through the corridors of the UN, teaching us diplomacy, protocols and introducing us to relevant personalities in the administration and other delegations. His contribution to achieving the vital UN resolutions that led to a lasting peace on Bougainville should not be underestimated. A true champion of human rights."

Mike Forster
Representative to the United Nations - Bougainville Interim Government; Conflict Resolution Manager - Bougainville Interim Provincial Government and Personal Attaché to President Kabui – Bougainville Autonomous Government.

"Scott Leckie's autobiography could not be more timely. The right to housing is the most striking example of the negative impact of global neoliberal economic policies on human rights in general, and economic, social and cultural rights in particular. Scott's life as an advocate for the right to housing is a shining example for future human rights and housing rights defenders."

Manfred Nowak
Professor of International Law and Human Rights
Vienna, Austria/Venice, Italy

"I appreciate the title HOME for all that a 'home' entails and requires in the broadest sense. The amount of humans on the planet without a home is one more condemnation of how our global inequality and injustice systems operate inside borders and between Nation States. Since I met Scott in 1986, I have never not known of him working, writing, and supporting the struggle for homes for all. This book takes the reader on parts of Scott's life journey working to achieve this. An important takeaway is how this work and struggle play out in the global and regional human rights systems we humans—via our very complicated (to put it politely) Nation State system—have created. An equally, if not more important takeaway is when these human rights systems do not succeed (more often than not for reasons outside their control, and "above their pay grade" in our global inequality and injustice systems), Scott takes the reader back to grassroots struggle and the dignity and strength of people across the planet, no matter how daunting the obstacles. Scott tells this story his of life journey and the struggle for a HOME for all, abiding always by his credo: *Get it done but keep it fun.*"

Grahame Russell
RightsAction
Toronto, Canada

"Home is an inspirational account of what passion, principled commitment and intellectual courage can achieve. Scott's work has transformed countless lives and left a profound imprint on the United Nations human rights system itself, shaping its standards and practice on housing, land, and property rights. Through rigorous research, tireless strategic advocacy and litigation, and visionary normative drafting, he helped move economic, social and cultural rights from the margins to the centre of international responses to displacement, urbanization, and post-conflict recovery. His book captures not only a life of remarkable impact, but the enduring force of ideas translated into action."

Khaled Hassine
Legal Advisor, Secretariat of the United Nations
Sousse, Tunisia

"HOME beautifully chronicles Scott Leckie's extraordinary journey but even its vivid pages fall short of capturing the true depth of his decades-long commitment to building a better world. This book stands as a testament to new generations: reject materialism and radicalism, and instead find the courage to be brutally honest with yourself and then channel that inner strength into making life better for others."

Pablo Rueda
Co-author of *One Earth, One Politics: Building Our Shared Path
Toward World Citizenship*
Punta del Este, Uruguay

"I first heard of Scott long ago, in what now feels like the "golden era" of peace support operations—before Brexit, before Trump, before COVID-19, and before Ukraine—when I was searching for restitution solutions for Roma families in Mitrovica, northern Kosovo. It was there that I came to understand the power of bringing together housing, land, and property (HLP) rights to respond to urgent needs and to protect those most vulnerable people who had endured both structural injustice and direct violence. Years later, as I began launching an HLP rights programme in the hopeful Myanmar of 2015, I reached out to him with little expectation of a reply. Since then, I have had the privilege of working alongside him to advance the HLP rights of vulnerable communities and minorities in Myanmar, persevering through the 2021 coup and the many hardships that followed. Scott is the kind of person who does not bend to the harsh winds of history. He endures, persists, and continues the work when circumstances would discourage most. Hope, after all, is a form of resistance. In these troubled times, he embodies a quiet determination that refuses to abandon the possibility of a more just and brighter future. *Home* is the story that tells it best. Gracias, amigo—¡hasta la victoria siempre!"

José Arraiza
HLP Rights Advocate
Madrid, Spain

"With over four decades of "good trouble" under his belt (and hopefully many more years of good trouble to come), Scott Leckie shares his life lessons in his new memoir, Home. Scott tells great stories from his eventful life that reflect his unparalleled passion for and commitment to the human right to housing. His tales from throughout the globe are also filled with fun and adventure—lots of it. And they tell of the deep human connections he has made wherever he has travelled. For Scott, there is no "us and them" as he pursues housing rights for everyone, everywhere."

Andrew Scherer
Professor of Law and Policy Director,
Impact Center for Public Interest Law
New York Law School
New York, United States

"It's been my pleasure to read this, and my honor to have travelled parts of this journey alongside Scott as my colleague, collaborator and friend. And what a journey (so far)! Five decades in the making. Driven by his curiosity, fuelled by his passion for humanity, surpassing his numerous milestone achievements with audacious humour and righteous conviction, and a mind fully open to parsing the lessons punctuated throughout this memoir, Scott's narrative reminds us all of the roles we could play as *good troublemakers*."

Dan Lewis
West Coast International
Vancouver, Canada

"Scott Leckie has travelled the world promoting the human rights of fellow humans who lack shelter and protection. His personal journey and stories are full of humanity, achievements and setbacks, good humour, and the connection we all share. A fun read about how to get things done, while having a blast along the way."

Brian Gorlick
Ex-UN Official & Lecturer, Refugee Law Initiative, University of London
Stockholm, Sweden

"The author once schooled me in Ken Wilber, keeping faith with rainbow rooms and mountain air while I muttered about enforcement clauses and airports and concrete everywhere. I wanted proof. He showed me the land maps of Palestine. Meanwhile the grandees of "international law" polished their phrases as power vaulted the railing and made off with the silver. We have lived through the great inversion. Charters glowing, bombs falling, billionaires carving up the commons like a Sunday roast. And still the ordinary punter works ragged for a door that locks and a bed. This book calls that possession out. The world is not the private estate of the well-lawyered and the heavily armed. It is not vacant land for the loudest claimant. It is stubbornly held in common. There is home for us all. It holds us. And if that sounds unruly, good. There is no country but earth."

Michael Morehead
Lawyer
Sorrento, Australia, Earth

"I first encountered Scott in my early years at the United Nations, when I was a young human rights lawyer trying to understand how the system could be made to work for those most in need. What struck me immediately was his fearless self-belief, his mischievous humour, and his stubborn refusal to accept that injustice was inevitable. *Home* tells the story of that same restless commitment. It is a vivid and deeply human account of decades spent pushing the boundaries of international human rights practice in pursuit of one simple idea: that everyone, everywhere deserves a safe place to call home."

Anne T. Gallagher, AO
Director-General,
Commonwealth of Nations

ALSO BY SCOTT LECKIE

Uncle Bill (2027)

Psychotic, Despotic (2026)

Killionaire™ (2026)

Shrewd Little Sleuth (2025)

World Citizenship: Origins, Obstacles, Prospects (2025)

Exploring the Rights of Climate Displaced Persons
(with Shaun Butta, 2025)

One Earth, One Politics: Building Our Shared Path Toward World Citizenship
(with Pablo Rueda, 2024)

Until a Democracy Died: Housing, Land and Property Rights in Myanmar
(with José Maria Arraiza, 2023)

Housing, Land and Property Rights: Residential Justice, Conflict Zones, and Climate Change (2023)

The United Nations Principles on Housing and Property Restitution for Refugees and Displaced Persons, the Pinheiro Principles: A Commentary
(with Khaled Hassine, 2016)

Repairing Domestic Climate Displacement: The Peninsula Principles
(ed, with Chris Huggins, 2015)

Land Solutions to Climate Displacement
(ed, 2014)

The Climate Change and Displacement Reader
(ed, with Ezekiel Simperingham and Jordan Bakker, 2012)

Conflict and Housing, Land and Property Rights: A Handbook on Issues, Frameworks and Solutions
(with Chris Huggins, 2011)

Housing, Land and Property Rights in Burma: The Current Legal Framework
(with Ezekiel Simperingham, 2010)

Housing, Land, and Property Rights in Post-Conflict United Nations and Other Peace Operations: A Comparative Survey and Proposal for Reform (ed, 2009)

Housing, Land and Property Restitution Rights of Refugees and Displaced Persons: Laws, Cases and Materials (ed, 2007)

Economic, Social and Cultural Rights: Cases and Materials (with Anne Gallagher) (ed, 2006)

Returning Home: Housing and Property Restitution Rights of Refugees and Internally Displaced Persons (ed, 2003)

National Perspectives on Housing Rights (ed, 2003)

When Push Comes to Shove (1995)

Destruction by Design (1994)

From Housing Needs to Housing Rights (1992)

HOME

A Life in Pursuit of the Right to Adequate Housing for Everyone, Everywhere

Scott Leckie

INDIES UNITED
PUBLISHING HOUSE, LLC

For
What could have been...

TABLE OF CONTENTS

Foreword

My good friend Scott Leckie was going to call this remarkable memoir 'Mr. Housing Rights'. He chickened out when someone who (thought they) knew better advised against it. I'm not sure about that, for this early nickname neatly captures what Scott is: a housing activist, scholar, and intellectual entrepreneur extraordinaire. I suggested 'The Originator', as a former Special Rapporteur on the right to housing once described him to me. Scott also rejected that too, sadly, for I think it conveys the same notion. Mind you, I can't fault his final choice of title which draws attention to his energetic lifelong quest to ensure that everyone, everywhere has a safe and adequate home in which to live.

The reader of this memoir will find that its subject is a highly original human being, one of the most effective advocates and great characters of the international human rights scene. I must, therefore, confess that I was somewhat surprised when Scott asked me to write this foreword. Sure, a foreword would be nice. But why one by me? What has a boring, former judge from the Antipodes got to say about such a rich and varied life as is here described? Having read the memoir in various states of astonishment, bewilderment, and blushing admiration, or sometimes just blushing, I am glad that he did, for I have quite a lot to say.

I am a relatively new friend of Scott's and his redoubtable wife Kirsten Young, whose pivotal role in his life he generously acknowledges. I am, therefore, not one of the many people who have shared his long and eventful human rights journey. He and I met through Kirsten, whom I knew through a mutual friend. I immediately felt his strong gravitational pull, surely a most valuable possession for an advocate for very hard causes. Housing justice and human rights were the usual subject of our conversations. He taught me much that I did not know as he will the readers of the memoir, although it is not designed to be a pedagogical work as such. Like the book's back cover says, it is the story of the joyous highs and devastating lows of an eccentric human rights life (as you can see, Scott thinks a noun without an adjective is a thing undressed). The pedagogical content is there though, smuggled in amongst the numerous vignettes and deliberately folksy life lessons. Memoirs of human rights defenders of any kind are quite rare, and there is much to learn from this one both because it is just such a memoir and because it is truly unique.

Scott is a very open individual who fully exercises his right to freedom of speech and expression in this candid memoir. Inevitably there will be not enough candour for some and too much for others. He speaks in his own vernacular. You won't find much human-rights speak here. He takes us through his life's work in the slums of Santo Domingo, Bangkok and Manila, the creation of UN mechanisms on the right to housing, the wars in Kosovo, Iraq and Burma, natural disasters in Bangladesh, Japan and Maldives, 'peace' in the Republic of Georgia and Sri Lanka, the occupation and much worse in Tibet and Palestine, independence in Timor Leste and Bougainville and the climate-caused catastrophe in Kiribati. It is the story of Scott's own gradually widening interest in housing rights, in housing, land, and property rights and in climate change and displacement. His evolving path of thought now seems so natural and linear but it is really the product of a mind that is courageously self-reflective. While Scott describes events in these places which posed profound human rights challenges, he foregrounds his own deeply personal and humanitarian responses. You will see one more evolutive step in his hopes for a world that is without borders although not without government—a 'oneness world', one that is indeed one.

I have skin in the game with this foreword because I grew up in public housing and have worked all my life in the housing justice and human rights field in several capacities and still do. I support the premise of the memoir that having a secure home is indispensable for a flourishing and dignified life. This is my lodestone too. As a judge and scholar and earlier as an activist, I have sought to understand, explain and apply the right to housing. In doing so, I have drawn heavily on the International Bill of Rights, as well as the work of UN Charter and treaty bodies and Special Rapporteurs who have interpreted and elaborated this right. I consider the body of work which they have produced to be one of the UN's greatest contributions to humanity.

Scott can justly claim to have played a seminal role in the production of this work and in making that contribution. He tells with elan the story of how he helped create the Special Rapporteur on the right to adequate housing and wrote drafts of foundational UN reports, resolutions and statements that came to be officially adopted. Throughout the world, millions of people who go without adequate housing hang onto these links in the protective human rights chain for dear life. His behind-the-scenes insights will be fascinating for anyone interested in how idealistic human beings who are all flawed try to make human rights law that is not. Scott also tells, from his point of view, the story of the rise and fall of a truly great NGO, the Centre on Housing Rights and Evictions, which he established. The narrative drips with equal amounts of joy and pain, but also much fun and humour, as there is in the memoir generally. I especially like the long list of alternative acronyms for COHRE that Scott and his colleagues used to workshop, my favourite being Change Our House Rent Easily.

More than ever today humanity needs realisation of the right to housing for everybody. You will find here the remarkable story of a human rights advocate who played a seminal role in explaining and promoting the right and in creating the international instruments and institutions that are necessary for achieving that objective.

The Hon Kevin Bell AO KC
(former Judge of the Supreme Court of Victoria, Australia)

Preface

Speak up, speak out, get in the way. Get in good trouble, necessary trouble.

—John Lewis

American civil rights legend John Lewis gained fame for many things, in particular his courageous walk on 7 March 1965 across Selma, Alabama's Edmund Pettus Bridge on "Bloody Sunday," when white state troopers and citizens viciously beat dozens of Black marchers demanding their human rights a full 100 years after the end of the bitter war that was meant to end slavery. More than 50 marchers were injured that day, many of whom required hospitalization.

Though these tragic events took place when I was just two and a half years old, somehow, the moving images of what occurred on that bridge are some of my earliest memories. I also have distinct memories of two other events around the same age. One involved me climbing onto a chair and reaching across the kitchen counter and then eating half a kilo (one pound) of raw mincemeat (hamburger meat) for a reason I have yet to decipher. My other memory relates to the first of many conversations I had with a little boy that looked exactly like me who lived underneath our Los Angeles home in the crawl space who I called Fondi and with whom I would apparently converse for hours on end as I gazed into the dark underworld covered by our home. Fondi looked just like me, I used to tell my mother. More on those memories another time.

In what was a singular moment of the Civil Rights Movement, I vividly remember watching the carnage unfold on the black and white television screens in our LA home, on the other side of the country. Unable to grasp the ruthlessness or meaning of this historic moment, somehow the screams coming from the television and the gasps by my family sitting with me in our living room, made this memory stick in a way that undoubtedly influenced the life I was about to lead, despite the fact that I had no real understanding of what took place that day other than the cruelty meted out by the men in uniform against the marchers.

Perhaps the deep Southern roots of significant elements of my family made such events more prominent in my memory than others. With a paternal grandfather, aunts, uncles, cousins and others hailing from deeply rural Alabama, as well as regular childhood visits, the idea of "the South" was always present. However, there was no balanced discussion of its abhorrent history. In my childhood, any focus on the racial origins of the Civil War and its role in legally ending slavery barely arose.

When we took trips to the South to visit family when I was very young, it was not the Edmund Pettus bridge or other historic sites associated with the Civil Rights Movement that we visited. Rather, sojourns to Stone Mountain, glorified stories of Jefferson Davis and the Confederacy, the heroic fight against the Unionists and frequent, dismissive remarks I overheard in small towns and diners that I decoded for the first time about the "lazy (N-word) living in his (N-word) shack in his (N-word) town" dominated my recollections of those trips. I had never heard the N-word before, but it was immediately obvious that it was wrong. It was only after leaving my California home for good at the age of 17 that I began to truly grasp the racist horrors of this region—and realize that some members of my own family were perhaps on the wrong side of history.

I recently finished writing a biography of my paternal grandfather which I called *Shrewd Little Sleuth* after the many newspaper references to him using the same slogan were uncovered during my research on this amazing man. In doing so, I researched the intriguing, yet disturbing, life and times of Arthur Bernard Leckie (ABL). I have discovered that my dad's dad who died just months before I was born was—as you will see if you read the book—probably murdered while working as a private investigator for Marilyn Monroe who died in equally mysterious circumstances just 36 hours after ABL's untimely death. I also found out that he was extremely close to the FBI's J. Edgar Hoover, both during his years at the FBI in the 1930s and for all the decades after Hoover fired him in 1939. I have numerous original personal letters between these two men, as well as hundreds of pages of internal FBI documents that were provided to me following a Freedom of Information Act search by the agency that Hoover built. These documents collectively reveal that although ABL was rather unceremoniously forced by Hoover and his lover/deputy Clyde Tolson to leave the Bureau he loved so much, he nonetheless stayed in touch with the FBI boss until his death in 1962, a full 23 years later. Hoover is known for many things, but one of the traits that has become increasingly clear with each successive biography were the extremist views he held in support of white supremacy. Hoover was a proud Southerner through and through, and I have come to understand that his G-man ABL may well have tended in that direction at least during his early years, though some California reasonableness must have eroded some of the harsher edges the longer he lived there.

Other than Mexican gardeners, housecleaners and a Brazilian exchange student, my upbringing was almost exclusively white. My family was white. My neighborhood was white. My schools were white and other than watching my favorite Black USC football stars win national championships for the mighty Trojans, virtually my entire reality was white. And yet, when Los Angeles elected its first Black mayor, Tom Bradley, in 1973, I was at a neighborhood party and heard comments like, "Oh no, the voting levels in Compton are higher than expected. This is terrible. There goes the neighborhood."

For whatever reason, I was dumbfounded and confused that people could think this way. It just didn't make sense. I had no real understanding yet of politics, but the ten-year-old me instinctively thought it was fantastic that this guy won. He looked so cool and had the best voice I'd ever heard. It never mattered to me if he was Black or any other color though it apparently mattered to my neighbors very much. From what little I had seen on TV ads and the like, to me he seemed like a great guy that people really loved. Around the same time, I was waiting for my ride home from school and overheard a parent saying to their daughter, "Julie, I just heard the news. I am so sorry to have to tell you there is an Indian girl coming to your school", as if this was a horrible thing surely to result in pain and agony. Again, despite my limited interactions with people of color at the time, I was completely bewildered by views such as these. And besides, I remember loving that beautiful Indian girl from the moment I met her.

Every summer between the ages of 10-15, I went to camp for two months in Massachusetts on the other side of the country, where my eyes were opened to many things—like sex, drugs, and rock and roll. However, what I enjoyed most was befriending kids from Venezuela, Colombia, Mexico, Chile, Argentina, Nicaragua and other countries, despite the many entreaties to keep my distance. I loved speaking my rudimentary Spanish with those guys and learned so much from these kids, even if they were certainly from the elite classes of countries that were not always associated with the promotion and protection of human rights, especially in the dangerous latter half of the 1970s.

At camp, I made lifelong friends with some of the first Jewish people I had ever met, after witnessing only anti-Semitic jokes and racist comments growing up. Though I knew little of Judaism and the Torah, I learned quickly and then loved helping one of my Jewish friends study for his upcoming bar mitzvah. I even learned and then memorized a whole range of Hebrew phrases, many of which stick with me to this day. However, during a sailing race against another summer camp nearby, I learned another side of the Jewish story. I was in a Mercury sailboat with my Jewish friend Robert when an opposing boat cut us off, and one of their crew shouted, "Out of the way, kike!" I had never heard that word before but could tell it was far from kind and asked my friend what that strange sounding word meant. But before he could even answer the look on his face provided the answer; it was shattering and soul-destroying. I asked him again what it meant, but he was too shocked to even speak, and when he finally told me hours later, I just couldn't believe people could be so cruel. It was my first real experience of anti-Semitism right before my very eyes and it hit me to the core. He then told me that his grandfather had come to America and changed the family name from a very Jewish sounding one to another name that "sounded more American", as he put it.

I have countless additional stories from my childhood at home, school, camp, and in movies. But suffice it to say, despite the odds against it, I somehow knew we were all the same, all equal. Almost instinctually, I just knew from the start that there was no us and them. To me, this simply never registered, and when and if it did, it was only ever in the most positive way possible. My incredible privilege growing up in affluent southern California, travelling extensively and all the rest were things for which I have immense gratitude and, of course, I very much realize my good fortune.

But so much of my otherwise lucky youth was infused with sentiments that enraged me so much that I knew that as soon as I could I had to leave. Growing up exposed to various forms of racism and personally enduring multiple years of severe and often violent bullying, including being brutally subjected to an actual many hours-long torture session by a local politician's son on an isolated part of a field where we attended weekly football practice, and where I literally thought I might die, shaped me. Similar attacks occurred on multiple other occasions, each one perpetrated by another psychopath seemingly put on Earth solely to terrorize others. Even before I could define it, I knew I was destined to make my own kind of "good trouble," as John Lewis said. It was just a matter of figuring out how and where and when to strike. The following stories aim to articulate that journey.

For the past 40 years, in my own tiny way I have tried to be my own kind of troublemaker and plan to continue to be one until my dying day. Yes, as a child, I caused more than my fair share of bad trouble, likely in mindless response to the racism and bullying that surrounded my otherwise materially abundant childhood. However, after leaving home, I have worked hard to become the kind of troublemaker who creates the *good* trouble Mr. Lewis spoke of so eloquently. At the same time, sometimes I wonder how I mustered the courage to leave the home of my upbringing, let alone my neighborhood, town, and state. Considering the personal traumas and tragedies that piled up year after year in my youth, I'm still amazed I left home as early as I did, as an immature, skinny 17-year-old who routinely ran more than 150 kms a week in my quest to race ever faster, speeding off into the unknown horizons of the brighter world ahead. Then, less than five years later, I saw the writing on the wall, and at the age of 22 left the country of my birth for good many decades before the flood of thousands upon thousands of expatriates now leaving the US permanently to escape the ugly and racist fascism taking root there.

Beyond what I just mentioned, during my early years my favorite uncle, Uncle Bill, is presumably killed when I am 11 years old somewhere in the middle of nowhere along the banks of the Blue Nile of Ethiopia, a story I am now putting together in my next book to be called simply *Uncle Bill*. My first girlfriend is then killed in a car crash not long after that. I am mauled on three occasions by three different German Shepherds by the age of 14. Several times I nearly die from numerous diseases and even have to deal with being abused at some disgraceful Christian camp I was coerced to attend for one night by some sweaty-palmed fundamentalist molester whose name and face I still very much remember. The list goes on. For a kid from affluent Southern California, it was a lot to deal with. No wonder I hit the road as soon as I could—and chose a troublemaker's life of human rights work.

When you know suffering up close, no matter what form it takes and who does it to whom, it gets a lot harder to look away and do nothing when you know of suffering elsewhere, and two additional moments were instrumental in making me into the person who chose a human rights life. The first is a dog story involving what were presented to us as Lion Hounds. Our family was on the North Shore of Oahu in Hawaii. It was mid-afternoon on yet another perfect island day where all was indeed perfect, all was safe—until it was not. I was 10 years old at the time. It was 1973 and we were about halfway through our trip when we took a jaunt in a rented open-topped jeep and drove around Oahu through pineapple fields and lush farmland. We ended up on the North Shore, and my dad slowed the car, turning into an abandoned parking lot next to a permanently shuttered and empty tourist shop and a house surrounded by a chain-link fence.

My mom, sister and I were confused about why my dad would stop in such an unremarkable spot in an otherwise stunning part of the world. I asked, "Why are we stopping here, dad?" He replied, looking at my mom, "Don't you remember this place when we were here years ago? Don't you remember the amazing view of the valley beyond that hedge over there?" She had absolutely no memory of the place, which to me was far from surprising. My dad turned to my sister and me and told us that he was going to hop the fence and go check out the view to see if it was still as lovely as it once was. I was terrified but felt both tempted and proud that my dad was willing to climb over a fence just to check out the view, despite the "No Trespassing" signs and the unmissable "Warning: Lion Hounds" messages. I point these signs out to my dad. "Dad, it says not to trespass and that there are dogs guarding the place. Maybe it's not such a good idea to go in there." I saw the warning signs and heeded them. He saw the warning signs and ignored them; even saying "Everyone knows there is no such thing as Lion Hounds, Tiger." He called me Tiger forever. There is no sign of dogs anywhere, no barking and no food bowls, so maybe he was right after all.

I became immediately nervous when I saw him starting to climb the fence, especially after he again asked my eight-year-old sister and me to come in too. We both vigorously declined the offer and my sister exclaimed, "Dad, there are Lion Hounds in there! Come back!" I still remember the smile and laugh he gave us, telling us not to worry and how much we were missing by not joining him. He crossed the cracked concrete patio and disappeared through a gap in the thick hedge to find the vista point he remembered from all those years ago. For a moment, my sister and I, leaning into the chain link fence with our fingers grabbing on to the curved metal wires, just waited patiently for my dad to return. And then, with no warning the hedge began shaking violently and the terrifying screams of my dad became horrifyingly audible. He appeared at the gap with a look of fear and terror on his face, the likes of which I had never before seen. He sprinted toward us as fast as he could, but not fast enough. Two gigantic, salivating, and snarling dogs—extremely vicious Rhodesian Ridgebacks—bounded behind him, snapping at the air, and barking with violent intent, just inches away. Then, my dad reached the fence and tried to climb while his two kids, just inches away on the other side, screamed louder, crying uncontrollably in a state of complete terror. It was then that the clearly trained guard dogs got him.

Inches from our faces, these two huge hounds began trying to tear my dad to shreds, biting him everywhere they could—hands, legs, arms, bum, everywhere. I'm sure they were trying for his neck but they just couldn't reach it, thank goodness. Blood flew everywhere as my heretofore invincible dad—the man who had always seemed so powerful, so smart, and so indestructible—who once saved my life by blocking a high-speed, errant polo ball from hitting my right temple— was brutalized by two violent canines eager to do their job and guard the property. My dad would make some progress up the fence on the dog's side and then they would violently pull him down again. This happened repeatedly until a grumpy old man finally came out of a nearby building, and far too slowly and dismissively at last cleared the dogs away, and—all the while—yelling at my bloodied dad for stupidly hopping a fence with warning signs about Lion Hounds.

My dad slowly got up, barely able to walk, offered his apologies (the dog owner did not!) and he slowly climbed over the fence to join us again. We then drove to the nearest hospital we knew about with blood dripping from every one of the numerous bites he suffered, and I went with my dad when we got there. We went inside, and my dad, in his baritone voice, said to the nurses, "I've been bitten all over by some dogs, and am bleeding everywhere." Much to my surprise, the nurses laughed, then told him we were in the maternity ward. He was a great lawyer, and always went for the underdog, but sometimes a bit clueless in normal life, my lovable dad. Needless to say, had my sister or I joined him on the other side of the fence, there is no way we would have made it out of there alive—absolutely impossible based on what we saw that day. We read the signs, took the warnings seriously and played it safe. The one who didn't, came out bloodied, traumatized and in severe pain with lifelong scars. This life lesson has never left me. It certainly hasn't stopped me from doing dangerous or risky things. But in dubious settings, when the next close shave seems to be clearly near, the admonition always comes back to me: Warning - Lion Hounds.

Life Lesson No. 1: Take risks often but trust warning signs too.

About 12 years after the incident with the lion hounds, my close friend and I were trying to stay warm in a very dilapidated and isolated cottage deep in the English countryside in Essex near Colchester. As we warmed ourselves by an ancient fireplace burning extremely malodorous chunks of coal—our only heat source on a freezing cold -14°C day in the middle of a bitterly cold British winter in that noticeably uninsulated ancient cottage I once called home—my friend and soul brother Vangelis told me he had once died and come back to life. More than intrigued, I sat back and listened.

Vangelis grew up on Amorgos, the small and beautiful isle of love in Greece, right in the middle of the Cyclades. He was nearly as beautiful as his island home—some say even more so. Like another brother from yet another mother, cosmic soul brother of mine, Mystical Matthias, every time I'd walk down the street with the Voracious Vangelis, I'd get these seriously mixed feelings. I loved being checked out so much by every passer-by, but at the same time it would inevitably dawn on me that all of those desirous and seductive stares were not intended for me at all but for my walking partners.

Little Vangelis had enjoyed a pre-modern, idyllic life, growing up barefoot on a small island that took pride in its self-sufficiency—with limited electricity and no TV. He grew up fast, as other options were scarce. Every year, before Vangelis eventually left Amorgos for England and other places beyond in his twenties, and which led us to meet for the first time at a ten-day meditation retreat in 1985, he would venture to a neighboring island to acquire liter upon liter of olive oil for the months ahead.

At the meditation event, we walked on fire together at midnight on New Year's Eve as 1985 became 1986, hand in hand across some very hot glowing coals we had spent hours preparing with a huge end of year bonfire. Days before, without searching we came across a huge patch of hundreds of psilocybin mushrooms in the paddock of the estate where the largely silent Buddhist retreat was held, exchanged muted but gleeful smiles of mutual recognition, and gathered as many as we could fit in our pockets. We then sat on an old log in the woods and ate at least three grams each, maybe more. We dedicated the next eight hours—six of which we spent meditating—to some of the most intense experiences of our lives.

Before venturing forth like a modern-day Homer in search of his very own Ithaca, Vangelis the island boy lived on rocky and dry land that somehow provided everything the island needed except the huge amounts of olive oil its small population required. So, at the tender age of 16, he went off with his father in a small boat to a neighboring island, where olive oil was abundant. An annual trip to procure as much of the sacred oil as possible ensured a permanent supply of this holy elixir. The nearby island wouldn't have been far by motorboat, but in a small boat with only oars and sails, the journey could feel like an eternity. Though people don't usually associate the Mediterranean with storms, they can happen quickly and become very dangerous and severe. They reached the olive oil island for what was meant to be a two-day, one-night trip. After pulling the boat onto the deserted beach, they walked to the olive grove where a hermit-like farmer, the island's sole occupant, lived and asked if they could buy as much olive oil as they could carry back to Amorgos.

As always, he said yes, and they began transferring container after container of the liquid gold onto the small boat when the storm struck.

This vicious storm lashed the island and surrounding sea, making any open-water journey impossible. They asked the farmer if they could stay until it passed, and he—of course—invited them to stay as long as needed. Little did they know at the time, but one extra night turned into 15 long days and nights of waiting and waiting until the unusually rough seas calmed down enough for them to hop on board again and head back to the isle of love. After more than half a month of rest, they returned to the boat with renewed energy and sailed and rowed home in record time. As they neared their island after their surprisingly long journey, in an era without cell phones or any similar technology, they noticed an eerie silence, seemingly devoid of life, as if the island had been evacuated or struck by an unknown disease that had wiped out the entire population.

They finally made it to shore and still no one was to be seen or heard, and by now Vangelis and his Pop were getting scared. Where was everyone? How can this be? They unloaded the barrels of olive oil onto the beach and went off to explore what had happened, planning to come back later to retrieve their long-awaited haul. They slowly wound their way up the sole road towards the main village and still nothing; not a person, not a sound, nothing.

Now they were terrified that something awful had happened, and just then when they had almost given up hope, they heard the faintest ringing of a church bell. Fearing it was just the wind or that somehow the bell had been dislodged by natural forces and not a human, they slowly walked towards the church, and as they rounded the bend the screams began. "God is real! They are alive!" "Thank you, Lord, my prayers have been answered." "Oh my, our olive oil men are still with us." It didn't take long for the most beautiful man in the world and his loving daddy to realize they had arrived at their own shared funeral just as it was ending. The family and friends who had just said goodbye to two empty caskets suddenly saw these men standing before them, who were then able to say, as most of us never will, that they had attended their own funerals—alive and kicking.

I tell this story because, as I suspect you also know, attending their own funerals gave Vangelis and his father a new lease on life, a new way of viewing the 30,000 days we're lucky enough, on average, to have on this planet, and a wholly new way to relate to the world. Vangelis told me on countless occasions that the experience set him on the journey he has taken ever since: massaging the sick, giving acupuncture to those in need, and helping and herbily healing anyone who asks. In his own way, he made the world better for everyone who crossed his path—except perhaps a few beloveds who stopped serving as his number one.

Maybe we can all metaphorically do the very same thing; let our old ideas die as our new, expanded, inclusive, and worldcentric views grow ever deeper. As the Buddhists metaphorically say, the ego and emotions slowly wither the more one meditates. "If you die when you are alive, you don't die when your body dies." So, too, perhaps our seemingly embedded ideas and assumptions, especially about nation-states and nationalities—the source of so many human rights violations and human suffering—may be far better to lose than to hold on to. Prevention always beats cure.

Life Lesson No. 2: Have enough courage to let your old ideas die. Reassess everything and build again.

And thus, so too have I over the past several years considered my own life, including some of the many excruciatingly close shaves I have endured, like the worst illness I have ever faced just after starting this book, which against all odds I miraculously survived. When you come so close to death (yet again!) and your inevitable end, indeed much closer than Vangelis and his father did, you ponder the life you have led. You count the victories, the losses, and the draws. As a troublemaking human rights activist for decades, I recalled the rare occasions when my efforts won the day, perhaps saving lives—or at least reducing human suffering by a bit.

People who know me often feel that it is through my irreverence that I show my greatest respect; and this is usually very true. What people often miss is that my perceived irreverence is actually the deepest form of respect that I can muster. I try to create as much equality as possible, find common ground, and spark the beginnings of smiles—hopefully followed by a shared chuckle. I want to relate to everyone I meet in a quick and real a manner as I can muster. It makes all the difference in the world. Superficiality, formality, and the *status quo* have never been my way. I haven't worn a tie for around 20 years or so, maybe more. I refuse to use the formal 'you' in Dutch, German or Spanish. I most certainly refuse to not be myself in conversations with diplomats, billionaires, or stoners in a crowded concert hall. I've never really had a boss and absolutely hated it when I had to be one. Thankfully, somehow, I found a way that enabled me to never have to commute by car or public transport to work, never have to work in a cubicle or a high-rise skyscraper, and yet travel to all corners of the world to promote human rights. I refused to drive a car a single inch for a full 30 years until I became a dad living in a semi-rural area and was forced to out of necessity. Yes, I took taxis and rode with other drivers from time to time (everyone always asks…). I have seen the absolute best and the absolute worst of what our human species has to offer. You get me for what I am and I get you for what you are. That's both fair and equal.

I've forever gone my own way, for better or worse. If I had the chance to do it over, would I have chosen to be more mainstream, more obsessed with a regular paycheck, power or prestige, more materialist, more concerned with appearance over substance? The answer is no. I am certain I was so much more productive working as a troublemaking human rights activist than as a lifelong employee of some hierarchical organization or company. After all I have seen across all corners of our planet, the utter carnage done by fellow humans to other fellow humans, the hatred, violence, despair, and levels of anguish few outside of such places could fathom, how could I become anything other than the human rights renegade many have labeled me as over the years? *Get it done but keep it fun*, has always been my credo, and I wouldn't have changed that for the world. Work myself to the bone to make the world a better place, but throw a Frisbee to a friend, climb a mountain, jump in the ocean, embrace your true love, explore the unexplored, tend your garden and laugh as much as possible along the way—even though oppression, illness, death, and despair don't always make that very easy.

Life Lesson No. 3: Get it done but keep it fun.

Of course, I desperately wish I had helped more people, done more to achieve justice, and shown even more intensively that kindness and love beat cruelty and hate, especially to the human rights abusers among us. But even having only won the human rights battles in which I have engaged *sometimes*, on the other hand, what better life could I have led? What better way could I have spent my working life given my various strengths, and my many weaknesses? Using creativity, a bit of innovation, all couched in a sense of humor and the oneness of everything, including, you, me, and every human, I did my bit. I did what I could and will continue to do so as long as I am able. This is my eternal quest though it may look and feel different now from the days when I would travel every few days, give speeches at the UN, harass human rights violating governments and so on. Now, the aim is to universally embrace and understand the interconnections and interdependence between us all, one day (hopefully sooner than later) manifesting as world citizenship for everyone, notwithstanding where you were born, where you live now, and where you will go in the future.

Sadly, I will probably never meet you, although I hope I will. But even if we never meet, I can say without a doubt that I want all of us, including you, to share the same nationality, the same citizenship, with the same rights, same responsibilities and same obligations as everyone else. In building such a system of unified humanity, contrary to what many believe, we actually don't lose anything. We *gain* a new and bigger identity—shared by all of us— one bound to make our world a lot more livable and peaceful; something the world needs now more than ever. As Václav Havel so poignantly said: "Without a global revolution in the sphere of human consciousness, nothing will change for the better...and the catastrophe towards which the world is headed - the ecological, social, demographic, or general breakdown of civilization - will be unavoidable."[1]

Just as John Lewis was a troublemaker, so too were Václav Havel, Nelson Mandela, Martin Luther King, Petra Kelly, and so many others. In a way, everyone who seeks a better world, who points out injustice and intervenes when it appears is a troublemaker themselves. The chapters that follow will seek to unveil a few life lessons I have learned being my very own sort of troublemaker all across this beautiful planet that we all share.

To those who know me already, my apologies for leaving out most of the really spicy stories you probably already know. To those I am meeting for the very first time, I hope the collection of human rights chronicles I outline below will inspire you, make you laugh at the

---

[1]Quoted in: Arjuna Ardagh, *The Translucent Revolution: How People Just Like You Are Waking Up and Changing the World*, New World Library, 2005, pp. 397-398.

absurdity of life and then cry about the cruelty that humans continue to inflict on other humans each and every day. Above all else, I hope that the pages that follow will unearth for you the idea that a life dedicated to human rights and reducing the suffering of our fellow humans can be a pretty captivating one, indeed. Happy reading, my friends!

Scott Leckie
4 March 2026

Chapter 1

So, You've Decided to be a Failure?

Since the mid-1980s, I've been what some people have called a human rights renegade—maybe even a human rights outlaw—because of my often-unorthodox way of doing things. The vim that somehow powers me forward has been the rocket fuel that has kept me going ever since. When I'm lucky enough to add a booster shot of vigor to the mix the bad guys get scared; at least I hope they do. Since my earliest days as a human rights activist, people from Manila, Myanmar, Melbourne and beyond have called me Mr. Housing Rights, a name that first popped up in lovely Vancouver, Canada in the early days of my housing rights journey.

I've worked in more than 80 countries and carried out human rights work on another 35 or 40 countries beyond those that I have visited. I've been fortunate to live in over a dozen countries for sustained periods and could happily move to any country in the world tomorrow and quickly feel at home. Though moving between places and countries has become easy, achieving justice has not. Few of those one meets during a life of troublemaking activism will tell you outright that attaining a winning record in the world of human rights is simply impossible. You need to figure that one out yourself and find ways to live with this sad truth. Moving is easy, but winning is hard.

When I left the country of my birth, the United States, forever in my early twenties, the father of one of my best friends, a man who embodied the extremes of capitalist excess, 200 kgs, pudgy face, suspenders and all the rest, at least told me the truth, though I was certainly not ready to hear it at that stage. "What's next for you then, Scott?", he asked. "I'm leaving the US forever to work on human rights wherever this path will take me", I proudly replied with a combined scent of contempt, conceit, trepidation, and pride all merged together. This larger-than-life Billy Bunter of a man quickly chortled in his retort, oozing with derision, "So, you've decided to be a failure? What are you going to do, work with some international ACLU or some other do-gooder venture like that?"

Not for the first time in my life, I was speechless and couldn't believe these dismissive comments. As my mind raced through every expletive I knew, I walked away shaking my head in disbelief that anyone could have views such as these, especially the father of such a close friend. But as it turns out, this morbidly obese man, so proudly a lifetime member of a private golf club that for the longest time singled out and excluded certain ethnic, racial, and religious groups of people from membership, (I'll let you guess which ones), had at least one thing right, and that was this: The simple fact is that on any human rights journey, you may take the high road—and may as well make some good trouble, too—but more often than not, you will fail in your various quests; not always, but certainly mostly.

When you instinctively support the underdog or the little guy, you quickly learn that they are the little guy because the bigger guy—the one violating their rights—has set up the system to facilitate this. Now, decades after commencing my life of perpetual travel to human rights hotspots, as I reflect on what worked and what didn't, it's clear my track record fell short of my early hopes and expectations. Only recently has it dawned on me that many of the outcomes I sought to bring about or banish will have to wait for future generations' skills and humanity's evolution. I truly believed that by the time I came to the final phase of my human rights work, mass forced evictions would have been banished once and for all, Palestine and Tibet would be free and independent countries, women would earn as much as men, nationalism and racism (not to mention fascism) would have been consigned to the rubbish heap of history where they belong, and armed military invasions would have ended for good.

Coming to terms with these and other sad realities on our shared planet remains a daily challenge, one I may never fully transcend, no matter how far away from the main centers of human agglomeration I may choose to spend my final days. There is an immeasurable joy in realizing that all of us are members of the same wonderful human family, and for those of whom haven't reached that conclusion yet, I'd encourage you to get moving as fast as you can; you won't be disappointed when you reach there, I promise!

But at the same time, there is a rather daunting price to be paid in caring about the wellbeing of everyone, everywhere. Once this understanding pervades your worldview, it cannot be reversed, and why would you want it to? When you start caring about all of humanity, not just those in your immediate vicinity, you must find ways to transcend daily news announcements about human cruelty. Today, and every day, many people will be killed on battlefields. Thousands, maybe even more, will be tortured. Millions will go to bed with hunger pangs in their belly. Hundreds of millions will awake in dismal slums. And billions will breathe dangerously polluted air and face ever-growing threats brought about by climate change. Certainly, there are good news stories to report, but all too often our civilization serves up anguish and despair when compassion would have been just as easy and so much more preferable. I don't want us to live in a world like this. Don't we deserve better? Is this really the best the human race can do?

The recollections contained in this book have been doing the rounds in my mind for a while, based on my experiences as an international human rights legal expert and advocate since 1983. As I've discussed with so many of my global friends, my entire working life has been based on my very own personal 50-year work plan, and it still is. In your mind's eye, imagine a large brick wall, full of holes, cracks, weak spots, and far too easy to surmount, symbolizing an all too flimsy human rights system that, while in place, is rather risk-free to bypass for anyone who wishes to do so. And just to be clear, what we are discussing here is the antithesis of the type of wall so often touted by Donald Trump and those who follow his autocratic cult. No, here we are talking about a human rights *protection* wall, something that is built on our shared humanity. I imagine a wall that would perpetually protect each and every one of us from the countless abuses that are meted out daily by governments and private individuals against their fellow humans. That kind of wall.

My plan was, and remains, to creatively seek to fill those gaps and strengthen the weak spots. I aim to build this wall so high and thick that human rights abusers, wherever they are, will find it increasingly difficult to violate human rights laws with impunity—through either acts or omissions. As the wall strengthens, it will become ever more difficult for them to neglect the rights of their citizens, especially the still ignored poor and disadvantaged. In the end, this will contribute to the rule of law, enhance democracy, and lead to growing equality within and between nations everywhere. I'm at about Year 40 now, 80% done. Along the way, I discovered that for whatever reason I could rather easily identify human rights gaps in laws, institutions, and practices, and keep trying my best, each and every day, to fill them, strengthening the protection wall and expanding human rights protections for everyone, everywhere. And you know what, sometimes against all odds, human rights efforts bear remarkable fruit. Usually you will fail, but on occasion you win. The failures are devastating, but the victories are joyous and make it all worthwhile.

Life Lesson No. 4: When you pursue a human rights life, the odds are always stacked against you (and you probably won't become rich either). But when you win, celebrate like there's no tomorrow.

Apologies to those who find what I am about to say painfully banal but around the age of 19, I decided to dedicate my entire working life to making the world a better place, no matter what the level of pay and no matter where the work would be carried out. Having considered over a dozen potential career paths—ranging from the anti-nuclear movement to women's rights, trade unions, environmentalism, Green Party politics, and an array of others—I ultimately chose human rights. I felt this path would benefit more people, in more places, more often than any other option.

In working in the human rights field, it was never enough for me to simply recapitulate what had already been decided, strengthen victories already achieved, or to implement pre-existing laws. Rather, my particular efforts had to be designed to bolster and *expand* human rights laws in whatever way I could in line with my five-decade work plan. Having written my LLM (Master of Laws) thesis on the right to a sound environment in the mid-1980s, I eventually turned to the human rights issue that probably affects more people more places, more frequently than any other: the human right to adequate housing.

My housing rights life began at a precise moment in 1987. As I snuggled on the couch with a Dutch girlfriend, whom I had met several months earlier ice skating on an exquisite frozen canal after she kindly helped me to my feet after my hundredth face planting wipe-out. She worked for the Pacifist Socialist Party (PSP), and we were watching TV one cold night in Holland's fourth largest city, Utrecht, where the PSP held three local government seats. Much to my amazement a commercial came on the screen announcing the *International Year of Shelter for the Homeless*, a UN ceremonial year which for the first time was dedicated to finding housing for all of humanity. I thought about this for a moment, first amazed that national TV in any country would announce something this cool. Then it dawned on me that I'd seen the word *housing* in many of the human rights treaties I'd studied, but I'd never seen a single legal or academic article articulating precisely what this right meant under international law—or how it could be enforced. And so, I set out to write just such an article.

I slowly put my ideas onto paper, which became one of the first academic articles ever published that advocated for an enforceable human right to adequate housing under international law. Who could have imagined that those early efforts in the late 1980s would eventually lead to books, founding and directing several NGOs, and constant travel to work with slum dwellers, homeless people, refugees, and internally displaced persons all across the world? Throughout the process, I was able to contribute to a whole series of international standards on housing rights, forced evictions, restitution rights for refugees and displaced persons, and other themes to protect *you* and *your* lawful rights. These laws and rules are still on the books today. I was able to participate in actions that ended up stopping very large-scale planned forced evictions in a number of major global cities and conceived the terminology and the field of housing, land, and property rights (HLP).

There was a continual evolution flowing through these efforts that began with housing rights, focusing on the primary means by which these rights could be abused, namely forced evictions. At the most rudimentary level, it was clear that we needed to identify the most grievous violation of the right to adequate housing as a way of understanding the legal meaning of this right more clearly. This, in turn, morphed into work on the right to HLP restitution for refugees and internally displaced persons seeking to return to and recover the homes and lands from which they were forced to flee, often a core aim of ethnic cleansing. This work was influenced by the atrocities of the early 1990s, particularly the Bosnia-Herzegovina conflict from 1991-1995 and other acts of ethnic cleansing. I worked in places such as the Republic of Georgia, Kosovo, Timor Leste, Albania, Palestine, Sri Lanka, and Burma, designing laws and procedures to help victims of ethnic cleansing reclaim their homes, lands, and properties with varying degrees of success, after they were so brutally displaced by states that remain responsible for these horrible crimes. As I began getting more interested in preventing climate displacement, I knew a change was in store, but more on that later.

Life Lesson No. 5: Every single one of us calls Earth home. Far too many of us forget this.

With this book I have tried my best to give a sense of what a human rights troublemaker's life looks like from the inside. I have attempted to provide a truthful insider's account of the ups and downs of a lifetime built on compassion, infused with innovation and creativity, while finding joy amidst sorrow, wisdom amidst delusion, and boundless love in a world filled with too much hate. The following pages tell my human rights story, a story which begins with slums.

Chapter 2

Slums

Much of my working life has been dedicated to trying to improve and secure the housing rights of people all across the world, from India to South Africa, Cambodia to Brazil, Burma to Bangladesh and so many more. *Housing rights for everyone, everywhere* has been my credo for decades. I don't care who you are, where you live, what your religion may be or how poor or rich you are, I just want you to have a decent place to live throughout your life. My dream—apparently my impossible dream given the scale of slums in the world's cities today —was that by the end of my working days, the entire world would have eradicated homelessness, ended forced evictions, halted the theft of refugee homes, stopped discrimination against tenants and slum dwellers, ensured equal rights for women and men, provided security of tenure for billions of those still without it, guaranteed access to basic services like sanitation and water, and improved the underbelly aspects of life in slums. Alas, these hopeful dreams have yet to come true and with the greatest reluctance, I am tragically coming to accept that humanity as a whole will continue to fail in this quest, and perhaps will never succeed. And yet, throughout my working life, hope had an address, and that destination could be reached through a reliance on international human rights law, the United Nations and the rule of law and justice across the world.

Over the years, from working at the highest levels of the UN to working at the grassroots in communities with countless individual people and families living in appallingly bad slums, there have been important victories I know would not have occurred without my personal initiative. But sadly, the losses far outnumber the wins, and we remain collectively as far from solving the global housing crisis as ever, no matter what people may wish to believe. Despite the efforts of thousands upon thousands of people in every corner of the world, there are likely more slum dwellers now than when measurements began in the early 1980s. Predictions suggest that by 2050, one in three people may live in slums. What does this say about us as humans? What does this say about what we will tolerate, what we will accept as inevitable even though it most certainly is not? Are we collectively truly that selfish, that uncaring about our fellow human beings?

Life Lesson No. 6: Housing rights are for everyone, everywhere, full stop.

Some will say (and I have heard this from countless colleagues across the world) that far from being a problem slums are, in fact, actually the solution to the housing crisis. If the legal housing market won't provide and the state won't build the housing resources required, the poor will need to provide for themselves. In a way this makes perfect sense, of course, particularly in urban areas where land prices seem to never stop growing and thus where the poor are increasingly excluded. If left alone, and protected against eviction, a rudimentary slum shack built from recycled materials discarded by other slum dwellers can quickly become a more permanent home, sometimes even approaching a degree of the adequacy required by human rights laws. But from a policy or legal perspective, is this really the best we can do?

Having spent time in hundreds of slums worldwide since the 1980s —from Santo Domingo to Funafuti, Cairo to Mumbai, Phnom Penh to Belgrade, Cape Town to Porto Alegre, Seoul to Honiara, Bangkok to Manila, Accra to Delhi, Mumbai to Yangon to Hong Kong, and many more—I have seen slum life up close too many times to count. I have recollections of an endless stream of discussions with the people living there, and if I simply close my eyes and take a few calm breaths they all seem to come back to life, reminding me of their joy and their sorrow living in a slum they call home. And yet, far from being the preferred solution to global homelessness and landlessness, slums essentially are just a safety valve. They do provide dwellings of varying degrees of (in)adequacy for people, but at the same time they often just barely keep a lid on what could easily become a political powder keg just waiting to explode when the suffering they endure each day simply becomes intolerable for those who live there.

To make a very broad generality, slums are the best that slum dwellers can access with their limited resources and money. Some homes in slums are perfectly fine, but far too many are not and fall far short of any reasonable definition of adequacy. It's as simple as that; if those residing in the bad dwellings could get better housing, they would. Yes, remarkably they often make the most of slum living, extolling the virtues of knowing everyone in the community, knowing every winding path, every muddy lane, every shop, and so many more things built by the people themselves incrementally improving their houses year after year, brick by brick. All of this is true and the infamous "resilience" of slum dwellers that the well-housed elites love to spout as evidence of how amazing slums are is true, as well. But given the chance, I believe that the overwhelming majority of those living in slums would live in better places if this were possible for them. The problem, thus, is one more of resignation and acceptance, rather than choice, and this is the core of the issue that needs addressing in the future.

Life Lesson No. 7: Protect slums, yes. But don't over-romanticize them. Most slum dwellers would move if they could.

After visiting my first slum in New Delhi in 1988, a shockingly poor, grimy, and rather tragic place full of lepers, amputees, greatly deprived elderly people and countless barefoot children which I would have never entered had I not been with some of India's greatest social activists, I was so moved that I vowed right then to take some sort of action, though I didn't know quite what I should do. How could so many people in so many places be forced to live in such dire conditions? I was staggered, just as you will be should you ever enter a slum which is an experience only a tiny minority of well-housed Westerners have ever thought to do. How could government after government keep failing to ensure housing rights for everyone, especially those without the means to achieve these rights on their own? I had to do something, but how and what to do remained elusive. I wrote books, UN reports, worked as a UN consultant, made films, and linked up with a whole horde of housing activists from around the world, but this never felt like enough.

Several years ago, our planet of an endless number of slums became more urban than rural, with city dwellers outnumbering those living in the countryside for the first time since the dawn of humanity. Despite the well-known resource, environmental, social, economic, and cultural consequences associated with urbanization, the slum, housing rights and security of tenure crises that accompany city growth continue to generate an ever-expanding presence of low-income neighborhoods, often devoid of the promise of human rights. These informal settlements exist and continue to grow—not due to the so-called "free ride" of which some mistakenly claim the urban poor allegedly partake of—but because formal housing, land, and property sectors are simply inaccessible to lower—and, increasingly, middle-income groups.

At the same time, the global real estate boom of the past 30 years has made many property owners wealthier than they may have ever imagined, and societies across the world are bifurcating into those who own and those who don't with dismal consequences for political stability and the promise of housing for all. This in turn has played a key role in limiting access to the "legal city" for the new urban poor. The growth of slums and informal housing is the predictable outcome of decades of state neglect of housing, coupled with increasing reliance on market-based solutions for securing the housing needs of the poor. This is despite the clear evidence accrued over the past century that the market (or real estate developers) alone has never—

and will never—provide adequate, affordable, accessible, and secure housing to all lower-income groups in any society.

Life Lesson No. 8: In no country will the private real estate market ever build enough housing for the poor and lower-income groups. Don't believe the hype!

In many respects, state-built or subsidized housing programs have often fared no better, as few governments have made a truly concerted effort to build or subsidize adequate low-income housing that consistently meets international standards. At the same time, without strong governmental involvement in housing through both supportive laws and financial resources, prevailing economic models will not improve slums. Globalization, free trade, international investment, the growing migration of labor, and "property rights" alone cannot transform slums into vibrant, rights-embracing communities without proper support and backing.

Indeed, some might argue that the continued growth of slums during the past several decades can actually be sourced to prevailing neo-liberal economic arrangements that clearly favor cities over the countryside, as well as aiding those with access to international finance, education, and credit. Persons with access will prevail, and those without it will eventually call the slum their only home. This combined failure of both State- and private sector-led approaches to provide a sufficient number of homes that the poor can afford, and economic conditions which facilitate neither investment in housing for the poor nor the conferral of rights linked to people's housing, land, or property status are some of the key reasons why so many of the world's citizens remain as slum residents today.

Whether referred to as bidonvilles (French-speaking Africa), the ghetto or the hood (North America), bustees or chawls (South Asia), favelas (Brazil), barrios populares (Latin America), or simply as slums, these usually self-built, low-income, and frequently— technically—illegal neighborhoods are a now central part of the urban landscape in the Global South and increasingly in the Global North as well, though the homes may look different the relative economic reality remains the same. Whether we like it or not, broadly defined slums are home to a growing share of the population. Despite the poor conditions and negative media portrayal of slums, failures in governance, law, and policy by national and international institutions have resulted in a world where one-fifth or more of humanity lives in slums.

While slums are unique and multi-faceted—like any other neighborhood—most low-income settlements in Latin America, Asia, Africa, and even those located in the so-called "developed world" share certain common characteristics. Beyond the poverty and relative social disadvantage ubiquitously present in slums, these communities face challenges few would choose to endure, including insecure tenure and eviction threats, physically inadequate housing stock, overcrowding, and inadequate sanitation facilities are common challenges. Some communities also face inadequate and unaffordable water supply, poor drainage, sporadic electricity, and a lack of public services such as waste disposal, drainage, and emergency services. Additionally, they suffer from pollution affecting water, soil, and air, as well as violence and insecurity. Slum life is hard.

The term "slum" itself dates all the way back to 1812 where it was synonymous with "racket" or "criminal trade", and this perception of slums as criminal havens and zones of illegality unfortunately continues to pervade common connotations of lower-income neighborhoods, which in turn assists in marginalizing slums even further from the political mainstream.[2] The portrayal of slums and slum life in popular films like *City of God, District 9, City of Joy, The Constant Gardener*, and *Code 46* have contributed to a skewed view of slums, overlooking the need for enhanced human rights protections, drastic housing improvements, and the daily struggles of billions. Never forget that the vast majority of slum dwellers are hardworking, peaceful people seeking a better life—forced into illegality because the legal housing sector finds no place for them.

Slums would not exist if there were legal ways for everyone to find a decent and affordable place to live. As a result, most slums are in many respects technically illegal. Land is often occupied without legal

---

[2]The first published definition reportedly occurs in the convict writer James Hardy Vaux's 1812 *Vocabulary of the Flash Language*, (Prunty, *Dublin Slums*, 2). See also: J.A. Yelling, *Slums and Slum Clearance in Victorian London*, London 1986.

title, dwellings violate housing codes and regulations, and dwellers often tap electricity without authorization. Children may go unregistered at birth, and people may build drainage canals or public toilets contrary to public health and safety rules. In effect, thus, quite literally hundreds of millions of people alive today live their lives in conditions of informality, technically contrary to whatever statutory codes may be in place. And yet, it is clearly true that: "[L]aws are unjust when the poverty of the majority of people makes it impossible for them to comply with them. If for most urban citizens, Governments should either reform legislation or eliminate unrealistic laws when basic daily tasks—building or renting a shelter, earning an income, and obtaining food and water—become illegal. Urban legislation should be more flexible in adapting to the great variety of circumstances and the rate at which these can change."[3]

Life Lesson No. 9: Slums may technically be illegal but those living there most certainly are not. No human is illegal.

More than 35 years ago in their now classic work *Squatter Citizen*, Jorge Hardoy and my friend David Satterthwaite very accurately asserted that: "If present trends continue, we can expect to find tens of millions more households living in squatter settlements or in very poor quality and overcrowded rented accommodation owned by highly exploitative landlords. Tens of millions more households will be forcibly evicted from their homes. Hundreds of millions more people will build shelters on dangerous sites and with no alternative but to work in illegal or unstable jobs. The quality of many basic services (water, sanitation, garbage disposal, health care) will deteriorate still further and there will be a rise in the number of diseases related to poor and contaminated living environments including those resulting from air pollution and toxic wastes."[4]

Unfortunately, as remarkable as the prescience of their prediction has turned out to be, in fact the situation is even worse than they

---

[3]Hardoy & Satterthwaite, *Squatter Citizen: Life in the Urban Third World*, Earthscan, London, 1989, p. 35.
[4]Id, Hardoy & Satterthwaite, 301.

imagined. As UN Habitat's *The Challenge of Slums - Global Report on Human Settlements 2003* indicated 15 years hence: "It is almost certain that slum dwellers increased substantially during the 1990s. It is further projected that in the next 30 years, the global number of slum dwellers will increase to about 2 billion, if no firm and concrete action is taken."[5] Several years later, UN Habitat's *State of the World's Cities* report warned again that "Slum settlements are already home to almost one billion people, or one-third of the world's urban population, and over the next two decades the cities of the developing world are expected to absorb 95 per cent of the world's urban population growth. Without a renewed commitment to the needs of our urban era, matched by resources, the world's urban transition will see a further expansion and entrenchment of slums, and the spread of urban ills."[6] They add: "Already, one of every three city dwellers is a slum dweller, with slums emerging as a dominant and distinct type of settlement in cities of the developing world."[7] Bearing in mind that the developing world's urban population is set to grow to more than four billion by 2030, combined with the fact that well under 20% of all new housing stock in the developing world is constructed within the formal, legal housing system, the world's slum population is clearly destined to grow at an alarming rate.

Throughout my adrenaline-charged human rights life, I journeyed countless times deep into some of the world's worst—and supposedly most dangerous—slums, spending time with thousands of slum dwellers and the amazing grassroots organizations representing them. I never kept a formal count of how many slums I visited over the years, but it is surely in the many hundreds if not more than that. Other than a few guns here and there, a few knives and a few bad vibes, I rarely felt any threats or danger in these communities, something which will surely surprise many who have never set foot in a slum. Usually I felt community, a sense of hope, and even joy that something better was coming.

I could recount many stories of slum adventures in Nairobi,

---

[5]UN Habitat, *The Challenge of Slums*, xxv.

[6]UN Habitat, *The State of the World's Cities Report 2006/2007*, Nairobi, iii.

[7]Supra, *The State of the World's Cities Report 2006/2007*, 11.

including one with a wild survivor of the Rwandan genocide at the wheel, with whisky bottles being passed around and a strange mix of joy and terror among the passengers. I could share adventures in São Paulo and Porto Alegre, where slum visits were accompanied by local activists providing fine weed and white powder offerings in grimy women's bathrooms as samba played on. I experienced scary tales in South African townships, combined with attempts at re-igniting a lost love, as well as secret meetings with courageous local slum activists in Tunis who told us about dictator Ben Ali running their country into the ground. I thought slums couldn't get worse until I worked in Accra, Ghana—where I spent time in a huge slum in Agbogbloshie commercial district—where we fought to protect tens of thousands of residents from eviction, only to later learn it's one of the most polluted places on Earth. Maybe in this case, relocation would have been preferred! In Cambodia, where I worked on many occasions, the slums were often in staggeringly poor condition, certainly far worse than in neighboring Thailand, but this was to be expected given the brutal history of the Khmer Rouge genocide, the Killing Fields and frequent political instability. Local activists told me that property prices in downtown Phnom Penh rose so quickly after the 1990s that business crony friends of the government would, as hard as this is to believe, sometimes allegedly show up in the middle of the night with dozens of trucks loaded with tons of soil, and then proceed throughout the night to drain and then *fill in* small inner-city lakes, and then claim the new "land" as their own, making millions of dollars in the process.

The state of the slums, in otherwise wealthy Hong Kong, shocked me. I worked with the local group SOCO, which showed me the horrible plight of tens of thousands of slum dwellers. This included the incredible Walled City of Kowloon, but especially the brutally, yet accurately labeled "caged people" high-rise encampments which have to be seen to be believed. These individuals lived in two square meter bunk beds in rooms with 40 or more people, caging themselves in to protect their lives and property. These were mostly very elderly men and women with nowhere else to go, and a true tragedy that should have never been allowed to occur in such a prosperous place. Even the public housing flats that dominated such a huge percentage of the housing stock were often in extremely poor shape and the contrast between rich Hong Kong and the poor majority in the province was and remains staggering.

These and countless other slum experiences taught me about how many people live and how someone like me, living comfortably in the rich Global North, could at least try to be a force for positive change. Some of these visits, of course, clearly stand out and it was my time in some of the slums of Santo Domingo, Bangkok and Manila that come readily to mind now.

Life Lesson No. 10: Slums are generally a lot safer than you may think – go and visit one and you'll see that the people who live there are people just like you and me.

Dominican Republic - La Cienega-Los Guandules

The delightful little sparkle in the eye of the Dominicana employee of Iberia airlines, somehow exuded hope, for this was surely not the first time this excellent airline had lost a passenger's luggage. Indeed, after a restless night fighting air-con rumblings with three pillows and obscure Tibetan meditation techniques interspersed with hand-rolled cigarettes and the free Cuba Libres on offer—none of which worked—wearing three-day old clothes, I made my way back to the far too hastily built and as quickly decaying airport. My trusted driver Rafaelito was, as always, at the wheel bounding towards the first bit of what most European and American tourists think is their entry point to paradise. An aspiring thief hassled me, and another and another. Saying a few words in Spanish, I almost forced them to know I was hip to their pending scam, and they departed as quickly as they had appeared, both of us smiling broadly each time.

I find my way down into the bowels of the terminal in a hurriedly built airport with loans given to a dictator they should never have been given to, and an area which the traveling public was clearly not meant to see. Dark, piercingly hot, and dingy to the extreme, led further and further away from anyone except the bag man. "No se, amigo, maybe problema grande, where you bag, yo no se", he said before I could let him know that I spoke Spanish slightly better than he spoke my Mother tongue. My bags eventually came into sight, amid mountains of hundreds of others (many of which had clearly been there since the lost bag room was built—lost forever), and I was glad. Just for a moment though.

I had filled my now tattered suitcases with human rights documents in English and Spanish, highly critical of the government and the authoritarian president, ready for free distribution in the capital's slums. This generally isn't much of a problem; border guards and customs officials rarely look too closely at the human rights handouts I always have in my bags, even in the worst of places. This guy looked pretty rough, however, and the tinges of fear skirt their way downwards into my belly. "Why you come to my country?" "You like muchachas?" "You want disco, 24 hours open?" says the man identified as Angel in broken English, who was anything but what his name signified. He goes through all my documents, even ones entitled "Dominican Republic: Eviction Capital of Latin America" and "UN Condemns DR Human Rights Record", that type of thing. He pretends to read them, seems disinterested, and before I know it, I'm relieved and sipping a very cold, icy, oh-so-good-tasting beer with Rafael at the airport bar in the open air. On the road a little bit of alcohol almost always makes the lovely look lovelier and the horrors look less awful. In this case, it's a bit of both. We eventually make the 30km drive back to the capital where half the population live in shacks amid palm trees. We do so safely despite the bottle of rum Rafaelito sips incessantly as he drives, holding it tight between his muscular legs as he avoids the many potholes along the way.

It's 1994 and yet again, for the third or fourth time I'm in the Dominican Republic, the DR, to find facts as they say in human rights parlance; officially known as a fact-finding mission. Sometimes we do these things publicly, letting the government know we're coming, allowing them the polite warning of our pending arrival. This time, we kept it our own little secret and so no news stories today, no press conferences, no cameras, and no diplomatic language: "We would like to emphasize that the government possesses legal obligations under international law, which they have undertaken voluntarily, to protect the housing rights of their citizens. In our view, the government has not entirely fulfilled its obligations and we feel much more could be done to protect these basic rights...." None of this today, so it's party time in gnarly Santo Domingo, frayed capital city, slum-ridden place that I just adore, but in a country mysteriously known as a place for tourists seeking rapture by pretending there are no slums, no violence, and no evictions.

As much as I love the place and its people, if there was ever a country that I have ambivalent feelings for it's the Dominican Republic. I recognize, of course, that the odds are stacked against it. This small nation has been repeatedly attacked, illegally invaded, and occupied far too many times by their big lawless neighbors to the north. It has been governed by too many kleptocrats for much of its history. It remains marginalized by corporate greed. Hedonistic tourists, in their "I did the DR" T-shirts, have taken over many of the once pure palm frond beaches. And so, some days I absolutely love the DR, others not so much. It's not just the *turistas*, though.

What really stands out each time I am there are some of the completely transformed Dominicanos who went to New York and other American destinations to make it big, became Americanized, made some money, and then returned to the island of their birth. This was in an era well before the brutal mass deportations by the United States today, but nevertheless these Dominicanos who had returned were visibly and palpably more superficial and individualistic than their compatriots who had remained behind. It all too often seemed as if the worst of American selfishness and deluded "exceptionalism" had rubbed off on them in only the worst of its forms. The once ubiquitous smiles of local Dominicanos seemingly lost forever, these returning expatriates somehow became hardened during their stay in the land of Uncle Sam, as if a part of their soul had been drained away without them even knowing. They are almost too easy to distinguish from other Dominicanos, and rarely anything like my friends who push that inimitable and vivacious Dominican spirit ever onwards. Spirit gone, boundless joy gone, even the constant dancing gone. It's become that American tune, sung too loudly; it's now just me, me and only me. It's sad to see, but sometimes they seem to be everywhere, as if they learned what they thought they needed in Nuevo York and happily brought—what they deem as knowledge—back to the hot place they once called home.

So, in the 1990s, if you take the tourists, mix them up with returnee

Dominicanos, a ruthless dictator, human rights violations, oppressive poverty, and massive slums across all corners of Santo Domingo you get a sauce that covers everything, but which is far from tasty. However, when you can get beyond this, transcend the dirt, the poverty and the despair, the DR is as good a place as any, in many ways much better.

You can find a general enjoyment of being alive there just about anywhere, in spite of everything. The near worship of the ubiquitous merengue music—the movement of the hips—and the casual joy of waving to a pal, is ever-present. This place will always retain a special place in my heart, to be sure. Anything for a laugh, a handshake, a wink, and a smile. Que lo que, compas? That's the DR I know and love. And even ole dictator Balaguer at the time (blind and in his 80s when I worked there) was ruthlessly joked about at every opportunity.

On each of the many working visits I made to the DR, I worked with the amazing crews of three NGOs who did extraordinary work on behalf of the slum dwellers there. One was COPADEBA or the Committee for the Defense of the Rights of the Barrio. Another was Ciudad Alternativa or Alternative City, and the third, a legal aid group called CEDAIL. I absolutely loved working with these fine human rights defenders. People like grassroots leader Chichi Ceballos, his fist in the air at seemingly every meeting we attended together. And then there was Father Jorge Cela, a voluntary resident of a seriously bad slum and a decades-long supporter of dwellers' rights, inspired many—when you could get a glimpse of his work through the constant clouds of smoke from the chain-smoking priest. Another housing rights hero, Ana Selman, was completely dedicated to protecting the rights of slum dwellers but was nonetheless—as were we all—terrified when travelling with me and Grahame Russell of RightsAction as we wound for hours in a leaking boat down the polluted Rio Ozama, which courses through many of Santo Domingo's worst slums. We recorded a bit of that trip on a handheld recorder during which time Grahame did his best imitation of Colonel Kurtz in *Apocalypse Now* endlessly repeating, "The horror, the horror, the horror...."

I worked incessantly on the human rights situation in the Dominican Republic, throughout the 1990s. During this time, half of the larger island of Hispaniola hosted numerous international guests who celebrated the five hundredth anniversary of Columbus' accidental landing there in 1492, which initiated centuries of occupation, colonialism, genocide, and so many additional crimes. In the five-year run up to the 1992 celebrations, Balaguer wanted to "beautify" Santo Domingo by removing as many of the slums as he could guide his bulldozers into. Beyond this, he constructed a huge structure called the Columbus Lighthouse which bizarrely projected a massive Christian cross of light into the sky every night as it got dark, reminding the people of both God and Columbus—and that he alone was in charge of the country. Slums surrounded the location where the Lighthouse was built and those communities that weren't yet bulldozed had walls built around them so visitors coming into town from the airport wouldn't be able to see the true legacy of this megalomaniac. I tried to meet with the president on many occasions but he never offered an invitation. I saw him once walking in the city's nicest park, surrounded by at least 100 soldiers guarding him and leading his way. Billboards of his alleged "accomplishments," often meaning the decimation of the poor, were strewn throughout the city, always with the slogan "Brought to you by Balaguer" in big and bright letters.

Life Lesson No. 11: Universally speaking, dictators are bad for housing rights—all rights for that matter—but democracies don't always get it right either.

The mass, violent and forced evictions began in earnest in the late 1980s and it was these blatant human rights violations that led the local NGOs to get in touch with me to seek my assistance at the UN. During a discussion with Australian law professor Philip Alston, a member of the UN Committee on Economic, Social and Cultural Rights at that time and soon to be its chairperson, he suggested I go to the DR and prepare a report on the forced evictions there. This facilitated the first of many visits, usually flying directly from Holland on my then-beloved Martin Air, where smoking was allowed, or sometimes through Madrid, which had closer ties to Latin America than most of Europe, where I lived at the time.

The feeling of the hot tropical air on my skin after such long periods in the cold and dark of northern Europe was just so refreshing until it became oppressive which usually didn't take long. I generally stayed in the same apartment in downtown Santo Domingo and became good friends with a guy there named Juan, with whom I would always sip Cuba Libres immediately upon arrival, practice my Spanish and get all the inside political gossip of what had happened since I was last in town. I still remember landing in Santo Domingo for the first time and seeing old Air Cubana planes that had just arrived from Fidel and Che's Cuba, the next big island to the west. It confirmed I was right in the middle of the action—just where I wanted to be.

Rafaelito was always there waiting for me at the arrivals hall, this time, and every other time I flew in which always immediately put me in a good mood. This guy was so damn suave and from his demeanor and the way he dressed, gold chains, grease in his hair and all the rest, he wanted every woman on the island to know it. He always got me to every single one of the hundreds of destinations we went to together over the years, never late, never crashing, always drinking, always laughing.

I vividly recall the first time we drove together and when I saw up close the slums of the city as we rolled into the center of town. Crossing a bridge and seeing the community of La Cienega-Los Guandules for the first time, I could have never guessed that this place would figure so prominently in the work I would do in the coming years. And what a place it was as you can see on the cover of this book. Home to more than 70,000 souls, all of whom lived in conditions most people reading this simply could not imagine having not been there in person, as it is with all slums, I suppose. But it was their home and they wanted to stay there as long as they could. Located in the infamous Zona Norte, like many of Santo Domingo's slums, La Cienega-Los Guandules became a frequent stop for me whenever I was in town. This was especially true after I got the UN to issue a first-of-its-kind order to the DR government and Balaguer to repeal a presidential decree calling for the immediate eviction of the huge neighborhood. The UN decision made headlines in all of the main newspapers, usually quoting straight from our press release, and with huge letters proclaiming, "UN Condemns Government, Demands Stop to All Evictions." Remarkably, and especially so to those who believe the UN has no enforcement powers or real influence, Balaguer quickly cancelled the decree, and the community was saved. What a victory.

Going to La Cienega-Los Guandules after this decision with my Dominicano activist friends amazed me. After Chichi told them who I was, more than once the joyous crowd mobbed me, so thankful to this skinny gringo who had spent so much time and energy trying to save their settlement. This was surely one of the most satisfying moments of my entire human rights life, knowing for certain that my efforts, hundreds of hours of my very own personal exertions at (happily) extremely low and often no pay combined with the courageous efforts of COPADEBA and the slum dwellers themselves, led to this outcome. It helped prevent a violent forced eviction, saving the homes of more than 70,000 people. It made all the losses, all the failed attempts at justice worth it. It was so gratifying to know that it was the UN itself that proved to be the vehicle, the address of hope, for this little act of justice in an otherwise all too unjust world. Being a direct part of a UN decision that made a huge difference in the lives of so many was just so heart-warming. Watching law, theory, and strategy merge into reality in a way that benefited so many people who were certainly not used to benefiting from anything took my breath away.

Even though La Cienega-Los Guandules is poor, under-serviced (if serviced at all), a bit fragrant and sometimes rough, people there—and in just about every slum I have been in—took pride in their place on Earth, especially the women. Potted plants were placed in front of every shack, efforts were made to hand sweep the dirt paths regularly, and all the shacks were painted in bright tropical colors with excess paints donated by a local charity. In this slum, and slums everywhere, it feels like entering a perpetual building site, with people hammering, sawing, and nailing non-stop. There's always work to be done to build new homes or improve the shaky shacks billions of people call home. The people made the place look as good as it could against all odds.

Surrounded by crazy guys running cock fights, the never-ending boom of merengue music coming from every corner and avoiding some of the more than mangy, hairless, and scabies-ridden dogs that called this place, and every slum in the world home, a middle-aged woman invited me into her self-constructed dwelling for coffee to express her thanks. Her husband had died during the struggle to save the slum so she was in equal parts overjoyed to be able to stay and still heavily distraught that the love of her life was gone forever. I saw some movement through the wooden slats that made up the walls of her relatively spacious but rudimentary shack out back and asked if someone was there, perhaps monitoring us. Balaguer's henchmen started following me after this victory. My many TV appearances and newspaper interviews meant my normally incognito work was no longer as possible as it usually was. I ask the recently widowed woman if someone was there, and she says in Spanish, "Yes, it's my daughter, Josefina." I respond in Spanish, "Can I open the door and say hello to her?" She excitedly says yes and yells through the slats introducing me as the human rights foreigner guy who helped the slum at the UN.

I then opened the fragile door, loose on its hinges, and immediately fall in love with the most beautiful woman I have ever seen in my life. As I begin to melt and tremble, there was an extraordinary destiny-like quality to this moment and the sudden presence of a Kosmic kind of *Eros* that simply cannot be humanly manufactured. It was beyond love, certainly beyond lust, and clearly beyond anything I had ever experienced before. Speechless, legs wobbling, and trying to smile back at the most exquisite smile I had ever seen, I mumbled something, standing there thunderstruck in disbelief that this could happen to me when I least expected it—in the middle of a bad slum, in a rough town, on a steamy tropical afternoon just before the rain, with the music playing and fighting birds crowing in the background. I finally muttered in Spanish, "Josefina, this ... is... incredible ... it is just sooooo nice to meet you." She responded the same way, as amazed and wobbly-kneed as I was. In that moment, we both knew that somehow destiny had melded us together, bringing us mysteriously to the same place at the same time just to know that each other was out there, and that perhaps this was meant to be.

Time froze. We both speechlessly gazed into each other's eyes but neither of us could say anything. My mind raced trying to figure out what to do. I could see her mind racing, too. My friends began noticing what was going on and as I looked over at them briefly, they smiled in instant recognition that something very special was uderway. They finally intervened and told me we had to go to our next destination before either Josefina or I could come up with a plan to meet again but before we could a crowd formed and off we went to explore other parts of La Cienega. In the end, this relationship otherwise written in the stars lasted mere minutes, but I know, just as I suspect Josefina does, that some part of each of us remains forever within the other and so shall it forevermore be. May you, too, find your very own Josefina one day when you least expect it.

Life Lesson No. 12: Keep your eyes open because love and kindness can be found just about anywhere—and when you least expect it.

And it wasn't just La Cienega-Los Guandules that got my attention but countless other slums dotted across Santo Domingo, all of which deserved assistance. We worked with the "under-bridge dwellers" who were always threatened with eviction and who were given special mention within later UN decisions. We spent a lot of time in various resettlement sites that were always located way on the outskirts of town where the land was cheapest and the economy weakest. Former inner-city slum dwellers watched helplessly as their homes were demolished and they were relocated to the town's outskirts, where their attempts to start over often failed.

I remember visiting another resettlement site and entering the paltry homes with cracked walls, no jobs, and no hope. This site was not the result of an eviction but established after a brutal earthquake decades earlier, the people still angrily waiting to return home. At one point, even though we were obviously on the side of these earthquake victims and actively expressing our solidarity and support, people surrounded us, shoving their electricity and other bills into our faces, proving they had paid them and demanding respect. At one point, they got so riled up they began threatening our cameraman, so we quickly left before they lost control. If we ever needed proof that resettlement was anything but a panacea for displacement, this was it.

Beyond that, we worked in a whole range of other slums that occupy many of the precarious ravines of the city. It is in these places where you can find the worst slums. One of these was a place filled with some pretty rough gangs called Guachupita and in other insalubrious places found in the Zona Norte. In one such slum, a shack dweller took a certain liking to me and followed us around for hours, every few seconds pointing at a sick kid, a tumbledown shack, a dirty stream, a rabid dog. He would say "Check it out, hermano, check it out" in the only English he remembered from his stint in New York City, but what a perfect phrase to know in such a brutal place to live. Another day, Chichi took us to his half-built mother's house in a poor neighborhood, certainly better than the slum but still far from complete, signifying the long process slum dwellers endure to obtain an adequate home. They first improve their shack, then sell it to move to a better slum, repeating the cycle until—after decades of struggle—they finally build a home and maybe secure a land title, a process that can take 30 years or more.

Besides fighting the constant battles against evictions in the DR we carried out research with local University professors and discovered that the Master Plan of Santo Domingo was predicated on yet further, larger-scale evictions down the road, which again would lead to mass human rights violations. So, we fought this, too, and got changes made into the Plan.

After securing the UN's first-ever pronouncement of housing rights violations in the country in 1991 and creating a series of other precedents, such as canceling the La Cienega-Los Guandules decree, we convinced the UN to send a team of investigators of their own to Santo Domingo to witness the scale of the problems firsthand.

Before we knew it, a few months later we were back in town yet again to coincide with the UN visit. Instead of staying at my usual apartment, we stayed in the same fancy hotel where the UN investigators were staying, allowing us to lobby them constantly during their visit. Despite opposition by the government, the UN insisted that us NGO types were able to visit slums with them and to be present during meetings with government officials. This was openness and transparency writ large and our local Dominican partners and our team deeply appreciated this inclusive approach by the UN.

This didn't particularly endear me with the authorities in this then dictatorship and after all my media appearances I was a tiny bit paranoid at the airport that I might be hassled by the guards but they just waved me on through, smiles and good vibes in abundance, in a manner very different to how I was treated years later in Israel. Who knows, they could have easily been residents of La Cienega-Los Guandules themselves, and if true, that wouldn't have surprised me one bit. Think about it the next time you cross an international border into or out of a poor country and ask yourself where that woman guard arrived from this morning for her shift? What type of home did that guy sleep in last night? Are these uniformed officials representing the State actually slum dwellers like 50% of the other residents of this town?

I've been able to do more than my fair share of media interviews over the years and have had cameras and microphones shoved in my face and gooey make-up applied more than a few times. In one of these I remember—on what they told me was the most popular daytime TV show in the country—the producer came into the make-up room where they were preparing my gringo face for the lights and asked my name. I said Scott Leckie, and he replied with what I also thought was Scott Leckie. He asked me my story about the slums and the UN and all that, and then said again, Scott Leckie? in a question, which to me sounded like 'Sco Lehi'. I said yes. Just 30 seconds before my live interview, I heard him telling the interviewer my name. Instead of "Scott Leckie," in a classic lost-in-translation moment, he says, "El experto del derecho a vivienda, de Holanda, bienvenidos a Señor Ecko Guiy." And then before I can correct him or the interviewer, I see on the monitor of the live feed my face and underneath is written 'Ecko Guiy, experto de derechos humanos'. So, there I was not as Scott Leckie but as *Ecko Guiy* telling stories of slums, of human rights, the UN and my love for the people of this amazing land. Some good friends still call me Ecko Guiy to this very day.

I feel so at home in Santo Domingo, as I have the good fortune of feeling in dozens upon dozens of places across the world where I have been so lucky to have lived, worked, and visited. The rum bars, the narrow streets, the street vendors, the soul of the people are just part of life in the DR, as is the ever-present merengue, of course. Even in the touristy Plaza Colonial, slum kids still sell roasted peanuts, swinging their charcoal burners through the air, constantly swirling them around, to keep the coals hot and the peanuts warm.

And the single time in all of my many visits to the DR that I went to a place where the tourists usually go, way on the other side of the island, it was actually great. Travelling with my Dutch photojournalist friend, Sijmen Hendriks, we avoided other gringos and immediately befriended two local criminals. They tried to convince us to take their taxi, warning about the "mafia" waiting along the road to pounce on anyone not with a local. I had travelled enough to know this scam and let them know it. We all laughed and I snuck them into our fancy resort every day for the rest of the week getting them free Cuba Libres and Piña Coladas all day long which they very much enjoyed. They were both cane field workers by day and harmless petty criminals at night, so would stash their machetes in the deep undergrowth just outside the hotel so as not to arouse suspicions. When they'd ask us if we wanted them to climb a nearby coconut tree and get us one, we'd—of course—say yes. They'd scamper up the tree, twist off the best coconut, let it drop and then use their very sharp machetes to lop the top off, carve a little scooper out of the top portion and make a hole big enough to drink from. After the milk was done, they'd chop some more and we'd then use the scoop to get the delicious coconut flesh into our mouths just as fast as we could. Gracias Cruzito y Raul, hermanos por siempre! Que lo que? You sure made Ecko Guiy a happy man!

Thailand - Klong Toey

Thailand is one of the world's truly delightful nations and a place where I feel more at home than just about anywhere else. I have been visiting this extraordinary never colonized place for more than 30 years and was fortunate to have called its capital Bangkok home for seven wonderful years. Though Bangkok's glitz and glamour, its merger of Buddhist tradition with capitalistic modernity, and its open-minded, kind, and deeply calm way of being are pervasive, all too often its international reputation for freewheeling vice in which too many young mostly foreign men indulge is what people think of first when the name of this city is mentioned in casual conversation. Yet, this utterly naïve view captures really only a tiny part of one of the world's most extraordinary cities. You can visit and even live there as I have and virtually never encounter the tourist excesses carried out in this incredible town unless you actively seek them out, as far too many one-tine visitors and gnarled retirees tend to do. Once—and only once—I explored one of the famous seamy alleyways after two well-known human rights activists from other regions of the world that I was hosting insisted that they couldn't leave Thailand without seeing it all up close and personal. We were then briefly immersed in a sewer of toxic unhinged testosterone-fuelled masculinity all around us at such a level that I had to quickly flee as the horrors of the moment overwhelmed me.

Of course, Bangkok is anything but a bastion of purity; what big city is? But if you choose to avoid the limited places where carnal excesses are there for all to see, the true, far more prevalent and often enchanting Bangkok will emerge; the city of canals, of small and green, shade-filled side lanes, barefoot monks strolling in the early morning hours through the still largely empty streets, the city of smiles—some fake, most totally real—the city of such sublime food, the city of exquisite hotels and spas, the city of hidden sois (alleyways), the city of temples and the city of kindness and respect. Then there's the other city; the city of slums, the city of too much traffic, too much concrete, too much pollution and too many shopping malls. Bangkok has it all and there are few places anywhere on the globe that I love more than this City of Angels as it is known, and indeed much more so than that other City of Angels where I was born so many decades ago, LA.

Life Lesson No. 13: Home can be anywhere you allow it to be.

It is the mysterious nature of so many of Bangkok's stories that add tangible intrigue to this magnificent town, which keeps aiming at glitzy, but all too often falls just a little short. With that much constant heat and that much cement it would be hard not to. Indelible and strengthening democracy driven solely by the popular will of the population seems to be constantly kept at bay and never quite fully breaks through. Just as it seems to take hold and begin to provide the benefits, back the democratic genie is put into its tightly closed bottle, awaiting another try down the road. On top of that, military coups are a rather frequent occurrence in Thailand. Since 1932, some 22 separate coup d'états have taken place, an average of almost one every four years. During our time along the Chao Phraya River where we dwelled, in 2006, we lived through one of these coups. We found out about it when we awoke. I looked out the eighth-floor window and the streets were eerily empty. I then quickly turned on our TV and put the channel on a local station where we discovered a solemn screen with patriotic martial music being played. We turned the channel to another station and the same exact programming appeared. We changed channels again and the same. It was only when we found the BBC that we learned that a coup had just taken place. Fortunately, it was largely bloodless. It was presented and justified as a means of preventing a massive loss of lives, as clashes between two sides—the so-called Red Shirts and Yellow Shirts—seemed imminent at various hotspots across the city. Within hours of the ouster of the billionaire Prime Minister Thaksin Shinawatra, you would have been hard pressed to find any sign of the coup and things returned largely to normal, though with the military in charge. These processes have played out over and over again over the past century or so. This turned out to be one of the comparatively undisruptive coup d'états but it certainly didn't feel like it would be the last.

This truly unique city, the biggest city in a nation built around face, surface, and appearance, has a soft *facade* of smiles, hands together in a *wai* instead of a handshake, all orchids, all blossoms, and lime sodas. Bangkok, and indeed, all of Thailand is so overwhelming the first-time people visit, and few experiencing this can have imagined just how kind and gentle the people could be. But this city remains a huge urban agglomeration and no city in the Global South has yet to become perfect, and as with cities everywhere, the slums remain.

Indeed, more than a thousand slums provide community and homes to hundreds of thousands of Bangkok's poor. Compared to slums in many other Asian, African, or Latin American cities, these are generally "good slums" according to my friend Father Joe Maier who lives and works in the biggest slum of all, Klong Toey. Most houses there are connected to electricity and equipped with TV, radio, and even pretty decent drainage by local standards, at least. But still, these are slums and replete with all the good and bad that these areas always possess.

I first met Father Joe in India in the 1980s, and he's remained a friend ever since. He has lived in Klong Toey since the 1960s, working as a Catholic clergyman, though in many ways he acts more like a Buddhist. Joe's dedication to the poor is truly humbling to witness and whenever I am in Bangkok, I always spend at least a day or two of every trip with him in Klong Toey, marveling at his Human Development Centre and Mercy Centre complex which provides schools, medical care, food and social workers for street children and victims of domestic violence. People have written several books about Father Joe, or Khun Pah, as he is affectionately known. Over the years, his efforts have led to the construction of dozens of kindergartens, providing education to thousands of children who otherwise had no access, a process which also serves the dual purpose of being an effective anti-eviction strategy. It's a lot harder for the authorities to send in the bulldozers if there's a school in the way. Klong Toey is very close to the centre of Bangkok, squeezed as it is between highways, shipping ports and the river, and as a result has been threatened with eviction for decades as property values have continued to increase. Slowly but surely developers have been chipping away at the edges of Klong Toey, evicting a section here and a section there, but the core of Klong Toey remains very much intact. Some sections of Klong Toey are far worse than others, but most homes are in decent shape, though some new investment there would surely improve conditions greatly.

Before he once became deathly ill and his associates insisted that he move into a better dwelling, Fr. Joe lived in the poorest part of Klong Toey with the Catholic Thais who all worked in the nearby slaughterhouse, Buddhists being rather reluctant to do this work. That home of his there was, no matter what he may say, on the outer edges of human habitability. I went there a few times, and it definitely wasn't great, but I admired him so much for living there with the poor in exactly the same conditions as them.

Getting there meant risking a fall through a wonky walkway over a river so polluted that rubbish and detritus obscured the visible water. Rats would sometimes crawl over him while he slept. Some of his neighbors involved themselves in dangerous night-time activities. I asked Joe how he could handle living in such utter squalor for so many years and he admirably said "Well, if the poor live there, then I will live there." As simple and selfless as that. He was close friends with Catholic mystic Thomas Merton, and it was Joe who discovered Merton's lifeless body—after a very premature death—in his Bangkok home on December 10, 1968, the twentieth anniversary of the signing of the Universal Declaration of Human Rights, International Human

Rights Day.

Joe shared amazing stories about his social work during the Vietnam War all across the region, especially when he walked through an isolated part of Laos to a village suffering from a severe US bombing. The US military dropped more bombs on Laos than it dropped during the entire WWII period, lest we forget. Let's just say that the thousands of perfectly circular lakes one sees when flying over Laos did not form naturally. Joe and his fellow social workers came across a bend in the track and then reached the top of a hill where they found an abandoned mortar site, still full of both mortars and ammunition. I wonder what happened next.

In his later years, Joe became a fan of the Grateful Dead much to my joy. I'd been haranguing him for years about the amazing sounds that occur at a Dead show and after sending him link after link of some of their best shows, he *got it*. So much so, that it's all we seem to talk about when we're together these days in his greatly improved home, smack dab right in the middle of Klong Toey. The last time I watched Dead & Company play the song "Sugaree" in person was along the beach in Mexico in 2019 during what became their annual four-night run there every January. The second I heard the notes coming from Bobby and John's guitars, I called Joe on my iPhone from the middle of the pit, where I was with my pal Jaap—who came all the way from Holland while I came from Australia—just a few meters from the band, and yelled into the phone, "I have no idea what time it is in Bangkok, and I can't hear anything you're saying, but listen now, they're playing your song." Up I held the phone so ole selfless Joe, the Buddhist Catholic could hear his favorite song live, up close, and almost personal, right in the middle of Bangkok's biggest slum. "I'll meet you at the Jubilee", his most beloved line in that wonderful Dead classic. See you at the jubilee, Joe!

Besides Klong Toey, the poor community of Bangkok that I spent the most time in was the amazing neighborhood of Pom Mahakhan, right near the Golden Temple of Wat Saket and just a short stroll away from the regional UN Headquarters on Ratchadamnoen Road. After being in place for more than 200 years, the wooden homes and Bodhi trees were a living testament to a place with a history that was very much alive. Pom fought a valiant and long 25-year battle against eviction, which sadly ended in the demolition of this ancient community in 2018.

The whole time I lived in Bangkok from 2003-2009, I worked with the community and its main leader Khun Gob to help them resist the looming eviction threats. I was truly heartbroken when I learned of its demise. The local city government had responded very reasonably to the public criticism of their eviction plans, the UN condemnation of the potential eviction, and the growing public support the community had received from people far and wide. Every time I went there something new had been developed by the community themselves. One time, they had barricaded all the entrances, using the last section of the historical old and white city wall as a strong barrier against invasion. Another time, they had put up permanent and exquisitely ornate signs in both English and Thai in front of each house, each tree, each temple, very professionally done, outlining their historical importance to Bangkok and Thailand as a whole. We made a film about their struggle in 2004 that you can still find online, and which shows what an incredibly resilient and well-organized community the residents of Pom were. I hope and pray all of those wonderful residents were able to find a decent way forward and that they will never forget Pom, for I will certainly never forget them.

Philippines – The Grateful Dead Rocks a Quezon City Slum

When the world is at peace, when all things are tranquil and all men obey their superiors in all their courses, then music can be perfected. When desires and passions do not turn into wrongful paths, music can be perfected. Perfect music has its cause. It arises from equilibrium. Equilibrium arises from righteousness, and righteousness arises from the meaning of the cosmos. Therefore, one can speak about music only with a man who has perceived the meaning of the cosmos.
—Hermann Hesse, The Glass Bead Game

No one can live a life of work alone, and the non-work realms of life are just as important, and indeed, central to living not just a full, good, and very *examined* life, but a human rights life, as well. And when life offers up the opportunity to dramatically merge the work and non-work elements of life into a memorable moment of magic, how could anyone not accept such a compelling invitation. Music, mysticism, and mind-altering experiences are all key parts of this, at least for me. Besides my visits to so many countries for human rights work and the long hours spent behind screens writing too many books and publications, there is so much more. For everyone, there are— whether our personalities (or in some cases, religious beliefs) allow us to admit it or not—crucial moments of sex, drugs and rock and roll— thank you Ian Dury—that we will forever remember as some of our most beautiful moments. Not to be too crude, but even if you've had erotic experiences with far fewer people than the youthful you may have hoped, and your drugs are antidepressants, caffeine, or sugar, with Van Halen, ABBA, Barry Manilow, Milli Vanilli, or AC/DC occupying the top spots on your list of rock and roll favorites, these things are somehow a part of who you are. So, let's withhold any judgments here even if more interesting items in each of these three categories might be far more preferable. And yet, if your life feels like it has too few of these sensory and sensual attributes, or perhaps few or no experiences whatsoever with local culinary delights, reading novels, forests, jungles, biking, growing food, waves, mountains, kayaking, travel, family life, religion, oceans, art, running, walking, films, meditating, books, boats, sports, cooking and so much more, it might be time for a bit of extra-curricular exploration.

At this point in my rather frenetic life, though it remains very high energy in nature with a never-ending stream of projects always underway, it tends to be more localized, more stable, more settled. After decades of almost never saying no to the next job offer, the next trip, the next amazing adventure, my quest now tends far more towards *being* than *doing*, just as it is infinitely more towards becoming *nobody* than striving to become *somebody*. For me, having fewer and fewer possessions is a much higher ideal than acquiring more, and with each material possession I give away, recycle or discard, I feel more free, more at peace, more able to embrace the world and love all of its people. Days on which I use no electricity other than the solar energy generated by the panels on my roof and stored on the battery on my outside wall, spend no money, consume only food that I have grown, and use no plastic or fossil fuels in any way are the best days, and if I strive for anything it is days like those where the imperfections I leave on the Earth are as small as possible.

It is important to remember here it is not the poor who are destroying the world, it is the wealthy. For instance, in 2026, the wealthiest of the wealthy of the world and the 1% are responsible for more than 70% of the world's CO2 emissions, gorging themselves on empty pleasures, killing the Earth one CO2 molecule after another, most of them effectively giving a huge middle finger to the rest of the world, living the pathetic lie that "He who dies with the most toys wins." For these greedy creatures who fly on their private jets and drive their ugly Hummers, who thrive as they kill Earth, I feel both disdain and nausea but also sorrow and pity, tinged with a sense of anger that they should really know better. There is something clearly pathological about living a life dedicated to a never-ending future of *more*, never able to be satisfied with what they have. You can see it in their eyes. Deep down inside they know they will die. They know their lives are impermanent, and they even know there are other paths available but they're to a one too afraid to follow them. Their embrace of foolhardy beliefs based on fear and faith in the unprovable only gets them so far, so they live on deceiving themselves into believing that pure consumption will let them live forever, and off they go to consume for another day.

Sure, we all need some material things, but has it ever crossed your mind why it seems so different for the richest among us to just be satisfied with a certain degree of financial security, a certain amount of simple living in a good house, with good food and close family nearby, and maybe friends everywhere who give so much but cost so little? What they have clearly yet to figure out is that most of the things you'll remember, where true beauty and life's meaning emerge, have nothing whatsoever to do with money or cost as the indigenous peoples of the world so clearly show us if we are curious and willing enough to listen.

For me, one of those evenings that cost almost nothing, but which gave so much happened on a night when the music was perfected like

Hesse imagined. That was the night that the sounds of Jerry Garcia and Pigpen belted shatteringly loud along with the rest of the Grateful Dead through the ether in one of the gnarliest slums in Metro Manila, located right next to the Quezon City Municipal Rubbish Dump. The music of the Grateful Dead has been a part and parcel of my life since I first attended a show at the San Francisco Civic Auditorium with my Deadhead girlfriend, Lise Saffran, on December 30, 1983—a night that, without exaggeration, changed my life forever. From the first notes of *Bertha*, the opening song that night, I knew something special had hit me. The Dead is the only band to *never* play the same show twice—quite a feat. I lucked out hearing them open the always elongated and seamless second set with the inimitable *Shakedown Street*, followed shortly thereafter with the *Mind Left Body Jam* (which they played for the first time since October 1974). Then they played *Truckin'* (the first Dead song I'd ever heard years before on the radio), *Wharf Rat* (which became the first Dead song I ever learned on guitar —hint: the opening chords are really easy) and ended the show with *Day Job* (which many Deadheads consider their least favorite song). But I liked it. "Keep your day job till your night job pays...." it unfolds; I guess not enough Deadheads had night jobs that paid, though I know most wish they did.

Even with all my human rights trips, international moves, and adventures, rare is the day when the Dead's music hasn't graced my ears. Indeed, as I write this they are playing in the background. My life, like millions of others, has been enhanced, improved, awe-inspired—by the offerings of this unique band. In recent years I would travel to places like Mexico, Dodger Stadium in LA, San Francisco, or the Gorge in Washington State to watch their latest formation Dead & Company play. Not everyone gets it, but those who do, *really* get it and it seems to stick with just about everyone inducted into its unique way of making the music perfect.

One of the guys who *got* it was an extraordinary man named Boy Carrillo. Boy was a tireless activist in the slums of Manila, who when I met him was, much to my utter delight and surprise, already a Deadhead. Having travelled very far and wide across the world, I've found that Deadheads are almost exclusively isolated to the United States, with just a handful in Europe and other regions. Oddly, there's quite a few in Japan, much to my amazement when I found that out. So, when I met a pre-existing Deadhead in the middle of a Manila slum, there is no possible way I could feel anything else other than joy and a dose of magic.

Manila, what comes first to mind? Would it be that famous 1975 boxing match between Muhammad Ali and Joe Frazier memorably deemed a *thrilla* by America's Howard Cosell? Chicken Adobo? The world's kindest people? Smokey Mountain? People Power ousting dictators? Dictators using their power to crush the people? A Cardinal named Sin? These and other wonders pierced my mind as I entered the Philippine capital for the first time back in 1992 after some extraordinary days in Hong Kong where I visited all the dismal housing sites just about no one else sees when they visit the rich, once British enclave. After that first trip to the former US colony, I headed to Manila a few times until I realized my efforts wouldn't yield what I had initially hoped for. However, I partook in some seriously memorable moments in a country I will always love, especially for the incredible army of nurses this poor nation has sent worldwide to care for the ill—and many of whom helped heal me at Holmesglen Hospital in Melbourne in early 2021. I love you all my Filipina and Filipino healers!

The first time I met Boy I was at a housing rights forum, and the positive jolt I got from meeting this high-energy guy was fantastic. This bubbly wild man, with his gap-toothed grin and badass demeanor, was such a selfless activist. After sharing human rights stories, Boy and I became fast friends and then discovered his love for Santana and then the Grateful Dead. I was amazed at this, to say the least, for it's not as if the Dead had ever played Manila before. And so, at a certain point, Boy says "Hey, man, why don't you come to my slum tonight with whatever Dead cassettes you have, and I will wire the whole place up with our 20 speakers. We can have a wild night rockin' to the Dead." As if I could ever say no to such an offer.

Boy had worked all throughout Manila's famous slums that dominate so many parts of this city—Tondo, Commonwealth, Smokey Mountain, Pasig River and so many others. Tonight, though, we'd be heading towards his home slum next to the Quezon City Municipal Rubbish Dump, and we'd be partying with the heroic garbage men who lived and worked there. I grabbed my Canadian architect pal Graeme

Bristol and off we headed, bouncing along in one of Manila's millions of Jeepneys heading towards the adventurous evening. I'd brought four cassette tapes with me of Dead shows from the early and mid-1970s, considered by many to have been the best years of this band, not planning on playing all of them. But, in the end, we did precisely that.

Of all the millions upon millions of Deadhead moments across the world since they began playing in 1965, few could possibly have compared to this moist and steamy night in the depths of the Manila slum. Boy had literally wired up a big chunk of the community with some massive speakers, the sort they must have normally used to make community announcements or for political campaign speeches or religious gatherings. But tonight, it was Jerry's and Bob's guitars, Phil's bass, Pigpen's wails and Bill and Mickey's drums gracing a very grateful slum. I could not believe just how loud Boy was able to make these speakers blast and am quite sure they kept a lot of people awake even if their shacks were very far away. We drank local beers, ate some seriously good Chicken Adobo, despite being offered fresh dog meat cooked with a blow torch, legs splayed on a makeshift vertical grill. I politely declined, despite pleas that I was rejecting the best and most expensive meat of all. After all those libations, I frequently excused myself to hit the rudimentary outhouse. Every damn time, dozens of gigantic frogs awaited me—the biggest I've ever seen—the size of a ripe honeydew melon. Fear coursed through my veins, imagining they were a special breed with teeth, ready to bite anything hanging above their heads. They all gazed up at me whenever I returned, so it was like running the gauntlet every time, though fear of an errant bite receded with each subsequent visit.

When Boy pushed the bright red "On" button, it felt like he had activated—and cranked it up to eleven—the Dead's real Wall of Sound, designed by sound magician Stanley Owsley, in a nod to the Spinal Tap lads. "Hey Boy, how in the hell did you get it to be so loud?", I asked. His reply, a simple "In the slum, ours goes to eleven." I couldn't believe he knew that line! Remembering this epic night, which was preceded by a visit to a 1950's style American diner where Boy's wife, Estella, worked as a waitress on roller skates, I can still hear the opening notes of the epic version of *Morning Dew* of May 26, 1972, pouring from the massive speakers scattered across the slum. Holding a very cold bottle of San Miguel, the only intoxicant of the night, I shed a tear for the unfathomable beauty of the moment—dancing with my garbage men pals—and another tear knowing that, despite the joy, their chances of escaping the slum were nearly zero. As all of our legs began getting a bit too wobbly and the sound system began getting a bit too crackly in the wee hours of the hot and sweaty Manila night at 5 a.m., we called it quits—our bodies, our minds, our souls merging with one another, as we wound our way back to the road, morning dew-laden bushes sprinkling our sleeves with the beginnings of a new day.

Life Lesson No. 14: Great music sounds even better in the slum.

Life Lesson No. 15: If the volume knob goes up to 11, use that option.

Chapter 3

Law

"Let us remember: One book, one pen, one child, and one teacher can change the world."

—Malala Yousafzai

It may sound somewhat adolescent to even ask, but hasn't every one of us wanted at some point in life to *change the world for the better*, even if just a little bit? Despite all of the reasons not to feel this way, my faith in humans remains strong enough to believe that virtually everyone has at least once thought about how to make the world a better place, even if only to protect their children or improve their own circumstances. Such thoughts crossed the mind of Malala early in her life as she struggled to access education as a girl in the repressive community of her youth. Such ideas only crossed my mind, however, when I was 18 years old. Once I personally grasped this notion, my first thought was: how does one even begin going about trying to achieve this impossible dream? I had no idea, other than desperately wanting to reduce human suffering, expedite that change, and strengthen the tools needed to enhance justice for the poor and oppressed.

I knew the UN was probably as good a vehicle as I could find for these efforts; I just needed to figure out how to get there. Once I did, for many years I gave it my absolute all to bring to life new laws and decisions through the various human rights bodies of the UN and within scores of national governments with the sole objective of using the law not to entrench privilege or to preserve power, but rather to reduce misery and enhance justice. I may not have achieved my dreams of justice for all, but I did chip away making small differences along the way.

I always pursued the ideas I found in a book I happened across by coincidence in 1983 in an old and charming thatched roof house of my friend Jaap in the small Dutch village of Eerbeek. The book had been published in the 1960s or early 1970s and was called *The War of the Flea*. In my latest face-to-face moment with history, it was in this very house that Jaap's father had on three separate occasions hidden in a secret chamber from the Nazis during their ruthless occupation of the Netherlands from 1940-1945. All these decades later, standing in the secret hiding place that had saved Jaap's father's life, sent chills down my spine, a feeling I can still conjure up to this day.

The War of the Flea made the brilliant point that the liberation movements of the 1960s fighting against colonial domination all across the world were essentially wars of the flea; the tiny flea, so capable of hiding and moving at will, and able to harass and attack the dog sending it into a self-destructive frenzy and almost always winning in the end. Over the decades I saw my role as playing the human rights flea, not with violence but with innovation, creativity, stealth, boundless energy, and commonsensical initiatives. As the quiet and determined legal flea, I found myself pushing issue after issue from the edges of political concern into the human rights mainstream. Once these new ideas became entrenched in the middle ground, I would then pull back, let them blossom into whatever it was they would bloom into, and then do it all over again with the next issue I found worthy enough to spend time on.

Another strategy involved trying to change the language and terminology used within the human rights lexicon to describe certain human rights standards or principles I was working on by developing memorable names of new legal texts, as well as acronyms. Many of these, indeed most, appear to have stuck and these processes have helped to entrench ways of thinking within the social justice and human rights fields. The origins of many of these remain unknown, but I know and can assure you that these will remain secret forever. Simply changing the linguistic usage of how certain issues are described and defined in conversation and in law can make a very real difference in the lives of real people on the ground.

Beyond this, for years I tried to create all sorts of international legal precedents, many of which continue to bear fruit. Sometimes this would involve a simple procedural maneuver that had never been tried before. If it worked and was not opposed, the precedent was set. Other times it would involve inserting a single word or sentence into a UN resolution that once approved, would again constitute an important legal precedent that could be used by others. This was referred to commonly as "legislative authority." There were hundreds of times we did this successfully. I believed so strongly in the power of international law and the utility it could have in assisting reasonable governments to better protect their populations, that I helped create numerous institutions and political posts within the United Nations which remain in place, and about which the major media outlets of the world write about almost every day. I always tried to push the envelope and guided by reason and hope to make it easier for the non-committed to grab onto and embrace as their own. Sometimes I won, sometimes I lost. But no matter whether the wins outnumbered the losses or vice versa, there remains a part of me that is still amazed that I was able to achieve anything at all, let alone guiding so many new laws, ideas and perspectives through this opaque and intensely complex and heavily politicized system. As I work today on issues relating to world citizenship and promoting the idea of our need for a unified planet that I call a oneness world, I am hopeful that these ideas, too, will become increasingly embraced sooner than later.

Beyond using the legal strategies of the flea, part of the reason I was able to provoke so many positive changes within the human rights world was simply lucky timing. I had the good fortune of emerging into an activist just as the Iron Curtain was falling across Europe in the late 1980s. This historic time ushered in the dawn of a new political era. For a few precious years, perhaps peaking in 1998, this opening allowed the UN to fulfill its original purposes, as elaborated with the adoption of the UN Charter during its inaugural meeting in 1945 (where my granddad Arthur Bernard Leckie managed security). Between 1945 and 1989, initiative after initiative was made impossible because of Cold War considerations that resulted in progressive ideas being blocked by the US and conservative issues blocked by the Soviet Union. After 1989, everything seemed possible, and for a while it actually was!

People optimistically called the post-Cold War era the time of the *peace dividend.* It created such a tumult within the organs of the UN that diplomats from the now former Soviet Union and its client states often had little idea as to what they should vote for and against. As NGOs, we very happily filled this gap of uncertainty. In fact, for the few NGOs that knew how to creatively use the system to the maximum extent, we were literally able to move mountains that were once seen as perpetually immovable. In a way, civil society effectively ran the human rights scene at the UN for a short but glorious time and we were able to get things through, official documents approved, and decisions made that no one could have dreamed of a few short years before.

I tried to capture the essence of this in my keynote speech some years after this new era began at the 2002 Bodyshop Human Rights Awards Ceremony in London where we honored some amazingly courageous housing rights heroes from around the globe. I ended my speech by trying to capture the essence of human rights at the time, with the following sentiments which I even feel stronger about today, even if the world may not:

Though the images we see on the media may make us believe otherwise, we do live in the era of human rights: Because average people took a stand, we now live in a world where many practices that were once deemed acceptable are now prohibited— slavery, torture, discrimination, segregation....I never give up hope that one day the human suffering that we now treat as inevitable—including homelessness, slums and evictions—can be added to this list.

Today in 2026 it feels eerily like the late 1990s and early 2000s might have been the high point of the human rights project in many ways and we took to it like bees to nectar. Knowing that so much of what we achieved in those years remains firmly in place, still constituting vital pieces in the larger human rights law puzzle—even though problems continue, feels like a solid achievement, nonetheless. Seeing documents that I individually conceived of, wrote, re-drafted and then guided through the official channels now frequently referred to in courtrooms and Parliaments around the world, as well as in the demands of grassroots groups everywhere truly satisfies me. Each in their own small ways did change the world, not nearly enough, but at least we nudged things in the right(s) direction.

From the time that I took my first international law class from my beloved Professor Tom Hovet at the University of Oregon in 1982, his white crew cut hair perfectly suiting this kind man, and in whose memory, I eternally bow, I have been obsessed and in love with this legal regime, warts, and all. Of all the things Hovet taught me, including my first human rights law class, it was his response to a question from a typical American viewpoint that made all the difference. One fellow student, cynically asked: "Professor, there's no enforcement mechanism under international law so it's violated all the time, isn't it?" A good and reasonable question to which he replied, "Well, I'd say it is actually complied with 99.9% of the time because it's in the direct interest of any State to do so. When it isn't, you read about it in the headlines of the newspaper the next day—invasions, occupations, genocide, violence." From the moment I heard that, I was hooked and remain so to this day.

Life Lesson No. 16: International law is complied with far more frequently than it is violated.

During my last year of college—the first year I fully gave it my intellectual all, especially about human rights—my meager brain's efforts somehow led me to receive the lowest score on the initial exam of my first-ever human rights class. I was not off to a good start. This brutal result, presumably influenced by my rather intense fondness for a certain fragrant substance devastated me. But after the initial blow hit, far from discouraging me, this bad grade super-charged my learning desires. After that, it was straight A's all the way through. Hovet even told me that I had improved the most of any of the thousands of students he had ever taught since he began his academic life after working in the White House with President Kennedy in the early 1960s. This super-charged me even more, and probably put me onto the human rights path more than just about anything else.

Inspired by Professor Arthur Hanhardt to consider a life in Europe and Professor Dan Goldrich to ponder a career in environmental politics, as well as Hovet's entreaties, my problem at the time was simply that I knew I wanted a politically active working life at the international level, but I couldn't decide which precise pathway to choose to pursue this, not to mention how in the world I could possibly make a living doing so. Over and over again I kept asking myself: "Which one and how will I know when I've found it?" When I asked Hovet outright for advice, he simply and so wisely said, "When you know, you'll know."

Life Lesson No. 17: Remember Dave Wottle. If you start out worst, there's a good chance you might end up first.

I pondered all of the available options open to me in the mid-1980s. My first real human rights stint involved volunteering at the Eugene Council for Human Rights in Central America where I directly dabbled for the first time in actual human rights issues. My favorite part of this work wasn't exactly legal in nature. Rather, I loved it the most when I would ride my blue one-speed bike across Eugene every Wednesday morning before the sun rose to gather wildflowers and fern fronds in the nearby Douglas Fir forest. Then I would visit generous florists located on the opposite side of town who donated flowers for the tables at the weekly Hard Times Lunches we hosted at the Council, usually riding through yet another rainstorm to get there in notoriously rainy Eugene. All of this took a minimum of five hours beore I finally made it to the Council with my donated and foraged wares.

Life Lesson No. 18: If you can grow your own food, do so; it will make your day just that much better.

On those Wednesdays, I would have an incredibly overloaded bike rack full of huge amounts of flowers and fern cuttings, looking not all that different from the overloaded bikes you see all across India and Bangladesh carrying their harvests of jute and wheat. I'd arrive at the Council, always excited for the unfolding day, and set out to arrange 50 bouquets as best I could—always short on vases and resorting to empty chili pepper jars to make up the shortfall. Thanks to all the cool Argentines, Chileans, Nicaraguans, Guatemalans, Mexicans and other cheerful Latinos and Latinas, I still remember the moment on a given Wednesday when I discovered empanadas for the first time, and then fresh coriander leaves, a taste I could not believe existed in the universe until it graced my tongue with the that initial blast of flavor. I grow it now throughout all seasons of the year and eat it almost every day these days.

During that time at the Council, where I once hosted a surprisingly well attended poetry reading, which included the first-ever public reading of one of my now hundreds of painful attempts at poetry, combined with Hovet's class, my high grade and his encouragement, along with my very active years in the local Amnesty International section in Eugene, all combined to help in my ultimate decision to choose international human rights law as the path I would first pursue in my relentless quest to make the world a better place. Hovet was right, and almost without warning I knew this was it. Just a few days later, as if a miracle, I walked into the University of Oregon bookstore for the first time in over a year. Filled as it was mostly with textbooks and other publications I would never buy or read, on a whim I went to the law section and jumping out at me is a purple book called *The International Law of Human Rights* by Paul Sieghart. I simply couldn't believe my eyes and almost teared up as I reached down to leaf through it. I had very little money, but nothing was going to stop me buying this Holy Grail of a book that ended up changing my life forever. I was more convinced than I had ever been to pursue a human rights life no matter the cost or hardship.

With or without a decent income, it would give me half a chance to make things better while serving as a springboard to take me beyond the US—to wherever the human rights world led. I was open to anything, anywhere, just about any time. Needless to say, I had no idea it would eventually take me to every continent except Antarctica. Not a bad decision with 20/20 hindsight but pretty risky at the time for a poor, committed human rights renegade. But where to go first?

In the mid-1980s, there were very few international NGOs and even fewer human rights organizations. With no accessible Internet, research always involved the beautiful University of Oregon library— a place I loved. That building appears in the classic film *Animal House*, which was filmed at the U of O campus, though the school's name was left out of the credits as a condition for permitting them to film there. I knew getting an international human rights job was unlikely without a second degree or more experience, so I went to the library to find opportunities outside the US, where I could gain both.

At this time there were virtually no regular human rights publications, so I was overwhelmed with joy when after manually leafing through the card catalogue, I came across a thick journal-like publication called *Human Rights Internet* (named way before *the* Internet became a household word known to everyone). It was published in Canada by a married couple, Laurie Wiseberg and Harry Scoble, both of whom I met a few years later in Geneva. I became good friends with Laurie who was incredibly active in human rights hotspots all over the world all the way into her late seventies. Looking through the library stacks, finding and then holding an edition of *Human Rights Internet* in my hands for the first time was like finding my second human rights Holy Grail; a journal dedicated to international human rights, how incredible. I couldn't believe something like this even existed. It was like magic. I looked through its enchanted pages and—much to my amazement—at the very end I saw an advertisement for the University of Essex in Colchester, England and a new LLM Human Rights Law program that had just started the year before in 1984. I knew at that moment I just had to go there. It was perfect. A law degree. International Human Rights Law. Not in the US. Affordable compared to US universities. A program not all that hard to get into. I've got to make this happen.

Life Lesson No. 19: Stretch life, explore, expand, smile.

I quickly applied to Essex, got in and then just a few short months later in equal parts sadness and excitement packed up my room in the communal house I lived in called Stonehenge with some of the greatest people on the planet. After saying my tearful goodbyes to my beloved Stonehenge crew who saw me off at the Amtrak station just before what would be my permanent departure from the US, I trekked off to my parents to say a final goodbye. Little did they know that would be the last time I'd live in the US—a thought that now, as a parent myself, makes me incredibly sad for them. But as sad as they may have been, I was ecstatic.

After a few last days together in the house where I grew up, we went to a weird part of LAX on the opposite side of the main runway from the main terminal. This is where the cheap charter flights departed, including the Martin Air flight I was on to go see my many friends in Amsterdam before heading all across Europe for a few months prior to finding my way back to the UK and starting to study again. After rampaging across the continent that would be my home for the next 20 years for many wild weeks of excess everything, I took the night boat from Hoek van Holland. On the rough journey over, I unexpectedly met some Deadheads on board, took it as a good omen for the times that were to come, listened to the band all night long on the freezing outside deck on a battery-driven tape player and made it to England just as the sun was rising, sleepless, stale, crusty, chilled to the bone, and yes, still a little bit red-eyed and very unwashed. Though it's not easy spending the night on the open deck of a dark ship while traversing the rough waters of the North Sea at night, we managed—of course, we did.

I found a train and then a taxi to the brutalist concrete campus of the University of Essex and tried to get myself sorted. Dressed as I always did those days in a combination of hippie/glam/punk/cheap, earring dangling and mascara running down my cheeks, I negotiated the interminable maze of hallways full of some disturbingly pale fellow students which was indicative of the gloomy weather to come. I finally found the head of the program, law professor Malcolm Shaw. His mouth fell wide open upon the sight of me, in what to me appeared to be a thought process amounting to "I can't believe we let this weirdo into the program" swirling around unsaid in his professorial head.

Months later when he accepted that my weirdness wasn't all that weird and was at least partially balanced out by my unyielding dedication to justice, I proudly made dinner for him and his wife at my isolated ancient 400-year-old cottage where Vangelis told me his unlikely story. That evening where we tried to behave very differently than we normally did (with all smokable items kept well out of sight until he left), Malcolm told me that he grew up and went to school with none other than John Lennon in Liverpool. I was blown away when he said this, describing the writer of *Imagine* and so many more musical masterpieces as a *tear away* (a term I learned that day and which told me much about my rather strict professor!). After that, I thought he was a lot cooler. I still remember making my weekly phone call to my parents in California from a public phone booth on 13th Street in Eugene a few years earlier on that December 1980 day during my freshman year in college, and how hard it hit me when my mom told me about John Lennon's murder. It still hurts to this day imagining all the beauty that he could have produced in the intervening 46 years. Several years ago, I made my way to Strawberry Fields in Central Park in New York, dutifully paying my respects to a man who brought so many people so much joy and made life for all of us so much better.

Life Lesson No. 20: Living is better but harder with eyes open....[8]

I had a great time that year studying in England, learning everything I could possibly learn about human rights law. Ensuring that I was not too academically imbalanced, I found myself one day exploring heretofore never visited neighborhoods of my mind thanks to a gift kindly given to me by a Chilean refugee in London but did so at one of the worst places one could ever engage in such a journey, a small coastal town in deep decline called Clacton-on-Sea in mid-winter. Such excursions are now discussed rather openly, even on the nightly news and podcasts seemingly by the millions but at the time it was still very much an underground sort of thing. After our team of

---

[8] "Living is easy with eyes closed, misunderstanding all you see…", Strawberry Fields Forever, Lennon-McCartney, 13 February 1967.

explorers decided mid-way through that we had to rename the depressing seaside town into what we called Montley's Place, said in a strong Essex accent, in order to make it palatable to our very sensitive states of mind and save ourselves from what seemed to be mutually assured oblivion, it all seemed much more beautiful. The threat of terror receded and was replaced with a gallant, lovely journey to the mysterious inner worlds and beyond, especially after we got home to a roaring fire.

As I noted above, I lived in a dilapidated 400-year-old cottage with another student and a British family far, far away from the campus, all alone in the glorious English countryside with no neighbors for what seemed many miles. We froze our tails off there in one of the coldest winters ever—where the glass of water beside my bed at night would be frozen solid by morning. The army of mice who lived with us rent-free routinely emptied the rice bowl I used to stand my incense upright. We hosted a BAYW party there one night - *Bring Anything You Want* - and too many people did too many things at too high a rate and probably still remember the night they couldn't recall at the time...

Life Lesson No. 21: Anything means just that; anything...

That wonderful year of Britishness in Essex ended with a move to the capital culminating in a several-month stint living on the top floor of a house in Islington in London with the only bathroom in the house a distant four floors below, with foreseeable results. This was well before gentrification came and this was my humble abode with my girlfriend Kathryn while working as an intern with the still amazing NGO Survival International. After that, I went to live in Strasbourg, France, for the summer, studying more human rights law at the International Institute for Human Rights, located near the European Court of Human Rights, the world's most successful human rights court, by now having issued tens of thousands of judgments, most of which are fully complied with by the governments concerned.

There, I met some lifelong friends—Brian, Grahame, Charlotta, and others—who all went on to have stellar human rights careers of their own. I went to the same café every morning to drink my huge *café au laits*, into which I dipped the world's finest croissants, and ending it all with a nice hand-rolled cigarette and even sometimes a ruthlessly strong *Galoises* just because I was living in France. After a few days at this tiny, but magical place, I finally understood the famous romance for which France was so famous and I was changed forever. Once, that concept became permanently etched into my mind, I looked so much forward to re-visiting the place of its discovery, and all my fellow students always wondered where I went so early on my own every morning. A few days afterwards in another part of town, I became friends with one of those excruciatingly cool French guys who had as much a penchant for all things herbal as I, and this kind soul became my local connection that summer, scoring for me, and thus all of my friends, the best hashish I have ever had the good fortune of tasting. Merci, Laurent!

Life Lesson No. 22: Eternal love and friendship can take many forms and last many lifetimes.

There was some more travelling and then it was time to start thinking about where to live next, and for a whole host of reasons I chose the flatlands of Holland. Utrecht to be precise. I arranged an unpaid internship with the Netherlands Institute of Human Rights (SIM) and my human rights life became ever more real. While at SIM, I finished my final requirement for Essex, a 200+ page paper on the right to a sound environment, living off coffee, cigarettes, and other things for the months it took to finish. Using a computer for the first time only added to the stress that nearly destroyed me. This was right at the beginning of the computer age. Within minutes, the first time I used the computer allocated to me, I noticed sticky tape residue on the lower part of my screen, back when screens weren't in color and were in very low resolution. I asked a secretary why someone would put tape on such a sensitive screen. She told me that the person who used the computer before me didn't like the words going off the screen at the bottom when she scrolled up, so put tape on the screen to stop the words from falling into some infinite abyss where they would be lost forever. Hilarious. Some things you just can't make up.

It took me weeks to recover once my thesis was done, and even living in a very nice place with fellow human rights activists from

Argentina and Indonesia rented from Hans Thoolen, the founder of SIM, on one of Utrecht's most beautiful canals, De Nieuwegracht, couldn't break the spell of exhaustion mixed with anguish. Slowly life came back to normal, after SIM offered me a paid position and arranged for me to be able to officially attend my first UN meeting in Geneva—at the time, for me this was the biggest thing in the world. I had done it. I had figured out how to get inside the UN. My strategy was working. My very own peaceful war of the legal flea had begun and no one noticed but me.

So, in September 1986 at the tender young age of 23, off I went on the 12-hour journey on the slow train from Utrecht to Geneva to the first formal meeting of a process that eventually led to the full-scale revision of *International Labour Organization Convention No. 107 Concerning the Protection and Integration of Indigenous and Other Tribal and Semi-Tribal Populations in Independent Countries* of 1957. Out of the revision process grew what eventually became the greatly improved but still imperfect *ILO Convention No. 169 on Indigenous and Tribal Peoples* of 1989 which fully superseded the outdated notions that pervaded the tired *Convention No. 107.*

Sadly, 37 years after being approved by the ILO, only 24 countries of the world have ratified this important treaty. We can still hope that more states will ratify this text in the future. However, there is no doubt that the revision of Convention 107, combined with developments in the UN's human rights bodies, has fundamentally overhauled the rights of indigenous peoples worldwide. Yet, First Nations people everywhere, including the Boonwurung People on whose unceded land I currently live and where I wrote this book, remain among the most exploited, oppressed, disenfranchised, and subjected to rights abuses of any other group throughout the world. I often go to the ocean side of our narrow little peninsula where I reside these days and sit next to the Aboriginal middens that are mostly hidden from public view and feel the original inhabitants of this land in the soil, the waves and wind that engulf me on this incredible bit of coastline, which always guarantees I can be completely alone in nature with the ancient song lines of past millennia still audible if you listen closely enough.

Life Lesson 23: Sadly, changing laws and policies for the better doesn't always result in the hoped for change.

After having read hundreds of books and articles on every human rights issue I could find, studying and getting university degrees on these things, and a relentless will to make the world a better place, there I was, exactly where I wanted to be, working in a human rights organization in a foreign country. I might not have been living the dream of others, but without a doubt I was living *my* dream. I had been sent to Geneva to participate in a meeting where new international laws were being created. I couldn't believe my luck.

I felt awe in every way, all the way down to the dramatic entry hall and the odd green carpet that adorned the walls of the upper floors where the officials worked at the ILO Headquarters, an organization that was established at the time of the famous Treaty of Versailles ending World War I in 1919. I enjoyed moments of astounding beauty when meeting the people whose articles and books I'd read, hanging out in the offices of famous UN human rights workers, and even just eating in the UN and ILO dining halls. A guy called Roger Plant was in charge of drafting the report of my first ever UN meeting and I recall having great talks with him after I intentionally called him Robert Plant. He told me that stoned fans of Led Zeppelin would constantly show up at his front door in London thinking he was the frizzy haired singer who brought such incredible music to the changing world of the 1960s and 1970s, shouting through the mailbox "Come out and sing us *When the Levee Breaks* or *Lemon Song*!!" And with all of that, my official human rights life, my own multi-decade antidote to nationalism, violence, and ethnic hatred, began.

Life Lesson No. 24: When the Levee Breaks was a very accurate prediction of the future which we now call the present….

Little did I know at the time, but in less than five years, besides those international law bigwigs I'd read about while studying, it would be *me* who would be conceiving of, writing and lobbying tirelessly for new international laws and standards. I couldn't believe my good fortune of somehow managing to create this reality for myself. This work realm would dominate a large portion of my working life for many years to come, all the way up to now. My thought then was simply: Now I know what I want to do, but how do I make this happen when my days at SIM come to an end? Not just anyone can walk into the UN and pursue housing justice, after all.

Your Right to a Home

Way back in the mid-1980s, when I began writing about housing rights and other—what were then—very obscure human rights themes, including my law thesis on environmental rights, I had no idea or intention of founding an organization in a foreign country. I certainly never imagined it would become one of the world's leading international human rights NGOs, described by our first major funder, Larry Cox of the Ford Foundation, as the NGO that "sets the gold standard for work on economic, social, and cultural rights." And lo and behold, after a few years of writing articles and books and travelling around the world visiting every slum I could, meeting with community groups, NGOs, academics and others, I received more encouragement than ever to walk the housing rights path. A few short years later, after repeatedly resisting the idea of creating and running an organization, I finally relented. With no expectation of anything, no intention to grow into an NGO as such, and quite literally with no money in the bank, living in a foreign land, with no plan, no email, no staff, no budget and no clue about running such an operation, in late 1991 the Centre on Housing Rights and Evictions (COHRE) was quietly born in a hazy, pungent, smoke-filled, 12 sq. meter room, one cold Autumn night in Holland's fourth largest city, Utrecht. I eventually assembled a Board of Directors comprised of leading Dutch and Canadian human rights lawyers with whom I had worked for several years and a larger international advisory board of a wild gang of human rights dignitaries, arranged for the registration of COHRE as a Dutch foundation or *Stichting*, and all the other legalities associated with creating a not-for-profit agency, succeeded in raising my first institutional grant, hired consultants and off I went not really knowing where the wind would blow me.

Within a few short years, COHRE became one of the world's

largest and most effective human rights NGOs, with a staff of more than 70 working from 11 offices across the globe and an annually increasing seven-figure annual budget. By the time I decided to leave COHRE 15 years later, we had built this tiny thing designed to ever-strengthen the Protection Wall of my 50-year plan, into a thriving, essential and very well-funded, award-winning international NGO, recognized by everyone in the human rights arena not only as *the* housing rights group, but one of the five biggest international human rights NGOs in the world. By the time I took a sabbatical and planned my strategic departure from COHRE in 2005, we had amassed quite a track record. However, despite meaningful legal, institutional, and policy advances, frankly, we barely made a dent in the cumulative global suffering associated with slum life or the desperate efforts of millions of refugees and internally displaced persons (IDPs) to reclaim their former homes. We fought the good fight, day-in and day-out, but in the end human misery caused by the place so many people across the planet live, simply continued on.

Life Lesson No. 25: There is a tree in every seed

With an NGO in place, off I went to spend many frenzied years trying every legal means possible to be the troublemaker I believed was needed to force governments to simply comply with the international obligations they had voluntarily undertaken to ensure their citizens the full enjoyment of the right to adequate housing. In my first book on these rights in 1992, *From Housing Needs to Housing Rights*, I outlined my vision of precisely what needed to be done. Housing rights are found throughout international law, but the most important articulation is found within the International Covenant on Economic, Social, and Cultural Rights. The UN adopted this cornerstone treaty in 1966, and it gained the force of law in 1976. Article 11(1) of this incredibly important law says the following:

*The States Parties to the present Covenant recognize the right of everyone to an adequate standard of living for himself and his family, including adequate food, clothing and **housing and to the continuous improvement of living conditions**. The States Parties will take appropriate steps to ensure the realization of this right, recognizing to* *this effect the essential importance of international co-operation based on free consent.* (emphasis added)

What a ride those years were trying to get these simple but profound and promissory words to be taken seriously by States the world over! It was far from easy and almost sputtered to a halt before I had started when I proposed an article in 1992 to Niall McDermott, the head of the International Commission of Jurists, a leading international human rights NGO for their prestigious journal. The article was entitled: *Can Housing Rights Be Violated?* Far from receiving the enthusiastic response to such an original idea that I had expected, the stiff and stern Englishman just laughed in my face and totally dismissed my "ridiculous idea." If the head of a major human rights NGO was so dismissive, how was I possibly going to convince countries to comply with their own legal obligations?

Life Lesson No. 26: Can housing rights be violated? Yes, they can and yes, they are!

Trying to encapsulate the five thousand days and nights I led COHRE's global efforts to bring life to the heretofore dormant right to adequate housing would be impossible in a few paragraphs. Not only because the sheer scale of our work would necessitate another book— but more because so much of what human rights activists do often ends in failure. And, in a very overwhelming way, as I've mentioned before, this is one of the proverbial prices one pays for a human rights life. Yes, you are blessed to be able to at least *try* to help people achieve justice, fairness, and to access a roof over their heads, but you are also cursed by the simple fact that the little guy all too rarely wins. Governments as the key protectors *and* violators of human rights rarely change approaches simply because of the intervention of human rights advocates. When it comes to housing rights as such, one is always up against the forces of the market, the power of profit and property, and the deep vested interests that collude to keep housing and land prices high even if it means millions will be unable to access any housing at all.

But sometimes you do win. Sometimes, if you know precisely where change needs to occur, pick your battles carefully, and pull off the battle plan flawlessly, you can and do win. And while such triumphs themselves are rewarding, it is the use of those victories by the very people they were designed to assist, where *they* win, that make all the slogging, all the losses, all the late nights, all the politics worth it. To know, as I do, that so many of my early housing rights victories are still very much in place, only gaining in strength and frequency of use with the passage of time, stretching all the way back to 1991, more than makes up for the losses and countless moments when all of my never-ending efforts seemed to yield so little.

Life Lesson No. 27: No matter the chance of winning, always work just as hard as you can on every human rights struggle with which you engage.

It is these winning moments that make all the losses somehow worth it. In a way, all work that anyone, anywhere engages in is hard, but there are uniquely difficult aspects of a human rights life that most will not be immediately aware of. I can tell you, for instance, that I conceived of and drove the lobbying process leading to the adoption of the most detailed international legal statement on housing rights, *the UN Committee on Economic, Social and Cultural Rights General Comment No. 4 on the Right to Adequate Housing in 1991*. Those several pages of important text conceal, however, the extraordinary amount of time and energy required to turn that initial idea into a text approved at the highest levels of the United Nations.

I first publicly proposed the idea of a general comment on housing rights back in 1988, but with little action forthcoming by others, as is so often the case I realized that I would have to drive this process myself, and indeed, this was a big reason for establishing COHRE in the first place. The drafting of the general comment, the constant lobbying, travelling back and forth from Utrecht to Geneva many times, phone calls, faxes, letters, generating civil society support for the initiative, fighting arguments opposed to the idea of such a new international norm and so many other actions, involving hundreds of hours of effort, the vast majority of which were unpaid. Even those few hours that were paid involved financial remuneration barely above the poverty line. This might begin to give at least a small sense of just what it takes to turn an idea into reality at this level. So, yes, human rights work is worth it, of course, but it is hard and certainly not for the lazy or easily depressed.

After I moved the COHRE Headquarters from Holland to Switzerland, ending up in the one-of-a-kind corner office of a former travel agency seductively called Banana Circle, strategically located right across the street from UNHCR's headquarters in Geneva, and just two minutes from the entrance of the mighty UN building itself, the organization really took off. More and more people came on board with a rapidly growing budget that I almost single-handedly raised year after year dedicated to pushing housing rights initiatives everywhere. At one point we had more than 40 donors and offices in Geneva, Bangkok, Melbourne, Colombo, Accra, Porto Alegre, Buenos Aires, Duluth, Toronto, Nairobi and beyond.

Life Lesson No. 28: Branch out, but don't spread yourself too thin.

It's hard to keep working on human rights year after year without at least the occasional success, and fortunately we had our fair share over the years. Rewarding highlights included conceiving of, drafting and initiating movements to secure scores of new laws, general comments, resolutions, declarations, principles, guidelines and other standards which helped to fundamentally re-shape the international law on economic, social and cultural rights. These new international standards, relevant to everyone in every country in the world addressed housing rights, forced evictions, restitution rights, women's housing rights, water rights, human rights and income distribution and so many more.

Driving the processes leading to *General Comment No. 4*, and then *General Comment No. 7 on Forced Evictions* in 1997 and *General Comment No. 15 on the Right to Water* in 2005 were all memorable and each, in their own way, became and remain springboards for a whole range of actions supporting these totally reasonable aims. Winning a UN Habitat award in 2001 was a nice moment, as were the months I was fortunate enough to work with Anita and Gordon Roddick, Terry Waite and others on the Bodyshop Human Rights Awards. Anita Roddick, the Founder of the Bodyshop, was an amazing woman who I quickly befriended while working on the Awards, which that year were given to housing rights activists around the world. Shortly before she died out of the blue, she indicated her wish to support a new crucial but painful project of mine on a pictorial history of United States War Crimes, one of so many projects I started but which remains in the To Do pile. I had a series of calls and meetings with her about this project and then prepared a proposal on her request. A few days later, she called me back and proceeded to give an incredibly detailed overview of every book, every article, every film that had ever been made on US War Crimes, showing she'd spent hours on her own exploring the project right after reviewing my proposal. Truly extraordinary. No wonder she was so successful.

Around the same time, I was riding my bike home in Geneva along the beautiful path that hugs the shoreline of Europe's largest lake, when I came across George Soros taking a walk, all alone, soaking in the waterfront vibe. At the time, my friend Rob was looking for funding for a new alternative energy project he was working on. I stopped riding, leaned my bike against the retaining wall, and called Rob to tell him I just saw Soros walking by the lake. I mentioned the closest hotel to where I saw him was the President Wilson Hotel, right next to the Palais Wilson, where the League of Nations was founded—and where many of my friends (including the High Commissioner himself) now work at the UN's Office of the High Commissioner for Human Rights. I told Rob he should just call up the Wilson Hotel and ask to speak to one of the world's richest men. He did so a few minutes later and leaves a message. The receptionist thought nothing of it, and in an hour, Soros called back the complete stranger to discuss his new energy idea. Again, how extraordinary. He never did give old Rob any funding, but good on him for making the call.

Building on my work on the Bodyshop Human Rights Awards, and grasping the benefits of such forms of recognition, we established the COHRE Housing Rights Awards, which we gave out for a few years to honor some of the world's incredible and courageous housing rights heroes. The first award was posthumously given to American Rachel Corrie who was so tragically killed by an Israeli bulldozer as she selflessly tried to stop more confiscation of Palestinian lands by her country's closest ally. Those land stealers always seem to stick together. In 2026, they still do. Another year, we gave the COHRE Housing Rights Award to an incredible Indian housing rights activist from Indore, Rajeev John, who fought tooth and nail to protect slum dwellers in his city against violent forced evictions. Not long after he received the award, however, he was found dead hanging from a noose in Indore which the authorities called suicide, but which those who knew Rajeev called something else entirely. To Rachel, Rajeev and all the others who have died in their fight for housing justice the world over, I assure you we will never forget you or the spirit for justice that drove you in your quests for a better world.

Life Lesson No. 29: Human rights activists are killed every day. Take a moment and remember every human rights hero killed in their fights for justice for all. In one way or another they did it for you.

A lot of my human rights victories involved getting the UN to approve the establishment of new mechanisms and procedures designed to improve human rights protections the world over. My proudest accomplishments include getting the two most important UN human rights bodies to create the post of a UN Special Rapporteur on the Right to Adequate Housing and other Special Rapporteurs on Human Rights and Income Distribution, and Housing and Property Restitution Rights for Refugees and Displaced Persons. I wrote hundreds of pages of reports for various rapporteurs, including those for Justice Rajindar Sachar, the first UN Special Rapporteur on Housing Rights, from 1992-1995, and most of Danilo Türk's reports as UN Special Rapporteur on Economic, Social, and Cultural Rights from 1990-1992, several years before he was elected President of Slovenia.

As it turned out, in 1989 I was the first civil society representative ever to speak officially before a human rights treaty body, giving a detailed and perhaps far too lengthy speech on housing rights from the back of Room XI in the Geneva UN building to a packed room of the UN Committee on Economic, Social and Cultural Rights. It was one small step towards making this body and the entire UN ever more open to the views of the people these institutions were set up to protect in the first place. Because the language used in human rights discourse is so much more important than people generally realize, I recognized very early on that it was one thing to get new standards adopted, but another thing entirely to get them noticed, used, enforced, and even remembered by those who could benefit from their application. As a result, and as I mentioned above, I played around with catchy names for otherwise long-titled texts and little terminological ditties that I developed and that are now common parlance in human rights circles - the *Pinheiro Principles*, *HLP Rights*, the *Peninsula Principles* and others.

Life Lesson No. 30: Someone has to write all those laws, and sometimes that someone might just be you.

During the COHRE years, we used the vehicle of the United Nations to get through a whole range of additional reports and standards, all of which pushed the human rights envelope just a little bit further. I was asked by the UN housing agency, UN Habitat, to prepare a document designing what became the *United Nations Housing Rights Programme* (UNHRP), a program which I think remains in place. The huge report I prepared, which I now know was far too long for most UN civil servants to ever consider reading, outlined in precise detail hundreds of things UN Habitat and other UN agencies could do to improve the housing rights prospects of people everywhere. And just to be clear, before I started haranguing them year after year, UN Habitat saw no need nor took any interest in taking on human rights concerns which it viewed as too controversial and risky. It happily just worked on housing as such—without all those annoying and unwanted human rights issues, which they often saw merely as politically risky baggage. Mr. Housing Rights the constant troublemaker strikes again. The UNHRP and some other initiatives took care of that at long last, but not without a long, long fight to make it so.

Beyond this, the COHRE years saw me writing ever more UN studies, including reports that, again after years in the making, resulted in officially approved *UN Guidelines on International Events and Human Rights* designed to end the forced evictions that so commonly precede such events. I coordinated the co-drafting and adoption of a detailed set of *UN Guidelines on Development-Based Displacement* in

1997, designed to ensure that large-scale development projects finally considered the rights of affected people. Beyond these, designing official restitution institutions the world over which have provided housing solutions to hundreds of thousands of war victims and building a series of solid global human rights organizations with offices and staff from around the world, all made life during my COHRE years quite the whirlwind.

Life Lesson No. 31: Our citizenships might be different, but in the end universal principles recognize that we are all the same.

Throughout those 15 years leading what became a very large, but increasingly unruly international human rights NGO, I was fortunate to work with an extraordinary array of diverse, talented, dedicated and inspiring people from all corners of our Earth. From stern but sometimes even compassionate diplomats to gun-toting revolutionaries (and non-violent ones too), corporate suits, to anti-eviction resisters, dry but caring municipal government officials, courageous community-organizers and slum dwellers, NGO big shots, NGO bores, NGO assholes and NGO loonies, dedicated interns and so many others in the cities, towns, and villages across all corners of the Global South. I worked with them all, and then some. It was an honor as COHRE's Founder and Executive Director to have held housing rights discussions with innumerable UN agency heads, government ministers, and even national leaders and Presidents, from Malta to East Timor, and South Korea to Burundi and beyond. I was even honored to have the mighty Nelson Mandela himself write a foreword for one of my books *National Perspectives on Housing Rights*, published in 2003.

We celebrated the ten-year official anniversary of COHRE in 2004 at the beautiful Geneva headquarters of the International Committee of the Red Cross. If I think back, this night was in many ways the highpoint in the evolving nature of COHRE. I flew in from Bangkok where I was living at the time to give the keynote speech to the hundreds gathered to commemorate our official tenth birthday, though it was really our thirteenth, considering that it took a full three years before our official incorporation in Holland. I still have a copy of the speech I gave that night—to a much more crowded room than I had imagined. I highlighted COHRE's achievements, especially the fact that with over 70 staff hailing from more than 20 countries, offices in 11 countries, and programs and projects worldwide, the entire COHRE team was friendly with one another. We were all brothers and sisters in the service of slum dwellers, and that was a beautiful thing to witness and be a driving force behind. All these years later, I now realize that it was at that very moment, standing arm in arm with a big gang of COHREheads on the stage at the end of the evening, receiving the applause of the audience after more than a decade of leading the housing rights charge, that COHRE's perfect barrel-shaped wave was at its peak, lip curling, and the beginnings of collapse just visible at the outer edge.

I have been exceedingly lucky throughout life to have moved from wherever I was living at a given time when I loved that place more than I ever had. Now, when I look back at the dozens of places I have called home all across the world, I think back fondly on every single one of them as I always seem to have left them before it became boring, stale or simply no longer interesting. These same feelings overcame me that night in Geneva, and I knew then and there at that pinnacle moment, that I had better begin to prepare my departure. It would never be as good as this again, I remember thinking, and how right I was.

Call me crazy, but I feel the need to reiterate again that there is no possible way to do sustained, decades-long human rights work all around the world without a regular dose of humor and good fun to balance out all of the human rights nastiness out there. Care to look into my email inbox today or any day? If you did, you'd find great messages from truly great people, but mostly updates on the latest coups and wars, news of a previous co-worker human rights activist imprisoned on false charges, news of a popular leader gunned down by cowardly off-duty cops, violent mass-level forced evictions of slum dwellers, genocide, ethnic cleansing and so on. You need some humor and laughs to keep going amongst all the human-sourced evil that is brought to your attention day in, day out.

When I think of light-hearted moments during my human rights work, I recall a miraculous film we made in 1999, starring me and my

Soros-calling pal, Rob. We went back and forth posing as various horrible dictators and making rude jokes, with voices that made everyone—who had the good (or bad) fortune to see it—laugh uncontrollably. It was a fine cinematic masterpiece if I don't say so myself. When movie making became boring, we'd head across the street to the massive park in the middle of a huge apartment building complex where we'd created a 27-hole Frisbee Golf course. We'd all try to get in a round of FG every day or two, with yours truly holding the course record of 46 on a par 54 course. Eight under par, if only my real golf game reached such under-par levels.

Collectively coming up with alternative acronyms for COHRE became another of our favorite pastimes in between speeches at the UN—an activity that would sometimes pre-occupy us for days on end. We literally came up with thousands of these, page after page, all documented for posterity, but far too many were a bit too risqué to print here. Some of the tamer ones, which were equally laugh inducing, at least to us, include...

....Change Our House Rent Easily - Creatures Originated Having Religious Experience - Christ Overtook His Regal Excellency - Could Others' Heads Really Expand? - Crusty Old Hairy Retched Elephant - Christ! Oh Horrible Rotten Egg - Crescent Or Half Rarely Eclipsed - Currently Our Homes Require Exits - Cold Or Hungry Rat Exterminators - Could Others Handle Rare Encounters? - Coagulated Ooze Has Reached Equilibrium - Contagious Oscillating Halogenic Righteous Enunciations - Cut Off His Right Ear - Come On, Have Real Experiences - Culmination Of Highly Rigid Endeavours - Committee Of Horrible Right-wing Evangelists - Commission On Hedgefund Re-investment Ecstasy - Confessions Of Humiliated Rejected Entity - Collected Observations Of a Human Rights Executive - Care Of Her Royal Emissary - Could Our House Rent Expensively? - Clap Our Hands Reciting Ebulliently - Clowns On Horseback Rarely Entertain - Carrying Out Horrendous Roentgen Experiments - Crotchety Obnoxious Halitosis-Ridden Englishman - Colonial Overlords Have Ravaged Egypt - Cease Obfuscating Haitian Realities Elmer - Caustic Odour Hampered Raucous Event - Consistently Overworked Hookers Repeat Efforts - Considering Obvious Hope Really Ends - Charlie Ogled Hortense Regurgitating

Effusively - Cut Our Hearts Remove Entrails - Cast Out Hateful Retrograde Elements - Can Our Hortatory Remarks Endure? - Cornered Obelisks Hoist Resplendent Edifices - Cantankerous Ornithologists Have Ruffled Edges - Chocolate on Humungous Runny Éclairs - Chicago's Officials Harness Rank Effluents - Corporate Oligarchy Honoured Reasonable Exceptions - Crimes Of Humans Require Evisceration - Convoluted Oratory Hardly Risks Edification - Corpulent Oafs Hoe Rows of Endive - Commission On Humanitarian Rip-off of Everyone - Crusted Oatcakes Have Rigid Edges - Curvy Oars Help Reduce Energy - Carnivores Of Horses Relinquish Ethics - Clowns Of Heroic Radical Expressions - Clapped Out Horrible Rights Enterprise - Crappy Opportunists Hunt Riches Endlessly.....

You get the picture. I'll leave it to you to come up with better ones, and if you do, please send them along.

Life Lesson No. 32: Carefully Observe Human Rights Epiphanies.

We tried to keep things light because we worked on issues all day and night that were—simply put—extremely heavy. Few things are worse than being homeless or losing your home due to eviction and violence, and it was these things that we set out to change for the better. While I had no intention whatsoever to build COHRE into the goliath it eventually became, the process of creating a non-profit agency in a world dominated by profit-driven motives was far from an easy task. I had had no formal education on organizational construction or design nor really on any aspect of running any sort of entity, profit or non-profit in nature. I was a writer, a researcher, an international legal expert and human rights activist, not an executive.

Life Lesson No. 33: Lead in a spirit of service not ego gratification.

As an extremely reluctant leader, despite what some may have thought, I abhorred almost all the elements of organizational leadership and decision making, especially when people needed to be fired, which happened more than once. I foolishly thought that anyone who sought work with an international human rights NGO would be as committed, as dedicated, as hard working and as productive as I was. I greatly underestimated how much ego, arrogance, and money played a role in people's motivations. I found it difficult to believe that certain people were as supercilious as some turned out to be and how utterly lacking in charisma and charm some fellow humans could be. I optimistically assumed during the early days of building COHRE into the institution that it become that anyone drawn to this work would be self-motivated and grateful for the chance to change the world in an incredibly meaningful way, especially in COHRE's highly informal environment, where the seriousness of the cause was balanced by humor and in-house comedy and an easy-going atmosphere.

When people started actually complaining about our world's most flexible holiday policy (take as much holiday as you wish as long as you complete your contractual obligations) and that marijuana was evil and the work of the devil, I knew it was time to start planning my departure. Being forced by the inactions and actions of others to fire people and having to raise millions of dollars annually without any thought of gratitude or thanks by most within the organization served as the cherries on my departure pie.

So, after leading COHRE from 1991 to 2005 and now living very happily in far-off Bangkok, I decided to take a one-year sabbatical to finish writing and editing several books that I could never seem to complete, catch up on reading, and—most importantly—plan my future departure from the organization I had worked so hard to build into a human rights powerhouse. Beyond the incredibly rich and innovative outputs that COHRE produced—325 publications and films and much more—and the countless visits to some of the tens of thousands of slums strewn across the world, some moments of which I outlined above, running what became one of the leading international human rights NGOs took so much time, energy, and stress that I knew it was time for a change.

I'd moved from the headquarters in Geneva to Bangkok in 2003 where my partner had been offered her next exciting job by UNHCR. We were in the process of starting a family, and as I was about to become a father for the first time, I was determined to do it right. I knew that running a global NGO comprised of dozens of staff and associates, maintaining relations with our numerous donors and just keeping up the institutional growth that was so commonplace for so long became increasingly less realistic. In essence, what was always fun for a solid 15 years, suddenly wasn't fun anymore. After staying away from Geneva for almost eight months after our arrival in our wonderful Bangkok home, I finally started what amounted to commuting between Thailand's capital and Geneva for the next year or two, setting processes in motion to handover the reigns of this truly unique NGO, then head off into the southeast Asian sunset.

Life Lesson No. 34: Know when it's time to throw in the towel.

I'd again innocently thought and hoped that this process would somehow be smooth, however, how wrong I was. When I started flying frequently back and forth between Bangkok and Geneva, to save money for the organization I would sleep on a couch in my office. Sometimes my flights would arrive very early in the morning, well before any of the staff showed up for work. After one early morning arrival, I thought I would keep my presence secret for a few hours to see as much as I could about how things ran in my absence. Thus, I was shocked to see from my window that one of the COHRE staff, who had some very important functions in the organization during my long absences, along with five other staff, left the building around 9:30 a.m. just minutes after they had arrived for the day. They spent almost the entire working day at the seedy café next door, smoking, laughing, drinking coffee, having what looked like a fine lunch, and slowly rolling back into the office around 3:30 p.m., some six hours later. Then I watched them all depart the office together at 4:00 p.m., another hard day at work over and done. The dedication of these highly paid people to the housing rights cause was truly monumental! I was working 15-hour days, seven days a week and then I see this. Now I knew why so many reports were late and poorly drafted, why no new donors had been found, why so many publications remained unedited and why so much bitterness had arisen within the ranks when there was none before. I had to fly to New York City a few days later to meet with new donors and attend a board meeting where I sadly had to inform the board that I had hired the wrong person for a vital position and required a replacement. I also let them know that after deep contemplation I was considering both a long-needed sabbatical and would be considering whether or not to continue as Executive Director afterwards.

Life Lesson No. 35: If you create a new organization, never assume that those you hire will be as committed to it as you are.

Even with the emerging awareness that I would be leaving the organization I had started in Utrecht years ago, the countless responsibilities of being executive director still burdened me. The more I had to handle them, the less I enjoyed it. Choosing new staff, deciding where to work next, determining whether or not to send COHRE representatives into harm's way and making sure they had the right medical and travel insurance set up, ensuring that the millions of dollars needed for the next year's budget was all in place, being available to the world's media at any moment and so much more were just part of the daily grind that I once embraced, but no longer. Tasks like arranging accountants and audits, keeping the Board and Advisory Board informed, preparing annual reports, updating the website, and maintaining our global network were all things I increasingly lost interest in. It was things like this day-in, day-out, never a real break, never a moment where nothing remained on the to do list, and never a time when I could sit back and say, "I have nothing to do."

Changing the world remained my number one motivation, and my belief and commitment in that mission was as strong and unwavering as ever. It still is. However, the administrative side of running a large global NGO, especially while living a 12-hour flight away from headquarters on another continent and about to become a parent for the first time, all made me wish it would end sooner rather than later.

Life Lesson No. 36: Trust your gut; it's rarely wrong.

As exciting as these years were, and despite how much we were able to achieve, there were aspects of leading such a huge institution that forced me into positions I had never thought possible. I had to be a mediator, a psychologist, and a shoulder to cry on; happy to do the latter, the first two not so much. Indeed, if you were to examine my curriculum vitae, in particular the publications list, you will find that my individual outputs in the form of books decreased massively as COHRE grew. I had become ever more burdened with administrative responsibilities, fundraising duties, and sorting out things that others should have been sorting out, but which were somehow forced upon me as the comprehensively reluctant boss, a status I dreaded and vowed never to do again once I left COHRE.

I'm happy to take responsibility for my own fundraising, but when someone else's mortgage or school fees depends on me successfully prying loose tightly held funds from one of a very limited number of international human rights donors, it is a different matter entirely. I knew in the long run this was not to be. Little did many COHRE staff know or even if they did know, little did they care, that I would routinely toss and turn all night long wondering how I could possibly raise the money needed to pay all the salaries so everyone could pay their bills. But sleepless nights became common once the budget reached into the millions. We tried to get other COHRE staff to raise funds and sometimes they succeeded, but mostly it was left up to me and after 15 years of that, I was really starting to have had enough.

It wasn't just these ordinary pressures that all Executive Directors face, but the psychological counseling that many staff sought from me as the head of the organization. One time a dedicated but highly unstable staff member was in a meeting with me crying, screaming, and telling me all of his life's worries and then says to me "And look at you, you just sit there, saying nothing!" I wasn't really sure what else I was supposed to do but sit there and listen to see if I could do anything to make his working life better. I later learned that another staff member tried to help him meditate for peace of mind. When asked to recall a time when he felt truly happy, calm, and at peace to get things moving, the man began crying, telling his meditation teacher that he had never once felt those things. This was just heartbreaking. It reminded me of listening to Ralph Nader once who made the key point that people need to look after themselves first, before trying to assist others. Right you are, Ralph.

As I prepared to leave COHRE, having worked for so long and so intensively on housing rights and slum issues, the Secretary-General of Amnesty International asked me to draft the components of their new slum and eviction policy. This was both an honor and a way to ensure these issues would remain high upon the world's human rights and political agendas, regardless of COHRE's future. Given what happened to COHRE after I headed off to greener pastures, I'm glad I did. I presented the policy to Amnesty's senior management at their London headquarters, answered a wide range of questions, and ended my detailed and lengthy presentation with a relieved comment: "Aaahhh, thank the proverbial lord above, better yet, thank Gaia; now I can surf." This was a metaphor for my plan to leave the major NGO scene and move sooner than later to my next country, in this case Australia, for my next adventure.

I tried my best to explain my proposed policies, which they embraced in full, in the following ways:

It is 4:30am when José stirs and then rises in the pre-dawn, relative calm of his home. He first glances at his still sleeping wife, checks on his five children making sure they are safe in the two beds they all share, and then slowly pulls open the rusty metal door of his one-room, 16 sq meter shack, steps into the darkness, carefully closing the latch behind him. The daily, early morning walk to the toilet, just before his two-hour crowded bus commute to his market stall in the city center, is an obstacle course. A mangy, shivering dog lies on the left, a pile of discarded melon rinds on the right, and puddles cover nearly every step along the way. Winding his way through the unlit alleyways that criss-cross the self-built neighborhood, José's olfactory senses are activated long before his eyes can see his eventual destination. Twenty meters further down the muddy lane he reaches his long sought after destination – the communal WC; if only there was water and a closet. Carefully dodging several pigs that linger constantly in the vicinity—day and night—he tiptoes up a hazardous wooden plank and kicks the jagged door open, careful not to touch anything with his hands. As he has done for years, he surveys the place of his daily ablutions, perched two meters above a rank and putrid pool that utterly defies description. With light spare, he can just about make out the strategic footing he will need to employ to keep from falling through the floor into the pile of excrement below. A ripped piece of yesterday's newspaper completes the ritual and José—again safely down the rickety plank—heads home ready for the long day ahead.

And every morning around the same time José's slumber is broken in the very same city, just a few kilometres away, Marcia awakes to a very different reality. Each day, Marcia's electric alarm gently wakes her with a hum, soft and soothing music, calmly bringing her air-conditioned night under the snug sheets to a peaceful end and ready to start her hectic daily routine. Donning her smooth cotton robe, she strolls down the hall passing each of her three children's bedrooms along the way, asleep and warm in their beds, arriving within just a few steps at one of her home's four bathrooms – three of which have 'baths' and all of which are 'rooms'. She turns into the lightly ginger-fragranced, immaculate, and refreshing powder room, and presents her suburb's sewage system with her daily offering, followed by a flush, all the while taking deep solace in the fact that the roll of supple tissue paper is derived from sustainable, farmed forests which helps to protect the few remaining real forests from any further abuse. Relieved, she heads to the kitchen for the first of many cups of coffee during her busy, busy day at a downtown office tower. Around noontime, she will pass José's stall on her way to the new Starbucks—the first in the country.

José and Marcia. Two individual citizens endowed with reason and rights. José and Marcia - Two people with families, identical needs, and desires, sharing a common set of rights enshrined within a shared universal code based on the inherent dignity of everyone. And yet, it is in these shared concepts where the similarities of life between José and Marcia end. For these two of the world's six billion citizens life's daily routines, the minute-by-minute moments that make up the measures of a life, bring into sharp relief just how poverty and the enjoyment of human rights intersect, and, in particular, how one's residential status—the place where one lives—can be highly determinative in the overall enjoyment of a wide spectrum of human rights.

For José and the one billion others who call the slums "home," life in these ramshackle communities all too often means daily indignities, such as communal toilets and a lack of security, clean water, sanitation, and basic services—and a life with little hope of real improvement, a life with few enforceable rights, and a lack of human dignity. It can mean a life with the specter of looming violent forced eviction. Life in the slum almost invariably means a shorter life, a life with constant threats to health and wellbeing and persistent disadvantage in terms of access to education, employment and other basic rights. Yet, the slums that dominate cities in the developing world—and a growing number of developed countries as well—stand as graphic testimonials of persistently failing economic and urban policies and the unwillingness—and sometimes inability—of governments around the world to take all the rights of all citizens seriously. From Soweto and the Cape Flats in South Africa, Kibera and Mathare in Kenya, Agblogbloshie in Ghana, to Klong Toey in Thailand, Payatas and Commonwealth in Manila, Dharavi in Mumbai, Orangi in Karachi, from Iraq's Sadr City, Egypt's City of the Dead, to Rio's Josinja, the Dominican Republic's La Cienega-Los Guandules, and Zona Norte and beyond, the "slums" of the world are home to hundreds of millions of the world's poor. All told, well over 200,000 different slums provide the only dwelling options available to the growing population of the urban poor. Whether we know it or not, we have truly become, in the words of Mike Davis, a "planet of slums."[9]

I had no idea whatsoever how to arrange my departure from an organization I had led for so long and so I simply looked it up on the internet, typing into the search engine: *How to coordinate an executive director's resignation*, and I learned a lot. I put together a plan, made an agreement with the board and said my farewells. I have rarely felt happier than on the day I left. After my departure in 2006, I set up two new international NGOs, both of which I still run to this day some 20 years later. Displacement Solutions focuses on global climate displacement, and Oneness World Foundation advocates for new forms of world citizenship (or *jus gaia* as I call it) and global governance. These are the themes I address in my recent book *World Citizenship: Origins, Obstacles, Prospects*.

Learning so much from growing an organization from nothing into something huge, I have very intentionally kept both Displacement Solutions and Oneness World Foundation very small, super strategic and most importantly incredibly productive, but also fun. I listened to E.F. Schumacher when he said, "Small is beautiful", and I can assure

---

[9]Mike Davis, *Planet of Slums*, Verso, London & New York, 2006.

you, it is. Together both of these new post-COHRE creations have produced scores of publications, films, websites, podcast episodes, new international standards on climate displacement, philanthropic initiatives to build homes for the extreme poor of Bangladesh and so much more. I've continued to expand my work as a law school instructor, film producer, UN advisor, speaker and writer, and involvement on many, many issues all across the world.

As for COHRE, despite leaving behind a multi-million-dollar budget, dozens of incredible donors, a massively positive track record, institutional name recognition throughout the international community and other hard fought for attributes, COHRE closed its doors a few short years after my departure. In-fighting, turf battles, and according to some former employees even physical violence in the office necessitating police visits, lawsuits, mass firings, office closures and sheer treachery by alleged human rights advocates gone mad led to the demise of what was for a good long while an extraordinary springboard for global justice and the evolution of international law protections. Watching this beautiful creation turn toxic on itself from the other side of the world, with staff viciously jostling for any tidbit of power while donors and supporters left *en masse*, broke my heart. However, leaving when I did relieved me to no end as the signs when I left were just rumblings of discontent—long before the bitter battles that would ensue that I heard about from those still working there.

They say the longevity of NGOs is much like restaurants, where only one in ten survive after five years, and from my vantage point this seems pretty close to the mark. So many once great human rights NGOs no longer exist and had incredibly short lives as the imperfections of the people within them became too strong for the center to hold. I could share dozens of stories on this topic but let me just let you in on one.

A friend had set up a totally unique and desperately needed international NGO in Washington DC working on a peace and human rights issue that was of immense importance. One day, after returning from a week-long work trip, my friend walked into his office to find everything of value gone. The entire place had been wiped clean, and when the poor guy checked the bank accounts, they were empty as well—all of this was done by board members who couldn't resist the temptation of enriching themselves. So tragic, this sad tale repeats worldwide over and over again, and has effectively forced a degree of professionalization into the NGO world. While this may have been needed, it took away a good part of the unique characteristics that make NGO work so unique, enticing—and effective. It is a little like a wild bird becoming tame, never able to return to its true nature ever again. Combine the petty jealousies that pervade the NGO world, the often-brutal internal politics, the modest pay, the frustrations, the immense egos and arrogance, and the way ambitious people simply use them as steppingstones to higher pay elsewhere—and it's easy to see why so many NGOs fall by the wayside.

Life Lesson No. 37: All things must pass.

But was it worth it, you ask? Were all the human rights victories, the 15-hour workdays, the constant travel and jetlag, sorting out ridiculous staff problems with other staff members, constantly wiping urine off the floor in the office bathroom and all the rest worth it? I can offer nothing less than a resounding yes. Would it have been nice to see COHRE continue long into the future after my departure? Most certainly. But to see now the hundreds of COHRE publications still somehow alive and kicking on the Internet for all to use and access free of charge means that it still lives. In fact, I was just contacted a few days ago by a well-known US magazine asking to quote one of COHRE's publications from more than twenty years ago so the struggle continues.

Life Lesson No. 38: Small is definitely beautiful!

Though as an organization it no longer exists, in spirit COHRE very much lives on. To see COHRE still routinely cited in academic articles, human rights reports, legal briefs, and judicial decisions are wonderful reminders of what a great force for good it was. Seeing the organizations I have started since COHRE, along with the successful careers of so many who used COHRE as a stepping stone for further career advancement—heads of international NGOs, UN staff, professors, special rapporteurs, lawyers, activists, and others—helps keep the COHRE energy alive. Being lifelong friends with many of those who worked with COHRE is another great benefit of those years. But most of all, the collective will of everyone who worked for or was associated with COHRE continues on, especially the slum dwellers, homeless people and their families, grassroots community-based organizations, refugees, IDPs, and more. This will assuredly continue onwards until we reach the day when all of humanity has the full spectrum of their housing rights fully met—from the day they are born until the day they die. Only then, will the COHRE dream truly reach its inevitable end.

Your Right Not to be Forcibly Evicted

Late 1991 was a frenzied time of intense activity, including drafting and guiding to fruition the world's first UN resolution on forced evictions in August. Then, in November, General Comment No. 4, the first definitive legal statement on housing rights under international law, made it through the UN, and at the same time I had just started a new international organization focused on both themes.

As I alluded to earlier, if you have not worked within a huge political institution, it will be hard to imagine just how much is required to get a decision, resolution, or other standard through the UN system. One aspect largely unknown to the outside world involves the sheer physical endurance required to make them happen. This is especially true if you're an NGO without the administrative and financial backing most governments have at their disposal, especially the rich ones. States have a massive head start in every way, and catching up as an NGO requires incredible and sustained energy. Most diplomats stay in five-star hotels, are backed by skilled staff at their respective embassies, get their clothes washed for them and dine out at fancy restaurants nightly. Conversely, most NGO activists attending the very same meetings in the very same rooms, working on precisely the same issues organized under the same official agenda of the meeting concerned, sleep on the floors of apartments often with many other activists (the most I personally had to share with was about 15 other activists, with all of us sleeping wherever we could find a spot in a two-bedroom apartment) and eat whatever food they can access for free. This is especially so at the nightly embassy receptions where governments try to outdo all others, much to the benefit of the hungry activists. Most governments are happy to have NGOs attend their fancy events and all of us figured out quite quickly which embassies put on the best evening gatherings and what it said about each country's efforts at the UN. Russia always had massive amounts of free caviar (and vodka) on offer, the French did what the French do best, the Dutch handed out small squares of gouda cheese with the Dutch flag sticking out of them, and the Americans, well, they served dirty bowls of stale potato chips and Budweiser beer. NGOs covering the human rights bodies often had to wear the same clothing day after day and exist in a social and economic universe wholly different from the diplomats who they sought to influence.

The days are extremely long and hours of sleep very few, as unhealthy living spent inside a massive, windowless room, breathing stale air becomes the norm. Lord only knows what it must have been like in there during the worst days of COVID. Far too many nights, when there was not enough time to go out to eat or find a nearby reception, we would have to rely on a single vending machine for our evening meal, located in a very obscure location within the UN building. Far too many coffees were drunk and cigarettes smoked in the infamous Serpentine Lounge near the meeting room where everyone hung out as much as they could, as this is where the real work was done. In the early years of my UN advocacy, we did all this *without* laptops or iPhones; they hadn't really been invented yet. We headed to wherever we stayed during four- to six-week sessions, hoping they had a mainframe computer and dot-matrix printer (remember those?) so we could come back the next day with hands full of draft resolutions and speeches—ready to deliver and distribute.

It was under these types of conditions that I spent August 1990 trying hard to pass the first resolution on forced evictions through the UN's Sub-Commission on the Prevention of Discrimination and Protection of Minorities. Despite hundreds of hours of trying, it proved unsuccessful, though valuable lessons were learned. However, we did succeed in getting a resolution approved condemning population transfer and the implantation of settlers which came close to what I was trying to achieve but it was clear the UN was not yet ready to put the blanket ban on forced evictions that I was seeking.

At the next session a year later, in August—by far Geneva's best time of year—I arrived with draft resolutions in my bag, strong relationships with most members of the Sub-Commission who would eventually vote on these texts, and the unyielding energy of a 28-year-old human rights activist. I wanted nothing more than to end the brutal and all-too-common practice of forced evictions, especially mass ones against entire slum communities, which sometimes displaced tens of thousands of people in a single day—and in some cases—even hundreds of thousands, as in Lagos during the COHRE years. Since the Sub-Commission, and indeed the UN as a whole, had not historically paid much specific attention to these practices, developing sufficient awareness to get members to vote for a resolution declaring forced evictions a "gross and systematic violation of human rights"—especially the right to adequate housing—was no easy task. How many times did I have to tell the same sad eviction stories to literally hundreds of people that summer, especially the 26 independent members of the Sub-Commission, on whose votes we depended for victory? To increase our chances and protect my vocal cords, I prepared a detailed dossier on about 30 cases of mass forced evictions worldwide, which proved crucial in convincing the UN to act.

After four grueling weeks, the Sub-Commission officially had before it a draft resolution on forced evictions—for the very first time in its history. I was thrilled that things had finally found their way through the system resulting in an official UN publication with an official UN document number, ready for consideration and – if I was lucky – approval. When it came time to vote, we all expected the resolution to sail through and pass by consensus, without the need for a formal vote. Instead, when the Chair asked if there were any comments, the independent Sub-Commission expert who was from Algeria and who had been totally supportive during my lobbying efforts, raised her hand and went on a tirade about the need to add an operative paragraph on the "null and void" nature of Israeli settlements on Palestinian land. As much as we may have supported the self-determination of the Palestinians and agreed fully with the sentiments of the proposed amendment, this wasn't the place for it. We wanted the resolution to be entirely thematic and applicable to everyone, everywhere, and to not single out any particular country. Negotiations amongst other supportive members of the Sub-Commission, Cees Flinterman of the Netherlands, John Merrills of the UK, Rajindar Sachar of India, and even the inimitable chain-smoking Miguel Alfonzo Martinez, Fidel's right-hand man from Cuba, and others all found a way to insert the suggested amendment and keep the rest intact.

The Chair asked for further comments and then, much to my deep inner joy, proclaimed that the resolution was adopted! It officially called forced evictions *a gross and systematic violation of human rights, including the right to adequate housing*. All of my NGO, diplomatic, UN and other friends ran up to me hugging and congratulating me, knowing what a battle it had been to finally get this through this important UN body. All those croissants, the 20 coffees and 40 cigarettes a day, the nightly bottles of wine and the UN cafeteria, incessant fondue, and freebies I could gather at the nightly diplomatic receptions fuelled me along for a solid month. I finally got my first UN resolution through by a vote of 26-0. I couldn't believe it. It worked! I've rarely felt so good, knowing that the weeks spent in the Serpentine Lounge, overlooking Mont Blanc and Lake Geneva, resulted in an effectively new international standard—*Resolution 1991/12 on Forced Evictions*—relevant to every country in the world. Damn that felt good!

Life Lesson No. 39: Getting the world to agree on a new global decision will change your life forever.

This resolution spurred a cavalcade of additional worldwide attention onto forced evictions, and in the next few years, the UN's human rights agenda made more and more progress in addressing this issue. These new standards empowered ordinary people and slum dwellers to protect themselves against bulldozers the world over. During this time, I was asked to write UN Secretary-General reports on forced evictions, Office of the High Commissioner on Human Rights reports on forced evictions (then called the UN Centre on Human Rights), a new general comment on the issue and so much more. And, most importantly, all of these standards and reports were used, often successfully, by the very people they were always designed to protect, the slum dwellers of the world.

The UN was working as it should have always worked, and these standards built a body of law and practice, while shaky today, nonetheless continue to work to prevent planned forced evictions and I hope can still give just a little bit of solace to the people concerned and a slice of additional strength to the idea that wherever we are, our place on Earth is sacred, no one should be able to arbitrarily force us to move away. These rules are still too easy to violate, and for that matter so is the UN Charter and indeed every international law, and national laws too. Yet, formal decisions are firmly in place for that majority of people and governments who wish to comply, who wish to protect the housing, land, and property rights of their people and who wish to end the ghastly practice of forever kicking people out of their homes for no other reason than living where they live.

When most Europeans were on their month(s)-long lovely summer holidays, I spent nine Augusts in a row from 1990-1998, running around the Sub-Commission and became a veritable regular there, performing the role of a *de facto* assistant to several key members of this important UN human rights body. During one session, I single-handedly drafted more than 25% of all the resolutions adopted. That summer I stayed with a Tibetan activist who, as usual, had several of us staying on her floor, which was just a short walk from the UN. One of those staying there was an activist from Pakistan. One day I stayed in writing a bunch of resolutions and speeches and at one point a heard a gentle, almost inaudible knock on the door. Knowing how many activists were staying at our place, I tiptoed to the door and looked through the peephole trying successfully to not make a sound. Who did I see but the Asian "diplomat" everyone had told me was a spy for one of the most feared intelligence agencies anywhere, standing there suspiciously, checking if anyone was home. I immediately opened the door, which jolted him to his senses, and he literally ran off saying that this must have been the wrong place clearly flustered that he had been so stupid to get caught.

Those incredibly busy days and nights during August, as well as the February and March sessions of the UN Commission on Human Rights and the May and November sessions of the UN Committee on

Economic, Social, and Cultural Rights, became my routine during those hyperactive years. I would travel by train from Holland, spend months a year in Geneva on the floor of different friends' houses for free. All of them told me in their own ways that I was the only guest who happily cleaned their apartments (bathrooms included) and ironed whatever wrinkled clothing needed attention, shopped for them, cooked for them, and planned invite lists for nightly parties with people from every corner of the world, during those hectic early years of political craziness. As they say, those were *the days*....

Getting decisions through the Sub-Commission, as hard as it was, was much easier than passing resolutions through the UN's Commission on Human Rights. The Commission consisted of 53 UN member state's governments, many of which were far from being champions of human rights—to put it politely—unlike the independent experts of the subordinate body—the Sub-Commission. It was a similar type of work you had to attend to, but heavier, more burdensome, and meaner, much meaner and angrier. I hear it's even worse today for NGOs and civil society working within the UN Human Rights Council who find themselves often sidelined to the periphery in ways that would have never happened in those human rights glory years immediately following the end of the Cold War.

To anyone who doubts the UN's relevance, political significance, or power, just attend a session of the UN Human Rights Council. Watch the lengths to which countries will go to avoid having a resolution adopted against them for heinous human rights abuses and atrocities. The United States is so terrified of this body and the truths that are exposed about their own human rights record, that the Trump Administration withdrew from the Council in yet another pathetic act of hypocrisy. So much for the great human rights country.

If you think countries exposed at the Council meetings don't care about accurate human rights reporting made public at gatherings of this body, you'd be very wrong. Diplomats will fight tooth and nail to win the day and have draft resolutions mentioning their country rejected, in the process sometimes employing seriously seedy strategies. I once watched flabbergasted as the Chinese Ambassador in response to some very legitimate human rights criticisms chillingly said to the world something to the effect of "Be careful, if we were to march one Chinese person into the sea every second, the stream of people would never end..." Jeez. Another time a draft resolution circulated condemning human rights abuses in one of my favorite countries committed during its lengthy and bitter civil war. The normally small diplomatic delegation suddenly seemed to have increased six-fold overnight. This was due to the sudden appearance of heavily made-up women dressed as if they were in a club at 2am in revealing clothing and high heels, breathlessly using the sleazy tactic of begging vulnerable diplomats to vote against the resolution by suggestively flirting them into submission. Sadly, it worked, and the resolution failed.

Yet another time, a major human rights player whose vote we needed badly on what became the last time a resolution on human rights in Tibet was adopted at the UN, when asked by an activist there, if he would vote for the resolution to condemn China's human rights violations in the land of the Dalai Lama, "Yes, I'll vote for the resolution, but only if you come away with me to the Alsace over the weekend...." Fortunately, she didn't go but he still voted for the resolution in the end, thankfully. A couple of years later this very same activist was very nearly raped by a Middle Eastern diplomat during what was meant to be a working session on another human rights issue under consideration at the time. Little old Geneva can be a much more awful place than most people may realize.

Whether raunchy, tasteless, seedy, or just seductive and juicy normal levels of mutual attraction, those human rights bodies create incredibly sexualized environments—all the way from the worst of the worst ways to some of the most wonderful mergers of people from entirely different backgrounds that I'd ever seen. If you ask me, there's nothing wrong with two willing people who see the spark of mutual recognition and make some love out of the visceral hate which pervades too much of the human rights world. Spotting the seedy guys was easy and those sexist swines were often promptly hounded out of there and rightfully so.

On the other hand, being part of the true love and greater connection among us was beautiful, and if you ask me, the more love, the better. I know you're waiting for it, so here's one image of thousands I could give: There I was sitting at the very far end of the

Serpentine Lounge, trying to avoid people for a few minutes of peaceful rest. I look far off to the east at all the huge trees still there on the beautiful UN grounds, look a bit closer and see two hands, one on either side of a large pine tree, fully hidden from view. Then see another pair of hands suddenly appear on top of the first hands I saw, and in an instant, I knew that two fellow human rights NGO friends, both of whom I knew well, were hiding (rather unsuccessfully) behind a giant tree and going at it against a massive conifer outside in the wintery Geneva air while all the rest of us suffered the polluted political air inside. I pointed this out to no one, just smiling inside at what I knew was going between two of the most wonderful people I have ever known. What a lovely, short-lived couple they made.

The 1993 session of the UN Commission on Human Rights was as intense as could be, but I felt duty-bound to get this cornerstone human rights body to adopt a resolution on forced evictions for the first time since the founding of the UN in 1945. I hand-delivered my annual forced eviction dossier which I had spent months perfecting in the run-up to the February start date of the session, that year adding a bright purple cover so I could easily spot it on the delegations' desks, along with pre-publication copies of my upcoming book *When Push Comes to Shove*, which was kindly financed by the Netherlands Ministry of Housing and Environment, to every government in the room. I spoke to hundreds of decision makers about the importance of the Commission finally taking a stand against the ongoing mass slum clearance operations worldwide. It was yet another freezing cold winter in Geneva, the Clinton Administration had just taken power in the US after the dreary Reagan and Bush years and the positive Pandora's box of human rights possibilities was just starting to open.

Lucky for me, the Netherlands delegation was headed by my friend and soon to be Chairperson of the COHRE Board, Professor Cees Flinterman, a truly kind and committed man, indeed one of the finest and most selfless humans I have had the good fortune of knowing. I will never forget him telling me that a close professor friend of his died suddenly, leaving behind an unfinished manuscript in the back of his office closet that the man's wife had shown to Cees. Even though he had had nothing to do with the massive book that his fellow professor had started, Cees decided to spend the next months finishing it for him and posthumously publishing it. I mean, what a dude! At the Commission, his tireless lobbying, dedication to the cause, and ability to generate political support across the broad spectrum of the 53 voting member states of the Commission helped pass what became Resolution 1993/77 on Forced Evictions, one of my most cherished accomplishments. Showing its significance to me at least, of all the more than 100 UN decisions I facilitated or wrote, it is only *Resolution 1993/77* that adorns my office walls today.

Again, the US tried to undermine my latest initiative by seeking out other states to oppose the resolution—but failed and ultimately had to go along with the consensus to avoid being labeled as a supporter of forced evictions. Oddly, unexpected support came from a speech by Syria which strongly supported the resolution, perhaps not fully understanding its true significance. When the time came for the vote, however, even the US decided it wasn't worth casting a vote against it, and consensus again prevailed. The resolution sailed through 53-0. Knowing the likely outcome, I had prepared a detailed press release and ran to my journalist contacts on the other side of the UN building, most of whom (as did I) hung out most of the day in the infamous UN Press Bar, what a place! If those walls could talk. The next day, we received huge media coverage of this major step forward in newspapers all across the world.

The UN Committee on Economic, Social and Cultural Rights

When needed, we used the political human rights bodies as they were often called, like the Commission and Sub-Commission, to gain broader global political support for fighting forced evictions, as I just outlined. However, it was within what are referred to as the "treaty bodies"—which function more like a court than a parliament—where even more was achieved. Few who have never set foot inside the UN's main building in Geneva can imagine the interesting things that occur daily when the world's leading human rights bodies meet. This surreal scene was most evident to me during meetings of the Committee on Economic, Social, and Cultural Rights. Many of those moments, shall we say, cannot be printed here, but if you ask me to expand one day in person, I promise to reveal all.

And thank goodness for these surreal moments, because without them to the untrained eye these bodies can appear to be far less than inspiring. But this committee, which I attended with almost religious fervor from 1987-1997 and sporadically afterward crucially expanded the legal precision of the term *housing rights* and massively strengthened legal protections against forced evictions, showing what the UN could do to address the grievances of victims of one of the world's worst human rights violations. The Committee allowed these victims to testify directly before its 18 independent experts, making a powerful impact. During its early years, very few NGOs or others followed this new Committee. For the few of us who did, including myself and a future SOAS law professor from England named Matt Craven, who became a good friend, we had secret nicknames for each Committee member. All were respectful, of course, but most carried a touch of tongue-in-cheek humor and linguistic gymnastics. One time, one of the Committee members introduced me to her granddaughter who she rather vigorously encouraged to go out with me. I did it for the cause! Another time after giving a speech before the Committee, I tried to sound smarter than I was and clumsily misused the term *in lieu of* instead of *in view of,* as in "In lieu of the fact that housing....." Committee member Philip Alston came over to me afterwards and gently let me know of my linguistic errors and I remember that every time I say either of those phrases to this day, more than 30 years later.

This Committee was, simply put, amazing. This was especially so after the super-committed Alston became its Chairperson when the sky became the limit in so many important ways that actually supported the poor majority of the planet. I became friends with many of its leading members and for years before each session some of the members and me would compare our precedent-setting wish lists and see what was possible. This was the progressive development of international law at its most exciting—creating new rules and laws grounded in the terms of the Covenant and broader international law, beginning to hold individual governments accountable, getting media attention where it had not been before and so much more. I looked forward to and loved going to these sessions which were always held in what became to us the sacred Room XI of the *Palais des Nations,* every single square inch of which I knew intimately. At the UN, every chair in the place has single-ear grey plastic earphones, which you can place over your ear and listen to all of the six official languages of the UN—Arabic, Chinese, English, French, Russian and Spanish. I loved listening to all those languages when the actual proceedings were boring and learned a few choice lines of each of those languages that I don't generally speak, especially Arabic and Russian, that I still use when meeting mother tongue speakers of these exquisite linguistic creations to this day.

The precedent-setting victories we guided through this Committee over the years are far too numerous to list here, but they include:

• Securing the first-ever official UN decision recognizing housing rights *violations* due to forced evictions in the Dominican Republic;

• Helping *prevent* numerous large-scale evictions before they were carried out in cities like Santo Domingo, Accra, Bangkok, Durban, Lusaka, Manila, Panama City, Rio de Janeiro, and beyond;

• Creating a new set of State reporting guidelines, requiring States that ratified the Covenant to report to the UN on their housing laws and policies; and

• Contributing to new general comments on housing rights, evictions, the right to water, and other advancements, all of which are still in use today and frequently referenced in legal pleadings and judicial decisions. Notably, two of the three general comments—on forced evictions and the right to water—are based on themes not explicitly mentioned in the Covenant but have since evolved into legally recognized rights in various jurisdictions worldwide.

General Comment No. 4 on the Right to Adequate Housing, General Comment No. 7 on Forced Evictions and *General Comment No. 15 on the Right to Water* were all part of my 50-year work plan. Somehow, we were fortunate enough to get this hardworking Committee to play its vital role in making the world a better place.

General Comment No. 4 on the Right to Adequate Housing is significant in countless ways, one of which is simply that at the time of its adoption in 1991, very few people understood what the term *right to adequate housing* actually meant in international law or national practice. The scale of misunderstanding about housing rights was far from insignificant, and how this right was ultimately defined would have a massive impact on what was to be done to secure it for everyone, everywhere. Do governments need to build the entire nation's housing stock? Does housing have to be given away for free? Do homeless people automatically get free homes? Questions like these were thrown about all the time.

Believing that precisely defining these rights was a necessary precursor to enforcing them, I set out to push the Committee in 1989 to consider adopting a specific general comment on these themes. A few years of work, drafting the original text, and lobbying Committee members finally led to the approval in late 1991 of what is still the premier international legal statement on these vital rights. Several of the most fundamental provisions of what we called GC4 reveal just how important this norm is for any government that is serious about respecting and protecting the housing rights of its populace. For instance, it was in GC4 that we achieved *the* international definition of precisely what the term 'adequate' means under international law. GC4 speaks of the following seven criteria needing to be in place for a home to be considered legally adequate:

- legal security of tenure;
- availability of services, materials, facilities, and infrastructure;
- affordability;
- habitability;
- accessibility;
- location; and
- culturally adequate.

Each of these are expanded upon within the text and while it may seem rather simple and straightforward, before these components of adequacy were developed no one really knew what the right to housing meant, in international law or otherwise. It is also in this document that we find one of the first instances of the UN officially equating forced evictions with violations of human rights:

18. In this regard, the Committee considers that instances of forced eviction are prima facie incompatible with the requirements of the Covenant and can only be justified in the most exceptional circumstances, and in accordance with the relevant principles of international law.

Again, it might seem insignificant to the untrained eye, but officially recognizing that forced evictions violate the Covenant and should be subject to domestic legal remedies were massive victories for the housing rights movement—and something we should never take for granted. This required a long and daunting fight. We took on the challenge and we won. The next battle, six years later, struggling to get what became *General Comment No. 7 on Forced Evictions* adopted, was another multi-year effort, but finally in 1997 we got it through, and its key provisions remain as valid today as they were when it was approved a quarter of a century ago.

In many ways, *General Comments No. 4* and *No. 7* were relatively easy to get through the ranks of this important Committee given the fact that the right to adequate housing was explicitly included in Article 11 of the treaty. On the other hand, because the right to water was nowhere to be seen in the Covenant's original 1966 text, I'm sure *General Comment No. 15* on the right to water would have never seen the light of day without my years of lobbying for it and the work of COHRE staff to get it through. After years of planting the seed for such a decision, this process culminated in a dinner I hosted at my Geneva abode with two key Committee members, who arrived as skeptics but left as dedicated proponents. Once they were on board, it was all just a matter of time before it would be approved.

Beyond these general comments, a German human rights activist and I drafted the first version of what years later became the Optional Protocol Complaints Procedure under the Covenant. This protocol, at long last, established a formal quasi-judicial complaint process that allowed beneficiaries of the rights in this cornerstone human rights treaty to invoke it when they alleged their rights had been violated. The *Optional Protocol* was finally approved in 2008. Rather depressingly, as of 2026 a mere 26 of the 171 countries that have ratified the Covenant have also ratified the protocol. I can only hope that the 145 other States parties that have yet to ratify the complaints procedure will do so sooner than later.

Another great aspect of working with this Committee was bringing people from the countries appearing before it all the way to Geneva, allowing local NGOs and grassroots activists from ratifying States to testify *in person* as eyewitnesses to human rights conditions on the ground. I organized numerous fact-finding missions with COHRE to everywhere from the Dominican Republic, St. Vincent and the Grenadines, Solomon Islands, Latvia, Japan, Zimbabwe, Panama and so many others, and we would report back, both in writing and in person, to inform the Committee and the world about what we saw. But the real joy came when I could manage to raise the funds that enabled people to come from their cities and countrysides in the developing world to Geneva, often leaving their country for the very first time and tell their stories themselves. This took a lot more work than one would imagine and beyond the often-complex logistics of getting people from, say, Colombia to Geneva—the visas, the flights, the local accommodation and so much more—ensuring everything went smoothly, affording them ample time to speak and meet Committee members privately in the amazing lounges of the Palais des Nations, and securing decisions in what are called *concluding observations* they could use at home was always a gargantuan task.

Once this started happening at every session, and because this was previously far from commonplace at the treaty bodies, the international and national news media started covering what these committees were saying. I will never forget the huge ALL CAPS headlines we got in all of the papers of the Dominican Republic when the Committee called their eviction practices violations of human rights for the very first time. This was the UN human rights system making a difference in the lives of real people and I hope it remains as it was during the glory years of human rights, when NGOs, UN officials, and even diplomats worked together to move us closer to the unified and rights-respecting world we all seek but often find hard to manifest.

And it was in mobilizing the resources of the UN to pronounce more forcefully and eloquently on housing rights and forced eviction issues than ever before that these new laws, policies, and precedents could be used in normal day-to-day grassroots human rights actions around the world—thusly planting a seed in the stuffy UN corridors that could sprout and flourish beyond them. Indeed, whenever new international efforts related to economic, social, and cultural rights were underway, someone had to mention key housing rights and forced eviction developments at the UN. At one of these, I had been asked to prepare the background paper and first draft of what became the *Maastricht Guidelines on Violations of Economic, Social and Cultural Rights* in 1997. These, naturally, contained specific references to these themes because of how central a role the designation of forced evictions as violations of human rights had been in developing this whole area of law. My background paper, one of what is now an embarrassingly long list of outputs, is by far the most frequently cited academic article I ever published.[10]

In a totally different context but yet again where the results of my UN efforts to condemn forced evictions bore fruit at a national level, I'll never forget the day when South Korean President Kim Dae Jung and I met in his official residence in Seoul, at the famed Blue House where South Korean Presidents reside. After a 15-minute anti-eviction rant from yours truly, he issued an on-the-spot Executive Order to four government Ministers who were also present, effectively banning forced evictions in several municipalities, which I thought was a pretty kick ass effort from a man described as the Nelson Mandela of Asia. I gave him a signed copy of my book *When Push Comes to Shove* after his bodyguards spent a good three minutes leafing through it to make sure these words were safe for their leader, and apparently, they were after decisions like those!

Life Lesson No. 40: Sometimes executive power used in the service of justice can be a good thing.

Still on the eviction theme but in a very different way, in the one and only time I carried out a major project for the oil and gas sector, I was asked by British Petroleum (BP) to write a policy on involuntary resettlement in the early 2000s. Knowing it was unlikely I'd get another chance to have the world's biggest oil company adopt a policy banning involvement in projects with any form of displacement, I took the job. I attended several meetings in various locations and ultimately wrote a 300-plus-page policy stating—in a nutshell—that BP would

---

[10]Scott Leckie, 'Another Step Towards Indivisibility: Identifying the Key Features of Violations of Economic, Social and Cultural Rights' in *Human Rights Quarterly 20*, 1998, pp. 81-124.

fully comply with all international, regional, and national laws treating forced evictions as human rights violations.

The condensed version of the policy, which was formally called *Resettlement: Aspiration, Expectations and Guidelines*, contained incredibly progressive commitments, all approved by this huge oil and gas company dedicating themselves to the following: "Moving people from their homes and lands creates significant risks to the success of our business. Consequently, our aspiration is that *BP will never move a community against its will*." It notes further that "Our commitment to the respect for the rule of law implies a commitment to complying with international law principles and international best practice wherever BP does business." I'm not sure if BP still considers these sentiments their official policy, but I hope they do and that they have complied with these norms *in full* over the past two decades.

Saving Housing Rights in Istanbul

Ever since the world met for the first time in 1976 to discuss international housing issues at Vancouver, the world now meets every 20 years to debate and plan what to do in the coming two decades about the world's habitat problem. In between 1976 and 1996, the world of housing rights had transformed from an absolute human rights backwater issue into the forefront of evolving international and national law. Core elements of my 50-year work plan and the protection wall were falling nicely into place. Where there were once no UN pronouncements on housing rights and eviction issues, there were now many. Where there was no official sanctioning of an individual government because of housing rights violations, now there were many. Where States had to report on virtually nothing about their efforts to fulfill housing rights, now there were very detailed and precise guidelines on what they were required to submit to the UN for scrutiny. And where there was earlier no real pathway for grassroots housing rights activists and slum dwellers into the hallowed halls of the UN, now there was. Small victories on my slow journey in implementing element after element of my half-century work plan. By now it had become clear to me that as one person you could do a lot; never close to enough, but more than you would think. With the right analysis, innovative strategies in place, immense energy, good luck, peacefully waging the war of the flea, and even better vibes the sky was absolutely the limit, or so it seemed at the time.

Riding this wave, I was asked to prepare the background paper for the prestigious American Society of International Law for the upcoming UN Conference on Human Settlements set to be held in Istanbul, Turkey in mid-1996. This gathering would commemorate the 20th anniversary of the first-ever world conference on these issues, Habitat I, which was held in wonderful Vancouver in 1976. From what I've heard over the years, the construction plan of the stupendously modern Habitat I venues was running way behind schedule with just weeks to go before the event was to commence. It was doubtful that they would be ready in time for the tens of thousands of visitors coming into this incredible town from all around the world, and where I was fortunate enough to live in the late 1980s doing a stint at the University of British Colombia. Legend has it that a rather large amount of a certain substance was apparently offered to the construction workers to spur them into overdrive, and it was all done on time. The grapevine tells me this was measured in kilos, not grams. I'm not sure if this story is true or not, but I suspect it was—it was the freewheeling '70s after all. No such stories from Istanbul, alas; we'd all seen Billy's plight in *Midnight Express* too many times to be anything but squeaky clean in Ataturk's land, where prisoners walked the wheel.

It was a bit different though three years earlier at the UN's World Conference on Human Rights, which was held in Vienna in mid-1993. Rather straight but still delightful Vienna (often selected as the world's most liveable city) somehow had to deal with thousands of human rightsers rolling into town, more than a few of whom had brought illicit smokable goods with them, which combined with the copious amounts of Austrian wine, Sacher Torte and other delights made for a pretty wild time. I met and became close to one of Nelson Mandela's interpreters and spent hours drinking way too much one day with Kerry Kennedy Cuomo (RFK's daughter and Andrew's Ex) who kept sticking up for the US no matter how hard I criticized it, commenting over and over that I was an "angry self-hating American." I kept telling her in my oneness-infused rant, one can love the people of a country and still feel distressed about what the governments governing those same people do in their name. If illegally invading countries, starting unnecessary wars, actively opposing economic and social rights at the UN, being a global hegemon with the world's biggest military budget and over 800 military based around the world, persistently supporting dictators, and being the only country to use nuclear weapons made me angry, so be it.

I was angry then and I am angry still today whenever the big guy pushes down the little guy no matter who they are, whenever the powerful trample the weak and the rich quash the poor. I just wish everyone had that in-built anger within themselves because then we might be just that little bit closer to the better world all of us human rights folks are seeking. So many of us, even quite a few of the so-called progressives, simply cannot let go of their country-centric views, their eternal belief in legal fictions called nation states, and this example is just one of many that provided a little more proof that when one views the world and the human race as the basis for understanding life on our planet, points of view change and expand to all of humanity. What is wrong with that?

Fast forward three years to Habitat II, getting the job writing about our proposed housing rights treaty there turned out to be perfect timing. I'd already planned to use this huge global gala as a springboard for my next big housing rights initiative, that of a whole new *International Convention on Housing Rights*, figuring that it might be a bit easier getting a new treaty through Habitat II than through normal human rights channels or those at the UN General Assembly. Yes, the plan was to secure approval for a new treaty devoted exclusively to housing rights, outlining people's rights and the duties of governments to respect, protect, and fulfill these cornerstone elements of a full, meaningful, and dignified life for every human wherever they may reside.

This would be no small feat, yet at the beginning of the process, which was set in motion in 1992 or so, I was as confident as I could be that this might actually work. After all, everything else I had tried to get through the UN in recent years worked with only a small glitch here or there—general comments, resolutions, new procedural precedents, new special rapporteurs put in place, in effect building a whole new area of international law, the entire field of housing, land,

and property rights (HLP)—so why not a Convention governing all of the world on bringing housing rights home for everyone, everywhere? Bring it on! Under international law there is nothing bigger than a Convention, so I was definitely shooting for the stars. It's like getting a major national law adopted on a theme affecting everyone, but not just for one country but for all 193 of them. No small feat, indeed! But when I was 32, I thought, why the hell not, let's go for it. I actually wrote the first draft of the draft convention by hand and in pencil in a rather dark and very smoky bar called Sarasani in Utrecht located on the famous Oudegracht Canal which publicly and openly sold things that were not for sale in any other country in the world at the time. Ah, Sarasani, I miss you now more than ever.

Life Lesson No. 41: No matter which political party is in power, the United States will always be an obstacle to economic, social and cultural rights.

I signed the contract with the ASIL, and within a few months, I had churned out a book length report published by them in December 1994 called *Towards an International Convention on Housing Rights: Options at Habitat II*, which included the first public draft of the convention. This great confluence of events was yet another one of those mysterious synchronicities that defies ordinary explanation. Having dabbled in my mind about the idea of a new housing rights treaty for years already, I'd convinced the UN Special Rapporteur on Housing Rights, Indian Judge Rajindar Sachar, all of whose reports I helped write (as I did for a whole host of other UN special rapporteurs at the time), that he should support the idea of a new housing rights convention, which he vigorously did. In turn, I sat at my desk and within two days edited the draft convention into a final version that was ready for comments and critiques.

The Convention provided in Article 1 that "All children, women and men have an enforceable right to adequate housing which is affordable, accessible and self-determined, and includes a right of access to a safe, affordable and secure place to live in peace and dignity." Who could possibly oppose this? Article 6(1) outlined that "Everyone has the enforceable right to security of tenure over their housing, protecting all persons from *inter alia*, forced or arbitrary eviction, expropriation or relocation, in the absence of an alternative acceptable to those affected, notwithstanding the type of housing inhabited." Again, who in their right minds could be against this?

Most everyone who read the proposed treaty and commented on it seemed to really love it, so after some further revision and tightening, I asked Sachar if we could include the draft Convention in his final report, and again he readily agreed. We, indeed, got it into his 1995 and final report and then things really started moving in ever-stranger directions. We had my thick ASIL report, we had a draft convention in an official UN document, we had increasing media coverage of the idea, and we had Habitat II coming up. What could possibly go wrong? Surely, this is going to work.

In another unpredictable twist of fate—this time a bad one—during a preparatory meeting for Habitat II in Nairobi, Kenya at UN Habitat's headquarters, the US government unexpectedly took the floor at the crowded plenary session. Out of the blue, to everyone's shock and amazement, they publicly attempted to kill not only the idea of a new housing rights convention but *the entire notion* that housing was a human right at all. Remember, this was when a Democratic administration was in the White House, Bill Clinton at the helm, not some crazy rights-hating Republican such as those that occupy the White House, the US Senate, and the US House of Representatives today. A Democrat President (from the same political party as FDR who had famously proposed a *Second Bill of Rights* including the right to housing way back in 1944) and his State Department were pulling out all the stops to destroy the legal principle that everyone everywhere should have a roof over their head as a matter of rights. So much for the US believing in human rights and global justice, not to mention any hopes I may have harbored for a restful time of re-charge before what would in any case have been a very busy time in Istanbul when Habitat II rolled around. In fact, this turned out to be one of the most frenzied and intense working periods ever. Sadly, I could no longer push housing rights forward with my once seemingly limitless energy through a new Convention on Housing Rights. Instead, reasonable governments, civil society and I would have to fight to save the very existence of these rights, even though hundreds of UN documents and countless national constitutions already recognized them.

As I always remind my law students throughout the world in every course I teach, it is all too easily forgotten that all rights are made by humans and so too can humans take rights away, and not just in practice but in their recognition in law, too. And this is precisely what the US government had in mind. The country that criminalizes homelessness in countless cities, the country that allows private landlords to exploit over 30% of the population who are tenants, the country that has one of the lowest percentages of social housing among developed nations, the country whose economic policies foster slum growth rather than improvement, and the country where "property rights" dominate while housing is merely treated as profitable real estate, rather than a fundamental human need—that country was trying to sabotage the very existence of housing rights. I took this personally. This one country was actually trying to destroy not just housing rights *per se*, but all of my recent achievements in international law were going to be for nothing if the US prevailed, and I wasn't going to have it!

Thus began a lengthy and exhausting battle to save housing rights, a battle I neither wanted to wage nor spend time on with so many other fights at hand, but to this I knew I had to dedicate all my energies or else the future would be anything but rosy. It's one thing to oppose a new convention, but another thing entirely to oppose the very existence of a right itself. And so, the battle began within seconds of the US statement. I started running around the huge meeting room in Nairobi in a state of panic, my uncomfortable and ill-fitting suit becoming more ragged by the day. I went to the seat of every reasonable government there, urging all of them to give retorts in response to this unexpected US-led assault on the rights of the world's poor. I ran to the delegations where I already had diplomat friends, to the Philippines first, then to India, to Sweden, Holland and others from the EU, South Africa and a bunch of others imploring them to reply and publicly support not just housing rights but the Convention, too. I was by now used to running around such meetings and shamelessly begging for political support and as it had before, it began working again. In subsequent months I gave speeches, engaged in private discussions at numerous receptions, wrote editorials, held meetings, published articles, and secured statements from various UN human rights bodies in support of housing rights. All of this created a situation where, over the coming months, the US began to feel increasingly isolated and alone, much as they do today though for entirely different reasons.

This all occurred despite the increasingly desperate efforts of the State Department which led the US charge to destroy housing rights. We successfully refuted every single one of the US arguments about the non-existence of housing rights in venue after venue and article after article, and it started to look like we would win the battle. And yet, no matter how hard we tried to push the housing rights issue to the top of the agenda, this high-level assault on these rights by the US did probably contribute to the *International Convention on Housing Rights* ending up without its moment of glory in Istanbul as we had hoped. To this day, there is still a big hole in the body of international human rights law where this Convention should have been. I've recently been urging the current UN Special Rapporteur on Housing Rights to reactivate the Convention idea, and certainly hope he will. But the even bigger quest of saving housing rights themselves would itself culminate in this town where East famously meets West and we were ready.

I came to Istanbul supercharged and more than ready for the brawls to come. The issue had grown so large that, besides working the official room where diplomats discussed and drafted what became the *Habitat Agenda*—a major statement on global housing issues but not a housing rights convention—I was invited to speak at over 40 additional events. Most were standing-room-only gatherings, and I attended all of them despite my increasing exhaustion. I gave speeches on Tibet, speeches on the Kurds, speeches on evictions, speeches on housing rights, speeches on the UN, speeches about everything it seemed. When I was free and able to head back to the official meetings, going in and out of the committee room where the work was proceeding all day long, some dictator-wannabe UN security guard repeatedly harassed me. It pissed me off so much that I asked to see his badge number to report him at which point he reached out to grab my security badge and threatened to arrest me though he had no power or reason to do so. What a sad wanker. Reading my name very loudly for all to hear, he shouted, "Scott Leckie no good!" With all of the pressure I was already under, this was anything but a nice moment. I wondered what the future would hold for this angry security guard. Anyway, chasing after this diplomat and that and making sure the language protecting housing rights would remain in the final text was, as it always is, a daunting affair neither for the faint-hearted nor weak-willed.

I will be forever grateful to two governments, in particular, which can very justifiably take credit for saving housing rights during that summer in 1996, the Philippines and the Netherlands; the former where I had worked so often in the slums all across Metro Manila and the latter which I had called home for so long and where I had just become a citizen. As the process neared its end, when it became clear we would win the battle to save housing rights after sorting out the details, the US privately and reluctantly accepted it had no allies in its ridiculous and backwards attempt to undermine the international legal system.

At that point, the Dutch diplomat I had been working with for years on housing rights asked me to join her and a colleague at his hotel to finalize the housing rights sections of the Habitat II final document. This was government-civil society cooperation of the finest sort. We arrived at a very fancy hotel, at which point he showed us around and then unexpectedly left to go somewhere more exciting, leaving me and the world's most splendid diplomat alone in a ritzy hotel drafting the document that would end up saving housing rights. We wrote and wrote and wrote, edited, edited, and edited, and at about 4am we finally had the text ready to go for the final meeting before the document would hopefully be approved, adopted and ready to present to the world.

Some people think of me as a perpetual party guy, and in some ways I remain that, but at 4am anywhere, including Istanbul, it's time for me to head home, including during those rather wild years of mine. Yet, even in the poshest of cities I have never been much of a fan of strolling through totally deserted streets on my way to find a taxi or some other way home at such a late hour, lion hounds always howling in the back of my mind. I assumed that because Istanbul is in a Muslim country, which in my experience generally have less street crime than countries dominated by other religions, and because it was hosting this major international event, security would be tight even at that late hour. Alas, that was not to be the case.

The best diplomat the world had ever seen got all of our papers together and put them in her overflowing bag along with her laptop, diplomatic passport, and everything else, while I got my stuff together. Out we ventured down the biggest pedestrian shopping street in Istanbul which had been crowded wall-to-wall with people all day, but what was now completely empty, with no one in sight. We carefully walked for a few minutes down this now extremely unnerving lane without any trouble at all and then I spotted some guy lurking in the shadows but thought nothing of it. "How could someone be so callous as to harass us? We just saved housing rights", I remember thinking to myself. And then just as that idiotic thought that I'd hoped would somehow magically protect us exited my mind, it happened. With absolutely no warning or clue she was about to be attacked, the culprit brutally assaulted my diplomat friend with a very violent shove in the back, pushing her face first into the ground, while he ripped her bag off her arm and disappeared down a totally dark and even scarier alley way. I screamed at him, yelled for help, and chased him for a bit but then, unable to see anything in this pitch-black zone, thought better of it and retreated to find my favorite diplomat on the ground, shattered by the fact that this violent mugging happened just as we were about to celebrate the end of Habitat II and the success of saving housing rights. By now we were both scared and stumbled along this now terrifyingly empty street desperate to find a way back to our respective hotels and finally we found a taxi and off we went.

It was really only in the taxi that we realized that everything we had written, all that work, the perfectly crafted texts that were to be put into the final document based on months of negotiations, and approved by all nations of the world tomorrow were gone. We had no back-ups and no earlier drafts from which to work, nothing was left but our memories. So, we did what we had to do and back we went to my hotel room to reconstruct on hotel letter paper we found in a drawer there everything we had spent the entire day and night formulating, reformatting, and finalizing. It took us the rest of this gloomy Istanbul night to do this but when the sun rose and began climbing into the early morning sky, we had done it. From memory alone, we reconstructed the entire document, which to us seemed a perfect rehash of what we had done before and off we went back to the UN venue to hand it over to the Committee chairperson. We slept not a wink that night and visited a rather intimidating Turkish police station to report the mugging the next day, which was far from fun especially going without sleep, running entirely on adrenalin.

Life Lesson No. 42: Always keep a back-up!

In the end, it all worked out. The Dutchies and the Filipinos carried the day, along with the rest of the world, *sans* the US, and housing rights were saved once and for all. The final text was included in an official document called *Human Right to Housing* issued by what was called The Informal Working Group. Paragraph 60 of the *Habitat Agenda* ended up reading: "Within the overall context of an enabling approach, Governments should take appropriate action in order to promote, protect and ensure the full and progressive realization of the right to adequate housing. These actions include, but are not limited to: (a) Providing, in the matter of housing, that the law shall prohibit any discrimination and guarantee to all persons equal and effective protection against discrimination on any ground such as race, color, sex, language, religion, political or other opinion, national or social origin, property, birth or other status; (b) Providing legal security of tenure and equal access to land for all, including women and those living in poverty, as well as effective protection from forced evictions that are contrary to the law, taking human rights into consideration and bearing in mind that homeless people should not be penalized for their status...."

And then in Paragraph 98 we won the day again on forced evictions, something that the US also sought to undermine. That paragraph ended up reading "To reduce vulnerability, Governments at the appropriate levels, including local authorities, should: (a) Work with non-governmental organizations and community-based organizations to assist members of vulnerable groups to obtain secure tenure; (b) Protect all people from and provide legal protection and redress for forced evictions that are contrary to the law, taking human rights into consideration; when evictions are unavoidable, ensure that, as appropriate, alternative suitable solutions are provided...."

Little did the world know until now that those words were written on hotel letterhead paper by my diplomat friend and me after being violently mugged on the mean streets of Istanbul at 4 a.m. So it goes sometimes in this strange world of ours. Now some 30 years later, housing rights are solidly entrenched with more laws, policies, and procedures in place to protect them than ever before. They are still not nearly strong enough, and remain far too easy to violate, but they are there. The US did stop the Convention in its tracks, despite what this document could have done to protect the rights of billions of people across the world who are yet to enjoy the full spectrum of rights accorded to them under international law. But they failed miserably in their efforts to destroy housing rights *per se*, and that victory of ours remains one of the sweetest of my lifelong fight for housing rights for everyone, everywhere. We beat the US at its ugly game to harm the poorest amongst us and I have to say we were proud that we did.

CNN and a bunch of other media outlets interviewed me about this and some other issues and told us when the story would be broadcast. Our cheap hotels where the NGOs stayed not only had no TVs in the rooms but didn't carry CNN either, even on the lobby TV. Desperate to see the housing rights story, I came up with the insane idea of going to a nice hotel in Istanbul, the Marmara, to ask if we could sit in an empty room and watch CNN for a couple of hours to catch the story. Much to my amazement, these unbelievably nice hotel receptionists said of course we could use one of their empty rooms, but that it would have to be a suite. "Would that be OK?", they asked. Amazing. Of course, I said, and then they promptly guided us to this huge and ornate suite the likes of which I had never once in my life set foot in, and then after turning the TV on to the CNN channel asked if we would like a drink. I said, well, yes could I have a gin and tonic, please? My friend, activist extraordinaire Minar Pimple, from Mumbai, said he would have one too.

She said she'd be back in a few minutes with our drinks, and indeed very quickly she appeared again with these sumptuous and very strong G & T's which we sipped while we waited for me to appear on the CNN screens. When I did come into focus, mis-tied tie, messy hair, wrinkled shirt, and bloodshot eyes, visible for the world to see, we just laughed and laughed and laughed as Minar and I always do whenever we are together fighting the good fight wherever that may be. Before she left the room, the receptionist simply said, "Welcome to Turkey, the room and drinks are on us." I was dumbfounded and insisted we would pay, but she smiled and refused. Magic again reigns, I thought. First, we saved housing rights, and then this. Sometimes the world is wonderful.

Life Lesson No. 43: Dare to ask. If you don't, it won't just happen on its own (and that applies to free upgrades to business class, too).

Restitution for Refugees and IDPs

Before we move on to the next stories of this tale, those about war and warzones, let me briefly explain how my work evolved from housing rights and eviction efforts to housing, land, and property restitution for refugees and IDPs. I started working specifically on these issues in practical terms in the immediate aftermath of the Bosnian war in 1995, and then concerning the Republic of Georgia, Albania, Sri Lanka, Palestine, Kosovo, Timor Leste, Syria, Iraq, Burma and so many others where refugees and IDPs found it impossible to return, repossess and re-inhabit their original homes.

Some of these stories are outlined in detail below, but for the moment I just want to thank former Minister of Human Rights in the Brazilian government and UN dignitary, Paulo Sergio Pinheiro for his instrumental assistance in pushing the restitution issue further than I could have ever imagined within the UN system and international law more broadly. In the early 2000s, Paulo was a member of the famous Sub-Commission where I had guided my first UN resolution through a decade earlier, and in that capacity, he agreed to take on the responsibilities of working as the UN Special Rapporteur on Housing and Property Restitution. This work, besides resulting in a series of major reports and a percolation of restitution themes throughout the full gamut of the UN's human rights machinery, resulted in what became known as the *United Nations Principles on Housing and Property Restitution for Refugees and Displaced Persons*, now colloquially known as the *Pinheiro Principles*, a name I gave them immediately after their adoption by the UN in 2005. The name stuck and now the *Pinheiro Principles* are known throughout the international legal system as the go to document on anything to do with HLP restitution in all of its forms.

In many respects, conflict- and disaster-related restitution issues dominated my work from roughly 1998 to 2008. After which time, I shifted more and more into the world of climate displacement, though I did do several years of work on restitution and land grabbing issues in Burma until the military coup by the generals stopped all of that in early 2021. I wrote and edited several books on restitution themes both in the run up to and following the approval of the *Pinheiro Principles*. Seeing them applied in practice in so many post-conflict settings has been truly rewarding, even though they should have been complied with far more intensively than they have been thus far.

Nothing irks the bad guys more than the prospect of having to give back homes, lands, and properties they have illegally stolen from refugees and the displaced. You can imagine how deeply the vested interests resist the *Pinheiro Principles* when those seeking HLP justice try to apply them.

Life Lesson No. 44: Only shameless cowards refuse to enforce restitution rights for refugees and displaced persons

For the moment suffice it to say that for a solid 40 years of my working life I have been dedicated to ensuring that everyone, everywhere can have a decent home, be protected against forced eviction in law and practice, and, that if you become a refugee or IDP, you can demand and reclaim your home, land, and property when it's safe to return. I have tried everything in my limited powers as one person, working together with an extraordinary array of amazing fellow human rights activists, to make all of these things come true for everyone, including you. Yes, *you.*

Chances are I don't know you personally and probably never will, but that doesn't matter, for I know without a doubt that we share so much more than that which divides us. I know you want to be loved and to love. I know you love your children and your community. I know you get hungry if you do not eat and tired if you do not sleep. I know you want peace more than war. I know you wish you were just a little bit wealthier and I know you wish you had all forms of security all the time. As much as I want to know you personally, I know even though I have been to all corners of our planet and plan to be there again soon, were I to have just a few seconds of time to look into your eyes, I know what I would see there and hope that you would see the same.

We would share a look of acknowledgement, that deep knowledge of our commonalities and the beginnings of a teardrop of recognition, shed by both of us, as we let go of anything that divides us and embrace all that brings us closer. This is what I have done in fighting for decades for *your* home, *your* rights to stay there and *your* rights to reclaim it if it was illegally taken from you. I will continue this fight until my dying day and even expand it to include the literally billions who stand to lose their homes because of climate change. I will never stop. It will always be my fervent hope that the little informal multitudes of love that I may have generated over the years will grow and grow and grow, all playing indispensable roles in pushing our collective evolution just a step closer to the more perfect world we all deserve.

Chapter 4

War

We cannot help but believe that the old hatreds shall someday pass; that the lines of tribe shall soon dissolve.
—President Barack Obama
20 January 2009 Inauguration Speech

I hope these wise words of Obama come true one day, but it sure doesn't feel like it at the moment, no matter how hard so many of us may try to bring them to fruition. To be a human rights advocate, almost always working too protect the rights of complete strangers you'll never meet or know, you must be driven by an inherently selfless sense of justice, a correspondingly deep abhorrence of injustice, and an iron will to keep going against all odds to get the bad guys to stop with their madness—and hold them accountable and sometimes even put the worst of them behind bars. Injustice in any form appalls me but being a housing rights guy, the process of first displacing people from their homes, then systematically stealing refugee and IDP homes, lands, and properties from which they fled to save their lives and then, finally, financially benefiting from this war booty always riled me and still very much does.

When I speak with people who wish for nothing more than to return to their now stolen homes, sometimes just to have a look inside or to gather whatever family heirlooms may still be there, and they are prevented from doing so by the illegitimate current occupants, it drives me crazy with rage. I assume that if it happened to you, it would drive you equally mad. Imagine for a moment that some unruly masked thugs linked to a particular religious, political, or ethnic group arrived at your home, told you to leave or you would be killed along with your family, and then as you are walking away you look back and watch those same thugs taking over your home. Imagine that happening to you. What would your response be? To whom would you turn for support? Would you want justice?

I remember speaking to a very gentle Serbian woman in a refugee camp outside of Belgrade who had once gathered up the courage to visit her home in Croatia from where she had been displaced. She said she reluctantly knocked on *her own front door*, which was then opened by a very angry Croatian man who aggressively asked what she wanted. She told him it was her apartment and that she just wanted to gather her old photo albums, visible to her on the top shelf of a bookcase, containing the only pictures of her family, who had been killed in the fighting. He swore at her, threatened her with death if she ever returned and slammed *her* door in her face. Just heartbreaking. Where is the justice here? What if this happened to you? How would you feel?

And what of the elderly Palestinian couple I spoke with in the West Bank who told me of their visit to *their* home in what was now Israel. They, too, fearfully knocked on *their front door*, having noticed that the same curtains they had hung in the late 1940s still covered the windows of the beautiful dwelling which was now occupied by people who had been allocated the ornate home by the Israeli-government's Jewish Agency. To justify Israel keeping control over the thousands upon thousands of Palestinian homes belonging to the now nine million Palestinian refugees spread all across the world, the government established a custodial entity that populated those homes with Jewish Israeli citizens, paid no compensation to the original owners, and most certainly prevented them from returning to live there or even sell their property. This is what ethnic cleansing looks like in the real world. The elderly couple, then just a few short years from the end of their lives, just wanted one last look at *their home* but again were angrily denied entry by the aggressive current occupants who nastily told them to leave before they called the police. Where is the justice here?

It is for people like this that I have worked so intensively to make HLP restitution a reality. Getting justice for refugees and IDPs involves not only facilitating the right to return as part of a broader peace process, but also the right to re-inhabit and re-possess their original homes, eg. the process of HLP restitution.

Indeed, it involves every possible effort to reverse the grotesque practice of ethnic cleansing, and I have pursued this crime, trying to reverse it, in almost 20 countries, including Kosovo.

Life Lesson No. 45: If it's not yours, don't move in. If you do and the owner returns, have some dignity, show some respect and give it back.

Kosovo - Soot, Shambles, and Shokimobiles

So much about war is, indeed, about the small 't' *tribe*, obsessed over by all too often meek humans with little else to live for in a world that would be much better served by *Tribe*, with a capital 'T', in recognition that all of us, everywhere, are part of a single human family. Though I proudly support the Tribe vision of our world, I am most distinctly *not* a war zone junkie like so many of my UN and NGO friends, but sometimes there is no alternative and into the zone you go to lend a hand to shift the focus away from tribe to Tribe.

From the mid-1990s onwards I started finding myself in a whole range of places across the world where war had just raged ruthlessly and in some cases where the wanton violence of ethnic conflict was still very much underway. One of those places was the former Yugoslav Republic of Kosovo. Kosovo has endured war and violence for hundreds of years, most recently being severed from Serbia after an intense 1999 NATO bombing campaign in support of the Kosovar Liberation Army (KLA/UÇK) and the ethnic Albanian majority, who made up about 90% of the population but were tightly controlled by the Serbian minority. In percentage terms, thus, not all that different than South Africa during *apartheid*. The tremendous—and justifiable—guilt most Western countries felt for failing to intervene early and intensively enough in the brutal war in neighboring Bosnia and Herzegovina (1991-1995), which caused hundreds of thousands of deaths and displaced millions, weighed heavily on them. As a result, the pressure for NATO to intervene in Kosovo's ethnic conflict became so intense that it finally acquiesced and began bombing both Serbia and Kosovo in late March 1999. The bombing lasted until 11 June 1999 at which point the Serbs surrendered and talks began to administer the new country with the UN to act as the *government* until such a time that local democratic elections could be held.

Life Lesson No. 46: Big 'T' Tribe always.

Being largely a non-violent, universal responsibility, humanitarian, pacifist sort of guy, it would never be easy for me to square the use of force with the principles contained in the UN Charter and the famous renunciation of war contained in the legendary Kellogg-Briand Pact or the *Peace Pact of 1928*. But having seen first-hand what occurred in Bosnia and Herzegovina during that war and other failures to intervene to stop mass killing and slaughters in places like Rwanda and Cambodia, it became harder to oppose the use of force in Kosovo when its use could probably end even worse violence and needless death. I still remember learning of the existence of the famous *Peace Pact* at university, and was stunned beyond belief that on August 27, 1928, the representatives of 15 nations gathered together in Paris to sign the renunciation of war agreement that abolished war as a legally permissible means of enforcing the law or of changing it. But I was even more astounded to learn that in January 1929 the US Senate approved the pact by a vote of 85 to 1.[11] Can you imagine what the vote would be today? And just what does that say about the shocking decline of contemporary America? I sure hope the world uses the 100th anniversary of the Pact in two years as an opportunity to truly end war

---

[11]Oona A Hathaway and Scott J. Shapiro, *The Internationalists: How a Radical Plan to Outlaw War Remade the World*, Simon and Schuster, 2017, p. 129 and 283.

forevermore.

During the early stages of the Kosovo war, I was in Malaysia working with local NGOs on various eviction issues trying to explain the complex ins and outs of how non-legal housing groups could most easily use human rights law to their benefit. Every night I watched news reports, which for a couple of weeks featured a tiny UN team comprised of my wife Kirsten, UN superstar Sergio Vieira de Mello and a few others visiting bombed out homes, bridges, and government buildings, all documented nightly on international television. Having asked for but receiving no security guarantees from NATO, let alone from Serbian, KLA or other soldiers on the ground, Kirsten and Sergio were always in danger of being bombed themselves. Watching these scenes night after night stressed me out so much that I ended up with the biggest and most gruesome carbuncle the world has ever seen, in full public view on my neck.

Lucky me, I had to host an international meeting in Bangkok a week later with eviction experts who we had invited from all around the world, which became increasingly less fun as the creature on my neck got bigger and bigger, and more painful, with each passing day. Before too long this thing became a life form in and of itself, like an alien that I couldn't wait to expel from my cranial region. Luckily a Thai doctor friend, Dr. Somporn the Slum Doctor as she was known, and her trusty nurses skillfully used a scalpel on that multi-headed neck monster and forced it into submission. All of the pictures I have from a trip I made to one of my favorite countries, Laos, after the Bangkok meetings reveal a smiling guy hand-in-hand with his new Laotian Buddhist monk brother Kham exploring deep and dank Buddhist relic caves along the Mekong River with a massive bandage covering much of my neck.

Until I wrote this down right now, I'd always assumed that this unique medical condition, which I had never experienced before nor since, was caused solely by the stress of watching my beloved on CNN in a warzone every night, and I think it was indeed that. But then again, it has just dawned on me that it could have been somehow caused by something else entirely that I experienced a couple of weeks before in Kuala Lumpur.

Life Lesson No. 47: Packing advice: always bring hand sanitizer.

One night in the Malaysian capital, I was at a boisterous NGO dinner in an Indian neighborhood when out of the blue a horrifying scream came from the neighbors next door. Our host Johanna ran outside yelling "Uncle, Auntie, what's wrong, la?" Some loud screaming ensued while we waited for her to come back and let us know what was going on. I was the only man there, so when she came back and looked straight at me, I knew she wanted me to do something that the women there might have been a bit more reluctant to do. She said, "It's OK, la, but they really need your help now, la, hurry!" I rushed next door, smelling the strong incense before entering the small and tidy apartment, with hints of an Indian life all around, when an elderly and very frail woman wearing a colorful sari came into the living room and said, "Can you please help me, la? My husband has had an accident. He is so stupid, la." I am completely baffled and immediately scroll through the medical lessons learned stored deep in the back of my brain, getting ready to do CPR or some other life-saving maneuver.

But before I could recall whether the breathing part of CPR remained part of the procedure or if it was just repeated chest compressions, she ushered me into the bathroom, where I saw her husband wearing only a very loose, once white and now heavily stained lungi, with the lower half of his left leg completely invisible and missing down the opening of the toilet! Yes, this brilliant elderly man hated sitting on the new toilet seat so much that, missing his ground-level squat toilet, he climbed onto and squatted directly on the raised rim of the porcelain bowl, 40 cm off the ground, to do his nightly number two. He slipped violently, with fresh feces acting as lubricant for his leg, which slid far down the pipes and might have been stuck permanently had someone not arrived to handle one of the least appetizing tasks imaginable. And that was the fun job of helping this poor guy to extricate himself from the iron vice-like grip of what felt like a very possessive and hungry drain.

Examining the situation in more detail and trying to understand just what it was that was going on, I see a leg missing a calf and a foot, a growing amount of blood and even more poop. Realizing that no one other than me is prepared to do anything to help this gentle man who, when his penis started flopping around and became visible to both of us, actually said, "So small, so small, when I was young it was so big, but now so small." His wife scoffs very loudly and melodramatically rolls her eyes after he says this, and deeply embarrassed rushes back into the living room muttering under her breath in shame at her life partner and his ways. The guy's leg is stuck halfway up to his knee and he's worried this strange foreigner is going to judge the size of his genitals.

I quickly turn to his very worried wife because he is starting to moan in pain now, and I ask her if she has any oil. She confusedly asks if I would like palm oil, coconut oil, vegetable oil or corn oil? I tell her it doesn't matter and to just bring the biggest container she has because I am going to need *a lot*. These were the days way before COVID, SARS or anything like that, and no gloves of any sort were available, let alone face masks; and I could have very much used both of those, believe me.

Once I had the oil in hand, I poured copious amounts over the visible part of his leg and into the toilet mouth, and then tried to gently retract his appendage to no avail. It was totally stuck and it really must have put this man of advanced years in a lot of pain. I tried again, more oil, more pulling, constant repositioning but still no luck. Then again and nothing. I was just about to call it quits and start looking for some kind of crowbar and on the fourth attempt, more oil than ever, and pulling and pulling and pulling, out it popped; lots of wounds and scratches, lots of blood, and yes, lots of you know what. He hugged me over and over again and wouldn't let go he was so grateful. I was so happy to help but washing my hands and arms, *make that sterilizing them*, was my most immediate concern. I stood at their sink for a very, very long time washing, re-washing, scrubbing and scrubbing until they were just about raw trying to get everything off. I thought they were clean, but maybe, just maybe, it was that fine event that somehow brought on the crusty carbuncle on my neck two weeks hence. Who knows? This kind couple who had left Malaysia precisely once in their life to, of all places, Australia, went to get me a gift before I left. Though I repeatedly said that would not be necessary they handed me what I was told was one of their most prized possessions that was prominently displayed in their living room, a mass-produced boomerang purchased in the airport departure lounge on their trip to the Lucky Country, fake Aboriginal dot painting adorning it. They meant so well and I was honoured to receive their gift. Bless their sweet and tender souls.

Just a few days after NATO suspended its bombing campaign, 30,000 troops from what became known as KFOR—Kosovo Force—entered the country, including Kirsten and a few others from the UN—who rode in from neighboring Macedonia, now called North Macedonia, on a KFOR tank. She was to spend more than year in Kosovo working with the UN government there, the UN Mission in Kosovo (UNMIK), with her long-time boss New Zealander Dennis McNamara who was the head of one of the four UNMIK pillars that made up the basic structure of the UN-led government, so never short of work during those hectic days.

When I was still in Laos, I received an email from the UN asking if I could come to Kosovo immediately to work on housing, land, and property rights issues. How could I possibly say no? Had Kirsten not been there, I might have declined, but what happened in Kosovo in recent years really moved me, so I said yes without thinking. I rushed back to Bangkok, then Geneva to take care of our apartment and tend to countless administrative affairs, and then I was off—first to Zurich, then Croatia and then Skopje in Macedonia. At this point, we were renting three apartments simultaneously, which made matters a bit complicated. We had a glorious flat in Geneva, another in Sarajevo, and finally a third in Pristina that Kirsten had rented shortly after her arrival there. These were hectic times to be sure, but at least I knew where I'd be staying in Kosovo and that soothed things a bit.

Our UN team met up at the Zurich airport departure lounge for the big trip in. After stopping in Croatia's capital, and wandering the streets of Zagreb, I again tasted the Balkans. Air Croatia then got us to Skopje Airport, with US drones laying all around along the sides of the runways, further augmenting the feeling of war in the air. The arrivals hall was incredibly hot and thronged by desperate Kosovar Albanians and Macedonians in an utterly unruly and decrepit terminal. This region had been through too much.

Out we finally stepped right into the oppressive 40°C summer heat of the Balkans that was far fiercer than I had anticipated. We spent the night in a rudimentary guesthouse of sorts where the husky owner harped on constantly about the war next door, the killing next door, the brutality next door, the danger next door, the evil next door. Next door being Kosovo, of course. A day later, before going *next door*, we made our way to the UN office in Skopje and arranged some spots on what they called the UN shuttle, a bus that ferried in UN workers from all around the world right into the middle of the action in Kosovo just a few hours away. A rather rickety local bus carried just five or six of us UN staff in the back, squeezed between a pile of obviously well-used mattresses, broken desks, outdated computers that looked like they came from the 1970s, and other essentials needed for setting up a whole new government. This was not your ordinary, run of the mill UN humanitarian mission where the UN distributes food parcels, sets up refugee and IDP camps and generally tries to prevent human rights abuses. No, this was much bigger. This was governing, and we were the government. We cannot screw this up!

Life Lesson No. 48: The liberator may be seen as the occupier much sooner than you may think.

These were the early days of what became the government of this little territory, fighting hard for independence, first seen as liberators by the local population, and then—quicker than you might imagine— as occupiers. The KFOR soldiers, acting as border guards, pretty much waved us through and there we found ourselves in Kosovo for the first time, a place that was to become my home for several very eventful months. On the bumpy ride to the capital Pristina, besides seeing rudimentary graves all over the place, mounds of freshly dug earth still showing, houses were burning everywhere we looked. The NATO air war from above might have ended, but the war on the ground most definitely hadn't. I watched one old woman desperately trying to douse the flames on what may have been her house with a bucket of water that had absolutely no effect, and that's when it dawned on me that I was watching a crime in progress. These were all Serbian homes. They had lost the war and were now being hounded out of the territory in a massive act of reverse ethnic cleansing being orchestrated by the very people NATO had ostensibly been trying to protect. So depressing. The bus went totally quiet as we all started realizing one by one what was going on. After watching the brutality meted out by the Serbs during both the Bosnian war and the Kosovo war, many found it difficult not to support NATO's air campaign, even though it was carried out without UN Security Council authorization. Many normally anti-war humanitarians saw it as the only way to end the mass human rights violations and blatant ethnic cleansing against the Kosovar Albanian community. It was crystal clear that none of the sides could be seen as unequivocally the good guys, but it was quite obvious that the Serbian side was guilty of far more oppression than the Albanians and as I always side with the underdog, I felt deeply for them.

I quickly scanned the horizon upon entering the sad sights of heavily bombed Pristina for the first time, looking everywhere for UNHCR signs and their main office. I had much more to look forward to than the others on the bus—a wife, a home, and many friends waited for me. The others were separated from their families, had few, if any, friends in Kosovo, and had the misfortune of dwelling in the rather depressing UN hotel housed in the infamous Grand Hotel, something that can only be appreciated after experiencing it, especially following the losses suffered during the war.

A few weeks into the mission, a UN friend and I who enjoyed food even more than me would hit one of the few functioning restaurants in the city located within the Grand. I can still hear his soft Canadian voice asking the disheveled waiter for a well-known Kosovo delicacy: "Do you have any cheese fritters?" pointing at the item on the menu, but they were all out. They were always all out. In fact, unsurprisingly, they were out of everything on the more than 200 dish-long menu. They only offered French fries and some kind of meat which had clearly been frozen for a very, very, very long time, so that's what we had. We went exploring after the meal, as this hotel was a visual goldmine for anyone who wanted to find an odd sight or two. We saw a sign for a disco and went through a door that had clearly not been used since the war ended. We found ourselves in the now decrepit basement disco and bar, horribly dingy and dark, and covered with dust and grime. This extremely spine-chilling place was bizarrely decorated with the entire front-end of a Mack truck, with full-sized nude female mannequins dangling from each side of the cabin, in some inexplicable display of debauchery. I sat for a moment on the heavily stained and burn-marked sofas, in the gloomy darkness of this once popular military hang out, wondering about all the horrible crimes that might have been planned there, over cigarettes and cheap whisky. This place had some seriously bad vibes, so we got out of there as quickly as we could to escape any evil karma that might have been inadvertently left behind.

Life Lesson No. 49: Visit abandoned discos at your peril. Chances are they will not increase your faith in humanity.

As my new colleagues left the bus and went off to the Grand, I asked around and found UNHCR's office in what appeared to be a crumbling government building. Seeing Kirsten for the first time in more than a month after the immense physical threats she had faced in the intervening period was so great and we headed off to what was to become my next abode, one of more than 60 very different places I've called home throughout my life. With so many buildings and homes in ruins and so much poverty across the province, we were extremely lucky to have great accommodation compared to what so many others were forced to endure. We lived in a small apartment complex with around 20 flats. While a horribly toxic chemical smell immediately engulfed anyone who entered, the flat we shared with another UN staff member was relatively intact, new, and luxurious by local standards. There were some seriously nasty bugs in the bed, the toxic smells never really went away, and there was rarely running water. We only sporadically enjoyed electricity and had no TV, but it was going to be home, so I made the most of it. One of the first things I did was to set up a little impromptu music system mostly run off batteries to ensure I'd get at least a bit of my daily dose of the Grateful Dead to keep me going.

In those extremely frenzied days and weeks immediately after NATO ceased its bombing and KFOR and the UN entered, simple questions like "Who does this apartment actually belong to?" never really crossed the UN's collective mind, even though this was one of the issues I personally had to work on. As it turned out, our apartment complex was owned primarily by Serbs, most of whom worked at the local airport. Our individual flat was owned by a Serbian judge. There was no illegal occupation here, but had the war not happened I'm sure the owners would have still been there instead of having fled to the relative safety of Belgrade. One of the owners felt he didn't need to flee, being of Turkish origin, but he decided to make some funds off the UN. So, he rented his flat out to them and moved with three other family members into the single car garage on the ground floor, which really didn't feel right, but that's the power of money, I guess.

The only reason the building was available, except for that single flat owned by the Turkish fellow was that virtually the entire Serb population fled Kosovo once the Albanians took over. Vengeance was everywhere. You fuck us over; we'll fuck you over. Tit for tat. *Quid Pro Quo*. You will reap what you sow. Call it what you want, source it to wherever, but it was playing itself out right before our very eyes, and yet again the UN was called in to sort out the unsortable. I only met the judge to whom we paid rent one time and I had rarely met anyone as terrified as he was that day. He usually received his monthly rent payments when a UN staff member visited the Serbian capital to meet him and hand over the cash. The one time I met him he was shaking like a leaf no matter how hard we tried to calm him down and settle his nerves, but who could blame him. It was probably the only time he came back to Kosovo since the war ended and I would bet on it that he hasn't returned since. He said he was there to collect some documents he needed that he had left behind but as the house was ransacked before we moved in, they were no longer there. Ethnic cleansing sucks and reverse ethnic cleansing sucks just as much, and he was definitely a victim of the latter.

We tried to create a sense of normality in this highly abnormal place, but it was never easy to get the front door to actually lock, avoid the noxious fumes of burning plastic and other rubbish that pervaded everything, gain access to water and electricity, and just try to have a degree of comfort. It finally dawned on me why the poor guy who sat in front of our building all night long every night was necessary. He was so delighted every time I brought him piping hot tea or biscuits in the middle of the often-freezing cold night. I was always happy to be friendly with anyone who kept a loaded Glock tucked into his ill-fitting pants.

Life Lesson No. 50: Ethnic conflict....awful

In those days, many of the still-standing houses were illegally occupied, including the one on the corner across from us. The new occupants simply tossed everything out through the windows onto the ground, scattering the remnants of the previous occupants' life like detritus around the house on all four sides. Violence was a common feature of life in Kosovo those days and within a day of arriving there was an attempted kidnap of a woman by human traffickers and the mass murder of 11 Serb farmers. Things were not going well during these early days of transition. With numerous books for sale in Pristina written by Enver Hoxha, the former Albanian dictator who seemed to still be worshipped by some, I feared for what this would mean for the future of Kosovo.

Life Lesson No. 51: You may find beauty, even in the midst of war.

There was not a lot of oneness around those days or even now more than 25 years later, but I tried my best to generate it with both my Albanian and Serbian friends. During the first days there, I stood around in the UNHCR parking lot amongst all those famous white land cruisers. A cool-looking local dude approached me and said "Hello, my brother, thank you for helping us." I smiled and when I saw the peace sign tattooed on his bicep, I knew he'd be a bro. Beja and I talked a long time and he told me he was a musician, but that the Serb Army had looted everything, including his beloved guitars, both acoustic and electric. He lost them forever during the worst fighting of the war. We hear about the big picture of war when we see it on TV or read about it in history books, but to me it is always these little stories of what happens to individuals who lose their homes, their dignity, their loved ones, and their prized possessions that the Big Powers who commence such wars often neglect to consider in their march towards calling the ultimate shots. I spent the following months looking everywhere to find a guitar that I could give to my new friend but with so little functioning I was unable to find one before I left for good. Beja, now in the majority, had been seriously harmed by Serb soldiers who ransacked his home, yet he remained peaceful. He was the only person in Kosovo, including UN staff, who truly understood the slogan on the badge I wear every day in places marked by hatred: an image of the Earth with the slogan "All One People." Like I said, not a lot of oneness there those days. In a place where there were very frequent attacks on Serbs and where ethnic Albanian thugs would publicly high-five each other in the street as they stood over a beaten Serb, a sense of shared humanity was all too dormant awaiting its eventual re-emergence.

Our food initially came in the form of not-so-delicious KFOR military rations, stockpiled in the pantry of our group house. With virtually every store in town empty or closed forever, there was little other food available, and, of course, the French rations obviously kicked the American one's ass. We drank some seriously horrible wine, lots of it, and getting news, emails, and the Internet was always a huge challenge, leading me to give up most of the time, belly all too full of a high carbohydrate diet, but digitally starved. Most of the time there was no cell phone connectivity, nor heating, so we had to rely on candles as the only form of heat when the weather turned cold as it inevitably did, extremely cold. After I left Kosovo in late autumn, the following winter brutally affected everyone there, including Kirsten who only had layers of clothing, blankets, a beanie, gloves and candles to sustain her during the nights when the mercury could hit -20°C or colder. How she survived this without getting sick, I'll never know.

The day after I arrived the work began in earnest, 15 hours a day; day in, day out, seven days a week for months on end. Reversing ethnic cleansing and creating the legal and other tools needed for real residential justice takes time and boundless energy! The rush of anticipation in getting to work in this war-ridden place was huge, despite my doubts as to whether I could really do this rather important job. For months, the world had helplessly watched as a million ethnic Albanian Kosovars were ethnically cleansed from Kosovo during the war, sending shivers of anger down my spine every day. I was one of the people entrusted to reverse this horrible injustice, and the feeling of being able to help with reconstruction and working towards building a new country was a true honor. I was daunted, but I was equally ready to work as hard as I could to bring some residential justice to everyone who needed it.

On that first day, and seemingly every day thereafter, the air was thick with throat-burning chokingly dirty dust, probably laced with depleted uranium from the countless tank-busting shells NATO had unleashed. Similarly, squawking blackbirds who would never be picked for the choir hovered above town all the time, giving the place a persistently eerie feel. The UN Headquarters was housed in the old and spooky Yugoslav Police and Military offices. We were the government now, after all.

At one point during my time in Kosovo, post-war agreements officially disbanded the Kosovar Liberation Army. 40,000 uniformed KLA guerrilla fighters marched proudly through the streets of Pristina, ending up in the football stadium next to our home, where KLA leader Hashim Thaçi addressed the crowd. After taking a bunch of pictures and talking with a few of the KLA members in uniform, I went to the roof of the UN hotel and watched much of the day's festivities from there, until a UN Security Guard yelled at me to get down, due to sniper threats against the UN. I complied, but only after taking a few more pictures of the overflowing stadium and KLA-filled streets far below. In another visit to the same stadium to attend the first major football (soccer) game since the end of the air campaign, one side of the grandstands chanted "Rugova, Rugova", followed by the other side yelling in unison "Thaçi, Thaçi." We asked an Albanian man sitting near us what they were yelling, and wanting to presumably make us think that sports was beyond politics, he lied saying they were old football chants from the time in the 1980s when Kosovo had considerable autonomy. We knew it was yet another sign that even within the Kosovar community there were considerable divergences of view as to who they wanted to rule this fledgling nation.

I walked over to UNMIK Headquarters for the first time, dodging far too many shell-shocked and unfriendly street dogs, burned out homes, rubbish strewn everywhere and some seriously odd characters. Before I could do anything else, I needed to get my precious UNMIK badge that made everything official and got me into all the UN buildings and meetings and which provided at least a modicum of protection. A fistfight nearly broke out between the cranky UN official responsible for arranging the badges and a de-mining expert who had definitely done the rounds everywhere engaging in some seriously dangerous and vital work to get rid of land mines and unexploded ordnance. UN administrative officials like all civil servants can occasionally be unpleasant, and I have had my fair share of run-ins with them over the years. But this brawl was so bad I had to intervene to get these guys to chill, even though the de-miner was clearly the one in the right. It came to be my turn, I gave all my information, and a badge was printed and ready for me to wear. Seeing that it had my blood type on it did not reduce any fears I had of working again in a conflict zone. Within the UN building, one official actually wore cowboy boots and having seen way too many of these places through UN glasses, said to anyone who wanted to listen: "Well you see, you got yer elections guy, yer electricity guy, yer water guy, yer security guy, yer factory guy, yer banking guy, you got all yer guys here and we'll be there next time too."

Across the street from one of the cafés I came to frequent there was some very prominent graffiti that read: "Thanks You Toni Bler, Klintun, Shirak!" scrawled by the local spelling bee champion on the main street of downtown Pristina. If one single image that repeated itself over and over sticks in my mind, it is numerous unidentifiable cars, screeching through the Pristina streets, filled with five or more unruly 20-year-old men, looking for trouble or Serbs, whatever came first. The KLA's liberation song was played at maximum volume all day long on Mother Teresa Street, the new name given to Pristina's main road, never to be a Top-40 hit shall we say. I guess those who re-named the street had neglected to read Christopher Hitchens' insightful book on the famous Albanian Nun, controversially entitled *The Missionary Position*.

We saw de-faced posters everywhere of Serbian politicians, many of whom shortly thereafter found themselves behind bars in the Hague, just as the former Kosovar Albanian President now finds himself there - equal opportunity war crimes, with no side immune as either victim or perpetrator. There were sad death notices on every tree and lamppost all around town, all in KLA red and sporting the pictures of those who had sadly died during the war. There were also the many - yes, many - ten-year old boys driving dented cars without number plates, smoking cigarettes and laughing as they nearly mowed into the pedestrians walking along the edges of streets. And the ubiquitous sounds of "*Sigora, scrapse? Sigora, scrapse?*" uttered by five-year old kids selling cigarettes and matches in beautifully arranged boxes, just like in old movies were an ever-present sight.

There were utterly putrid garbage fires all day and all night long everywhere, mostly burning plastic which made the already toxic air even worse. Rubbish bins were overflowing always and everyone seemed to just litter as the whole place went months without a single garbage truck playing its vital role in keeping the city clean. I actually wept tears of relief when I saw the first garbage truck roll by my office, not so much for the fact that it might have meant that the place would finally get a face lift, but more so that it symbolized the beginnings of a semblance of normality for the long-suffering people of the region.

But stability only arrived sporadically. One day some vengeful idiot climbed out of a car right near our apartment, went up to the window of a Serb-owned travel agency, pulled a grenade out of his pocket, plucked the pin and threw the ball of metal at the window of the company hoping to destroy the joint. Since baseball isn't a major sport in Kosovo, this dude's throwing skills were less than perfect. Instead of breaking through the window and destroying the premises in yet another act of ethnic hatred and violence, the grenade instead bounced off the window and exploded right in front of this numbskull, nearly killing him. He somehow survived with serious injuries. KFOR and UNMIK again had to pick up the pieces, in this case, quite literally. There was nightly shooting, the sounds of exploding ordnance and shouts of terror ubiquitous. The place was always tense. One of the few moments we could look forward to was visiting one of a small group of shops that were open and full of goods. My favorite was a hastily assembled pop-up storefront of the Bodyshop which had factory write-offs for sale, the smells of which were so much better than usual odours we had quickly become used to, especially the polluted air of the capital.

Given that the UN was the government and KFOR was the Army, the entire province was crawling with tanks, Humvees and Armed Personnel Carriers, as well as troops from all corners of the globe, all with different uniforms, different weapons, and different ways of being like a military man. I once watched an African soldier who looked totally lost sitting alone in a cafe just looking around and clearly not knowing where to go or what to do. I went up to him and found out he was from Malawi, out of his country for the first time in his life and that all of his luggage was lost. He didn't know what to do. So, he just sat there all day and waited, but no one came. I took him over to the UNMIK HQ to get a lift over to the KFOR HQ so he could take up his post as a UN Peacekeeper. There were lots of Fijian soldiers and police, as well, some of whom brought copious amounts of *kava* with them which probably made their stay a bit mellower than it was for the rest of us. Having spent a fair amount of time in Fiji, I would always give a *Bula!* shout every time I saw a Fijian dude in the distance which always made them feel at home. One time though, I must have shouted *Bula!* in as perfect a Fijian accent as I could muster, as the soldier turned around clearly thinking a fellow islander was there to hang with, and instead he got a boring white guy which quickly wiped his smile away. I felt so bad. I came across these two hilarious Zambian soldiers once who were both holding baseball bats and I actually thought they were on the way to a game. When I asked them where the game was and if they needed a sure-handed shortstop, they replied in a very strong Zambian accent, "Oh no brother, these are to fend off the dangerous canine creatures in these streets. Those canines will kill you if you don't hit them first."

And then there were the American soldiers, some of whom were among the nicest guys you'd ever meet, and who really did want to help end the suffering. But the US government itself, of course, couldn't help themselves and as they love to do, as a nation with 800 military bases across the world and counting, set about building yet another one, that became known as Camp Bondsteel within hours of arriving in the country, far from the prying eyes of the UN and others in Pristina. Apparently so much land was disturbed during the construction of this base that repetitive dust storms much worse than the usual ones blanketed the area for months until the main base was completed. And yes, though I never went there, the place actually had a McDonalds to keep the troops happy with their Big Mac and fries fixes and all the rest. The mere thought of a McDonalds existing in a country as poor, destroyed and violent as Kosovo at the time, just added to the surrealistic nature of things in this unusual place.

There were regular demonstrations for missing persons and prisoners of war, and there were maps in every room you'd enter - maps, maps, and more maps. In post-conflict zones, everything always seems to be about maps and I truly admired the incredible array of maps the UN produced which were extraordinarily useful and certainly ubiquitous. The girlfriend of my favorite mapmaker was one of the UN's spokespersons and she and everyone were so busy during these harried days that all of us would sometimes get tongue-tied. During one interview on the BBC, in response to a question about the massive displacement in Kosovo and its effects on refugees and IDPs, the spokesperson said that the UN was "burdening the load as much as we can." She didn't even notice the garbled phrasing until we pointed it out to her later. She survived the embarrassment, but some UN staff did not survive the mission, and we were all floored when we learned that a great Canadian UN staff member who lived in our building and worked for UNHCR, David Reilly, had tragically died in his sleep one night. Sometimes the UN lost staff this way, and other times staff was fired, but this always came with tremendous risk to the person doing the firing, especially in areas without the rule of law. A UN job for a local staff member can often be the highlight of one's career and even more importantly become the first stepping-stone of many for a ticket out—the beginning of an international life and eventual wealth beyond their wildest dreams.

I was here to try to sort out the question of housing, land, and property restitution, trying my utmost to ensure that *everyone* who was displaced or otherwise ethnically cleansed would have a legal way to get their homes back. Besides all the hatred and violence, one of the other things that I and the others dealt with was the simple fact that we needed not just to know the *de facto* reality of what was happening on the ground, even if this was totally obvious to all of us. We needed to know what the local law said on these matters and hence which laws might be kept, which might need amendment to bring them into compliance with international standards, and which new laws or policies might need to be written. I asked around for copies of every HLP law on the books and recall a rather heated argument on my very first day at work with a woman I'd initially and mistakenly assumed to be an Albanian Kosovar. She argued that Yugoslavia had the best legal system in the world, and that this was independently verified by a panel of the world's best judges and lawyers. It only dawned on me a few minutes into the discussion that she was a rather nationalistic Serb and doing all she could to stand up for what she believed in even if it did sound a bit far-fetched.

Life Lesson No. 52: Accept reality: Every place is the best in something, every place is the worst in something.

When you have travelled as far and wide as I have, know people from every country of the globe and embrace the never-ending truth of the oneness of humanity, you realize very quickly that no country has the best of everything; it's all a hodgepodge of goodness and badness, my yin to your yang, some things awesome, some OK, some horrible. Put the whole planet together and you'll find the best pieces of the puzzle here, and some there. If you add it all up, you'll eventually find the best of everything. Other than perhaps a unique type of cheese or other specialty food, the best of any system always mixes influences. This is one of the main reasons, my friends, we need to embrace our shared humanity, for if we do this, all of us will have access to the very best the world has to offer.

During these early days after the bombing phase of the war, no public buildings functioned, libraries were gutted, the university was shut down, and the Serbs simply didn't cooperate—even though we desperately tried to be fair. We were finding it almost impossible to access the laws we needed to find solutions to the housing crisis affecting all groups in Kosovo, in particular the majority Albanians and minority Serbs. In a moment of frustration at not even being able to get copies of the legal code we needed to do our work, I recalled walking past what appeared to be a law office a few days earlier, seeing scales of justice in the window. "Maybe they will have copies of the laws I need and I can even get the lawyers a bit of cash for making copies," I thought. I walked around a couple of corners in the afternoon heat, sweating heavily, and headed into the *Buro Advokati*. I couldn't find an interpreter, so with gestures I've grown used to using, even mastered over the years, I gesticulated at the young man sitting there: "Law books? Laws? Do you speak English? Deutsch? Nederlands? Español?" Continued blank looks, and I ponder another approach. But then what should have been obvious suddenly dawned on me; this wasn't a representative of the law offices at all. He wasn't a lawyer, but simply one of thousands of tough guys who had moved into Serb properties, taking advantage of the reverse ethnic cleansing which would eventually lead to almost 200,000 Serbs fleeing Kosovo. "It's OK, OK, never mind," I said, and glumly left the occupied office, still unclear as to what Yugoslav law said about the many complex areas of housing, land, and property rights as it applied to the then province of Kosovo.

Back in our office building I heard an eccentric UN guy speaking Russian loudly into his phone, waited until he was done and then asked him if he was, in fact, Russian. Vladimir, a Russian character straight out of central casting, said he was indeed a citizen of Mother Russia. I asked him if he could help me get the laws I needed, knowing that the Russians and Serbs were always very close, their Orthodox and Slavic histories always merging in their mutual mind's eye. Since the Serbs were so out of favor at this point, he seemed overjoyed that *anyone* talked to him at all—much less that I wanted him to help facilitate access to them for the UN—and that person was me. He immediately suggested we go over to the Serb Headquarters and there we would surely find the laws I needed. We rushed downstairs and hopped into his well-worn but still solid Mercedes, which made me think he'd been there quite a while. We tore through the mean streets of Pristina towards the only place in all of Kosovo where Serbs felt safe at this stage, the offices of what they still saw as the government of the province. This was both daunting and totally exciting in equal measure, squealing through the bumpy roads of a grumpy town with a vodka-reeking Russian wild man in search of the last remaining sad Serbs who still insisted they were in control, though they most certainly were not.

When we arrived, numerous KFOR soldiers surrounded the building to guard against a potential lynch mob, and countless coils of barbed wire blocked all but one entrance. In the near future, this building would become UNMIK Headquarters, with one regime replacing another. We passed through a series of security checks and with ole Vlad in the lead we were treated like royalty, the few Serb officials there very happy their Russian protector and his new friend Mr. Housing Rights had arrived. He asked them if they could get me all of the housing, land, and property laws concerning Kosovo and they very enthusiastically said they would and that they would even have them translated for me. I was overjoyed, my first task completed. But just as I felt the relief of finding this legal Holy Grail, I looked up and saw the huge portrait of hard-line Serbian leader Slobodan Milosevic on the wall, and immediately felt ill knowing too much about his crimes, doubting I would really ever get those promised laws, and indeed, I never did, not from them at least. After searching far and wide over a period of many weeks we did finally access the full HLP legal code, had it translated and then were ready to work on residential justice and law reform. One of our team even somehow found the national land cadastre indicating who owned which homes and lands that a caring civil servant had hidden in his home to make sure it was not stolen or fraudulently altered during the war. Imagine that.

Having gone through similar experiences in many other conflict zones where I worked both before and after my time in Kosovo, I was inspired years later not to confront this conundrum again and carried out a project with my friend and colleague Zeke Simperingham which few understood at the time. Together, we spent over a year compiling all of Burma's HLP laws into a 1,235-page volume so that when change came, a normal HLP code could replace the oppressive laws the Burmese military had used to hold onto the land it had seized for so long. The Swiss Ministry of Foreign Affairs generously funded this project, resulting in a massive tome that every embassy and NGO had on their shelves within days of its printing. It was printed in Bangkok and brought, unannounced, into the country by the hundreds. That was back in 2009, two years before the short-lived political reform process began and many asked Zeke and me over the years how we knew change was coming. The point was, we didn't know when it would come, but we knew it would sooner or later. Preparing during the bad times for the good times was the wisest course of action.

Later that same day that I hung out with Vladimir in Pristina, I visited one of the countless kiosks that dot so many cities in Eastern Europe. I began a conversation with the cool guy working there, asking him eventually if he was one of those who wanted what was called a Greater Albania, or a merger of both Kosovo and Albania into a new state or political alliance, a question I would ask everyone I could, just to gauge the sentiments of the street. This was the public rationale made by many Serbs seeking to justify the harassment of Kosovo's majority Albanian population. Most people just shrugged their shoulders, indicating that there were slightly more important issues to contend with. Embarrassingly for me, this muscled man, who quickly figured out that I thought he was Albanian, reached under his shirt and showed me a pendant on his necklace. I looked more closely and saw the famous Serb cross and quickly realized my mistake. He smiled and walked away probably muttering under his breath something like, "Stupid fucking foreigner", and I wouldn't have blamed him one single bit.

Life Lesson No. 53: Don't be a stupid fucking foreigner.

Kosovo was totally that kind of place. Everything seemed so obvious and fit perfectly into a logical societal framework, and then at a moment's notice, what we thought was the latest bit of understanding was stood on its head and then back again. One time, one of the really cool local Kosovar Albanian UN staff members in a private moment of honesty said to a couple of us: "I know this place could be better. The air is bad, the history is bad, it is ugly, the weather is bad, it's too cold in the winter, too hot in the summer, the food is awful, the people are mean, crime is everywhere, the culture is bad, the economy is bad, everything is bad.... I hate it, but somehow, I love it. We all love it so much, even though it is so horrible. I left one time in my life on a trip to Denmark. I was meant to stay for two weeks, but had to come back after three days, I missed it so much." And then he said "I cannot explain it but we all feel this way, we hate it so much, but actually we love it. My grandmother says it is the water...."

At one level, that's Kosovo in a nutshell, and I have to admit that at times I felt very much the same way. I dreaded so many things about this place, but at the same time I totally loved it. I loved how easily people smiled at me, especially the guy who made my daily kebab. He would greet me with a smile, make his amazing creation, and always apply the perfect amount of chili sauce, each and every time. I loved guys like Beja who were more plentiful than most people realized and I merged with this culture and these people, both Albanians and Serbs, as I always do, seeing the similarities outnumber the differences by millions to one. Even the many Albanians who I worked super closely with for months on end, travelling to every side of the country and back all the time, and who absolutely hated the Serbs (virtually always for understandable reasons - rape, pillage, plunder and abuse among them), all had this incredibly good side, which was irresistibly kind, generous, funny and utterly hospitable.

When I left after finishing my work and prepared to return to Geneva, I received some of the nicest speeches in my life at my farewell dinner from the many friends I made there during those frenzied months. The gifts—locally-made (ultra-strong) raki in an ornate bottle, KLA flags, one of those attractive traditional white hats the old men wear, and more—were filled with love and affection, which I returned in equal measure. Shukri, Shoki Seaad, Shazim, Lazim, Doogi and all the others, thank you - I hope you are all well! It's funny how close you become to people when working in such places, how you assume that you will stay in touch with them for years to come. But what almost always happens is that you only ever see one or two of them ever again, or in some cases none of the people with whom you shared such powerful moments in a place of so much tension and despair.

But still, there was no denying that this place was disturbing in some deeply troubling and structural ways, and sad to say it, it still is. Not only is Kosovo's official legal status still unresolved, but recently the then President resigned his position in 2020 and then turned himself in to the International Criminal Court; two powerful indicators of where things stand today. During the heyday of the Albanian victory thanks to NATO and friends, the same man who now sits in the Hague was leader then too. His car's number plate was light green and simply read: PM 001. This was very odd given that there was no official government other than the UN, no official Prime Minister and certainly no official way to get a license plate, but he surely had one. The whole Kosovo experience could almost be best described by talking about license plates—whether the mounds of them discarded at the border, the hastily removed police license plates we found in our office building or the fact that only the rarest of vehicles even had plates at all (except for UN cars, of which there were many).

As restaurants started re-opening, we spent a lot of time in such places, as they were far preferable locales to meet and work at than the cracked and often pungent buildings in which the UN had offices. No matter how crowded the good restaurants were—mostly pizza parlors —they always kept the best table permanently empty, ready to serve the KLA leader if he happened to show up with his entourage. You could sometimes spot the then-US Secretary of State Madeline Albright, admonishing the leader of the Kosovar Albanians, in a way that resembled a lover's spat, leading some to gossip that the two were somehow romantically involved, but I think the chances of that were extremely small for a whole host of obvious reasons. Not once in all the time I was there did I see the leader at these empty tables, and I feel like I ate twice each time I went to one; one pizza for me, and another for the missing boss of the KLA. Thanks to Pizzeria Monaco, Pizzeria Tony, Cafe Amerika, and all the others, I may have worked extremely hard but I also rather dramatically blimped out during those days. I must have gained at least 10kgs during my time there, having once been accused by a major UN official of being eight months pregnant, which did look about right – one needs plenty of reserves when you're trying to reverse ethnic cleansing!

I always seek justice and usually side with people rather than ethnic groups or governments, which is a foolproof way to stay above the fray—it's the world citizen way, after all. But there are times when you really don't know what to think. One day I was with a Kosovar Albanian translator who was showing me around the destroyed house of his best friend, which was inadvertently hit by a NATO bomb and, as is so often the case casually dismissed as "collateral damage." I was standing there with my mouth agape at the utter carnage and hear him say: "Even though the US bombed my best friend's house and killed him, he died right there," pointing his finger at a stained spot amongst the rubble, "I must never criticize the US for forcing the Serbs to leave my land...."

We then went to his house, met his family in the old social housing unit, which was designed for three inhabitants, but was now home to seven people—only one of whom had a job. On the way there, a ragged looking guy in his early twenties with his whole life ahead of him comes up to me and says: "Please, you are not from here, you can travel, can you please mail this for me when you are next out of the country?" He then pulls an old and rather tattered letter out of his pocket which must have been in there for weeks, if not longer. I say yes, take the letter and indeed did mail it for him from Florence on a weekend break we took to Italy to gorge ourselves on some seriously good food and Italian culture a couple of weeks later. This poor guy had no way to contact his family so had to rely on a total stranger to mail a letter for him from beyond the borders. There was no functioning postal service. He had both no money and no passport. He had no bank to go to even if he did have money, as none were functional. He had no phone and most of the time, as everyone, had only sporadic access to running water, electricity, and heating. These types of interludes with desperate people happened all the time, as they always do in places of war, despair and deprivation. At one point during my stay in Kosovo right in front of the EU building, a self-described 'real estate agent' came up to me before I went through security and asked outright: "You need a house? I get you one, very fast. You need tomorrow? I find one tonight for you, with my friends." He neglected to say that he'd have to ethnically cleanse some poor family in the process. This was not going to go smoothly.

On our way to the heavily damaged Pristina Aerodrome to catch a UN flight to Rome from this otherwise closed and passenger-free airport, we went through one of the many roadblocks manned by KFOR Soldiers from the United Kingdom. We chatted briefly to check if anything was happening in the area, given the still frequent violence, and they shared stories about the hatred, house burnings, and more. I interjected that the only solution would be putting Ecstasy or MDMA in the water supply, and they energetically shook their heads in complete agreement, smiles all around. At the airport itself, KFOR soldiers, also from the UK, ran pre-security checks. I mentioned the idea that, given the scale of damage at the airport and across Kosovo's public sector, perhaps NATO could pay compensation to promote justice and kick-start the moribund economy. However, let's just say my pleas fell on very deaf ears. I had a copy of the massive tome *Kosovo: A Short History* with me, which is probably more than 500 pages long, and the Brit who checked it in case I was hiding something inside laughed and said, "Not very short if you ask me mate, are you really going to read that whole thing?" I said yes, of course, I would, to which he dramatically replied, "No way!"

The destruction at the airport and everywhere else was staggering. I saw piles of melted metal on the taxiways at various evenly spaced places across the airport. I asked a soldier if he knew what those piles of once molten metal were. He laughed as if I should have known and said "Melted MIGs mate, fighter aircraft. We got 'em with depleted uranium shells and we melted those fuckers." "Holy shit," I muttered, genuinely shocked at what I saw. It was like this all across Kosovo with bomb damage at bus stations, at the nearby Yugoslav military base and just about all of the governmental administration buildings. Besides the miraculous MIG melt madness mounds, what was left of the airport terminal was a disgusting mess—walls full of missile holes, parts of the ceiling missing, and nothing functioning. According to one local, mercenaries who fought with the Serbian Army had left huge piles of faeces behind the smells of which were very much present.

Just before we headed across the tarmac to get on the plane, we were the very first people ever to get our passports emblazoned with the new official stamp of the UNMIK and Kosovar governments, which was pretty cool. A souvenir like that more than satisfied me, but the military types, both current and former soldiers, always traded odd items that didn't interest me at all, though they clearly got off on it. One guy would give another guy a bullet he'd found or a shell casing he'd picked up. Another guy gifted bayonets or knives to another guy, both of them admiring their new possessions in a testosterone-fuelled moment of mutual adoration, exuding precisely the same type of energy that led to the mess of war we were trying to end and clean up after.

Life Lesson No. 54: 'Depleted' uranium? Really?

Upon reaching Florence via Rome on the UN plane, we once again had everything we were used to in normal life for the first time in months: hot water—24/7, water from the tap at all, for that matter—electricity, clean clothes, amazing food, and a peaceful atmosphere. I mailed the letter the disheveled guy had handed me at a local post office. The weekend passed too quickly, and we returned to UNMIK land. We found our way through the streets of Rome to catch the flight back to Pristina on the World Food Programme (WFP) plane. This was the only flight into and out of Kosovo at the time and, of course, we stupidly left our passports in the hotel and missed the daily flight, requiring another night's stay. I promise we didn't do this on purpose.

A few short weeks later that very same WFP plane crashed straight into a mountain before reaching Kosovo and everyone inside was instantly killed—UN officials, politicians, soldiers, and the crew. It so easily could have been us. Our flight the next day from Rome was heavily delayed and I asked the pilots of this small plane what the delay was all about and they mentioned something about the gyroscope. The later crash on the mountain turned out to be due to problems with....the gyroscope. This wasn't the first time a plane I had recently flown on later crashed. Listing them all would take a long time—Swiss Air 111 (New York-Geneva), Necon Air (Pokhara-Kathmandu), Thai Air (Bangkok-Kathmandu), Bangkok Airways (Koh Samui-Bangkok), and far too many others. It's not the most climate-friendly way to travel but still the safest—albeit far from perfect.

Those poor Kosovar Albanians, I really felt for them. And then as quickly as I felt this very real feeling of the deepest possible compassion, we'd visit a suffering old Serbian woman living alone in her dilapidated flat absolutely terrified she would be violently evicted by local Kosovar thugs who were doing this *en masse* all across the territory. She begged us to help her, but all we could do was promise to report her case to the UN and that we would ask KFOR soldiers to visit her routinely. I could only organize her kitchen a bit, do her dishes, give her dying plants a bit of water and hug her and look deep into her eyes before we left, silently sharing this short moment of oneness with her. It was extraordinarily sad, so I went out and bought her several bags of fresh food. As I walked up and down the stairs again, in this building and countless others, I saw handwritten names scribbled in large, indelible ink on most apartment doors—all written by the apartment stealers who claimed homes that weren't theirs by force. How the elderly Serb woman was able to hold out, I'll never know. I made her a quick salad of tomatoes and cucumber and then we were off.

Later we visited the monastery where the well-known local head of the Orthodox Church, Father Sava, resided and reported the case to him in the event they would be able to assist, at which point this extremely articulate man brought out a massive binder full of brutal cases exactly the same as the one we had just seen. I travelled throughout Kosovo to places like the very tense Serb enclave of Mitrovica where I spent the day with Dutch UNHCR official Betsy Greve. We saw more carnage on both sides of the bridge that separates the two communities there. We went to Peç/Peja where we found UNMIK officials working from a partially destroyed building who were so happy to see other UNMIK people responsible for tackling the HLP crisis. It seems one of the UN staff at this office, in fact, had herself recently been evicted by local mafia types. We visited the sad spectacle of Kosovo Polje where the Serbs had lost a major battle hundreds of years earlier in 1389. This sacred monument had been completely ransacked, with Cyrillic metal letters that had once explained its significance strewn wantonly around. What was once a holy spot had become just another tragic endpoint of ethnic conflict, the remnants of pure vengeance. Every day, we would see people rolling down the street dragging carts behind them loaded with household goods, furniture, and other things. We wished, counterintuitively, that the items belonged to these IDPs or refugees who were seeking safety somewhere else, but a closer look almost always revealed that this was war booty looted from now-empty Serb homes. Sometimes, I would yell, "Nice stuff you got there, Shoki, how much did you pay for it?", knowing of course that all of it was stolen from someone weaker than them in this increasingly sad Darwinian environment.

Life Lesson No. 55: Beware of bridges. Sometimes they push us apart rather than bringing us together.

These were some of the first times I ran up against the dilemmas that were to continually face me throughout the entire time I worked in Kosovo. The UNMIK appointed me the head of the Housing and Property Task Force, and my specific task was how to solve complex problems like these in a way that was consistent with human rights laws, fair, equitable and doable. If you're interested in the many finer details of what came of these efforts, look online and you will find numerous books, academic articles, websites and so much more on what became the massive body of work of the Kosovo Housing and Property Directorate (HPD), the Housing and Property Claims Commission (HPCC), and finally culminating in the Kosovo Property Agency (KPA). This process conceiving of these agencies, designing them and lobbying to ensure their establishment took months, and was far from smooth. But in the end the HPD received tens of thousands of HLP petitions and resolved more than 70,000 HLP claims at last count, thus providing residential and restitution remedies to well over 200,000 people.

I wanted so much for a sense of normality to come to Kosovo, and this was reflected in the proposals I put forward for dealing with the HLP crisis there. It was clear that as long as things remained almost entirely outside of the legal realm, I didn't see any chance of the Kosovo nation, and in particular, the Kosovo economy, moving forward. When thugs can just knock on a door, throw the owners and their family out on the street with impunity, write their name on the door with a magic marker and call it their own, your country has a very big problem on its hands. And it doesn't matter which side of the conflict does this; it's horrible whoever does it. So given the way the war and the aftermath played out, it wasn't all that surprising that the HLP agencies I designed produced some unforeseen results. As history played itself out, the institution meant to restore the HLP rights of anyone subjected to ethnic cleansing became one of the few institutions where ethnically cleansed Serbs could seek the return of properties taken from them after the Albanians and NATO prevailed in the 78-day conflict.

Life Lesson No. 56: Things don't always work out as planned, but chances are they still work out.

Once UN official Dan Lewis—whom I started calling HST after noticing the many personality traits he shared with Hunter S. Thompson, the madman from Woody Creek—formally set up the HPD following my design, it became a key part of Kosovo's legal and political fabric. But in the beginning, it was far from clear that such a body would be put in place at all, as is always the case when anything concerning HLP issues are involved in the context of a conflict. Indeed, I had planned to have what became the HPD cover all HLP disputes and claims, but strong opposition within UNMIK against including commercial properties and farmlands meant the HPD would deal only with residential properties. Once the design was done, we got people to sell the idea within the UN, and the Kosovar and Serb communities, which was far from an easy task.

Both Albanians and Serbs reluctantly supported the HPD, fearing the potential loss of their war booty. Again, we faced opposition from the US, which resisted UN involvement in HLP rights, seemingly not having learned from their complete failure in Istanbul three years earlier. I worked very closely during this time with two centrally placed German officials who played major roles inside UNMIK. Thanks to the intense enthusiasm of German Green Party member Tom Koenigs—who later went on to head the UN's Afghanistan Mission—this new institution got off the ground. Another German diplomat played a vital role and was serious about the independence he was duty bound to show as a representative of the UN. At one high-level meeting on the HPD design, which I chaired, following a particularly undemocratic outburst by the US about them being in charge, this diplomat (much to my pleasure) stands up and says: "Yes, we are United here, but we are not the United States, we are the United *Nations*." Well, this shut up the State Department fellows, let me tell you, and matched my own feelings closer than he could have ever known.

While the lobbying was underway, we drafted the required laws and regulations with lawyers from the UNMIK legal department, including German Hans-Joerg Strohmeyer and American Milbert

Chin. Once ready, I presented the entire plan to UNMIK's highest-level executive meeting, with all agency heads around a large board table and live-streaming participants from the UN Secretary-General's office in New York, including Nadia Younes, who was sadly killed in Iraq just a few short years later.

We repealed two discriminatory laws used to disenfranchise Kosovar Albanians within these regulations and ensured that the three-judge panel—comprised of two non-Kosovo nationals and one local judge—would head the Housing and Property Claims Commission, guaranteeing impartiality. The first two foreign judges turned out to be Finnish and South African. The Head of UNMIK, flamboyant French politician Bernard Kouchner, led the meeting. I did my best to sell what would become the HPD proposal, definitely using all my convincing skills to get the UN in New York on board after they expressed some serious concerns about the UN engaging in HLP issues in a war zone environment. Everyone finally agreed to move forward and off we went to make it happen. I did scores of radio and newspaper interviews after the HPD was approved and then I could at least begin to relax a tiny bit now that my work was coming to an end.

In my last few weeks in Kosovo, besides getting the HPD off the ground, a lot of positive things started happening. KFOR undertook a massive program of cleaning up the hundreds of destroyed cars that were found along roadsides everywhere. A new bakery opened that actually made really decent croissants and *pain au chocolat*. A photography store reopened and I made a point of going there to buy anything I could just to help him out and increase his economic odds of success. Even though I normally simply hate shopping, here it seemed almost a political act.

During my final week in Kosovo, I spent three solid days walking around Pristina, taking picture after picture. One of those became my first magazine cover photo a few months later, appearing on the cover of *Human Rights Internet*, the very publication that had helped launch my human rights career 15 years earlier. While wandering around the UN buildings, some friends and I found a storeroom full of UN gear, including bulletproof vests and blue military-grade helmets, which we quickly donned and took photos of as if we were under attack—maybe tasteless, but it's a funny memory. The traffic lights, which had been out for months, started working again, and during a day out with the UK's Department for International Development (DFID), an official remarked, "Hey, we paid for those traffic lights." It was that kind of place.

One night there was an amazing concert put on by the UN called the *Return Concert* that brought in a bunch of international acts and was hosted by Vanessa Redgrave. The highlight of the night for me, by far, was when the incredible Canadian guitarist Bruce Cockburn took the stage. I was front row center amongst a bunch of excited and very under-entertained Albanian children who had obviously never heard of him. He only sang two songs, alas, but one contained his infamous lyrics, "Open up the windows, let the bad air out," which perfectly captured the bad scene of much of Kosovo. I had hoped that he would play *Going to the Country*, a song that still gives me so much joy whenever I listen to it, but I suppose its happy, upbeat form didn't match the less than joyous feelings in this cauldron of ethnic cleansing. Thanks for the tunes, Bruce, and for winking back that night after our brief oneness stare, you're the best!

The night before I left once and for all I made up a song of my own singing to the party crowd, "Hey everybody, how does it feel, to be driving down the street, in your ShokiMobile....." which referenced the little dudes, *shokis*, who we'd see every day driving their Mercedes sedans down the street, a memory that will never be wiped from my mind. We took a UN helicopter on the last ride out and landed at Skopje airport, which was still horrible, decrepit and smelly. Getting on the Austrian Airlines flight felt so incredibly luxurious after so many months in conflict-ridden Kosovo and that meal on the plane was like a Michelin Three Star place to my out of practice palate. I was in equal parts happy to leave, but also incredibly sad. I wasn't just sad about leaving Kirsten behind, who stayed in Kosovo for almost another year while I lived alone in Geneva. During that time, I started a short-lived band with two musical virtuosos named Squats 'n Ced. Our trio almost had an international hit called "Irritation." We also created "It," possibly the shortest song ever written or played, lasting just three seconds and consisting of a single note—written, I believe, by Squats.

But I was sad for Kosovo. I did what I could to push things in the right direction and worked incredibly hard to maintain the pressure for residential justice, but the depth of the ethnic crisis, the lack of oneness, and deep structural problems left my hopes lower than I had wished. I still love you all—my Kosovo friends, Albanians, Serbs, Roma, UN staff—and truly hope for good things in the future, even if the odds remain heavily stacked against you.

Iraq - Beware of Lion Hounds

Maybe plead is too strong a word, but in 2003 the UN certainly tried and tried and tried again to get me to come to Baghdad to do another job on HLP rights, but I always politely declined these kind invitations. I had just turned 40, and as cliché as it may sound, I no longer instantly said yes to every invite and actually began calculating the pros and cons of whether or not to go. I agreed to the job but only on the condition that I didn't need to travel. Something just didn't feel right. A few months before, I hosted one of my many wild parties for my 40th birthday, where I happily doled out dozens and dozens of ultra-strong cannabis brownies that too many people overindulged in —and which lasted far too long. To anyone who has ever had too many such brownies you will know what I mean. To those of you who are yet to have the pleasure, or rather, the terror of doing so, I advise a moderate approach.

Always the responsible party host, I had invited a very *experienced* (in the Jimi Hendrix sense of this term) friend to come over at 8 a.m. on the day of the party to take a brownie test, which discerned their strength and would ensure as best we could that no one would have either too much or too little. We calculated the perfect size for each piece after he had a mighty fine time for the next eight hours or so. We filled a massive platter piled high with dozens of little morsels of mental transformation ready for everyone who showed up to wish me well into my 40s, with an unmissable sign that said—**One Only**! I wore my favorite and brightest blue and red, love heart-laden tie-dye shirt that night. Besides the brownies we made a huge feast comprised of dozens of different delicious dishes. Most of the early arrivals did the right thing, had their one brownie and off they went into the stratosphere and stayed there all the way into the morning, as did I on this very memorable night during which no one slept. You only turn 40 once, after all.

The problems came with the late arrivals, the ones who had already been drinking or at another surely more boring get together, and especially the impatient ones. For those of you who have had the wonderful pleasure of the brownie experience, you know it takes a while to kick in and you surely must equally know that the effects are often infinitely stronger than just a puff or two of the very same substance. Anyway, lots of UN types, lawyer types, NGO types, Geneva banker types and other assorted stragglers that other friends brought with them came late and ignored my pleas and the sign to have just one. Before any of us responsible ones could stop them, some of these rabble-rousers started gobbling down 3 or 4 of these delectable delights when the first one didn't immediately bring them into space. Needless to say, the results were something most of those who failed to heed the call, will never forget. As I was taught by the Lion Hounds sign back in Hawaii, if there's a sign there you might as well at least consider taking it seriously....it might just be there for a reason.

Life Lesson No. 57: If the sign says 'One Only', it's best to comply.

Just after the effects of that fateful night had finally worn off, in early 2003 the UN hired me again to work on my forte—housing, land, and property rights—in Iraq following the second US invasion and military occupation. Sergio Vieira de Mello—whom I had met in East Timor and befriended—reluctantly headed the UN operation that aimed to counterbalance the US-dominated occupation. I had watched him on TV in 1999 as he traipsed through Serbia and Kosovo with my wife and a few other UN officials in the middle of that war. For what felt like the umpteenth time, the US couldn't help itself and decided to invade another country yet again. Built on a mirage of lies about white powders and weapons of mass destruction, the US shocked and awed the sovereign nation of Iraq in March 2003, just days after I moved to Bangkok—making everything so much worse than it already was. Watching the ultra-hawk US diplomat John Negroponte sitting with an embarrassed grin behind US General Colin Powell as he was forced to blatantly lie to the 14 other members of the UN Security Council as the world watched, live for all to see, holding up a vial of fake white powder as a prop to justify a war that killed hundreds of thousands of people the legacy of which continues to this day, made me retch. I walked past Negroponte a few years later on the street in front of the UN in New York and must admit that my pacifist ways almost didn't constrain me that day.

Though I had wisely departed the US forever almost 20 years before, I was again appalled that the country of my birth was once again so blatantly violating international law, mindlessly invading another nation, and spending billions of dollars that could have been used to provide adequate housing and access to high-quality healthcare for everyone at home. What about the *Peace Pact*? What about the *UN Charter*? What about international peace and security duties under international law? What about global reputation? I was pissed. The military build-up in the region was so huge that one of my flights from Zurich had to be re-routed northwards to steer clear of all those US military bases from where the invasion would be staged. When the US invaded Afghanistan following the September 11th attacks in 2001, I was in Italy, along the glorious Amalfi Coast, very jealously admiring Gore Vidal's most incredible home. The world went a bit crazy after 9/11 as the US bombed Afghanistan back into the Stone Age, hitting so many sites that they reportedly ran out of targets. As a result, our trip was altered once again. Imagine that. Look at both Iraq and Afghanistan now more than 20 years and trillions of dollars later and ask yourself if it was all worth it. Maybe the more than 60% of the American working age public who live pay check to pay check without any significant savings might have ended up better off had these invasions never taken place.

On 9/11 itself I was in my office in Geneva waiting to fly to Amsterdam accompanying a protected secret witness in a war crimes trial there, and just an hour before we had to head to the airport, I turned on my office TV and watched those planes crash into the Twin Towers. I called the whole staff together and we watched in horror as this unforgettable day unfolded. We reached the airport, which was just about the last place in the world we wanted to be that day, and news came that there were more planes still in the air that had been hijacked. We were sitting in the departures hall when we learned of the Pentagon attack and then news broke of what became the crash of the plane that was apparently heading to Washington DC, attempting to wipe out the White House or the Capital Building. Even though we were in Europe, and far, far away from the US east coast, the entire airport was eerily quiet, everyone was scared stiff and no one wanted to fly. But duty called and in we went into the metal KLM tube that would fly us quickly to Holland. You know by now that I literally love everyone, everywhere unless they give me a very good reason not to, but the fact that we were flying right over NATO headquarters and that about 30 young unruly-looking guys were on our flight all sitting together and looking around fearfully, made even Mr. Oneness a bit jittery. I chatted with one of the flight attendants and she said she had heard that 50,000 people had been killed in the World Trade Center attacks and that many thousands more would surely die that day. In the end, less than 3,000 died, 3,000 too many, but thankfully considerably less than we had originally been led to believe. She, too, mentioned her nervousness about our male contingent, casually adding, with a nod towards our friends up front, "and I hope we're not next." How comforting. Gotta love Dutch straightforwardness!

Thankfully, all went smoothly and we landed uneventfully at Schiphol, one of my airport homes away from home. Because I accompanied a secret protected witness at a war crimes trial, a van with dark windows met us at the plane, driven by a cool American guy. We discussed my fears about the upcoming US response to 9/11, which I knew would be brutal, just weeks before it happened. Needless to say, my concerns played out even worse than I imagined. Holland was as hushed as Switzerland, as I suppose the whole world was given the brazen and large-scale nature of these terrorist attacks. They checked us into a hotel under false names, accompanied us to our rooms, and told us not to leave until the next day. The van would pick us up again and escort the witness to the courtroom, where they would testify as Witness X about the many war crimes they had witnessed during their UN work in war zones.

When the eyewitness went off to the court, I wandered the streets of The Hague, a town I knew very intimately, having spent a lot of time there during my Holland years. I walked for hours that day and called a good friend in New York City who, like me, had founded an international NGO focused on economic, social, and cultural rights. We discussed everything known at the time (about what came to be known simply as 9/11). We discussed work he was then planning to carry out in Iraq, fearing correctly that the US would start bombing there again falsely using September 11th as a pretext, and how right he was. Shortly after we spoke, he and his colleagues went to Iraq to film ordinary life before the invasion, which graphically showed normal life in Baghdad not long before US bombs destroyed much of the city. I think Michael Moore used some of that footage in one of his subsequent films.

I kept wandering through The Hague, stopping off at different friend's houses and offices at the foreign ministry and the housing ministry. Then I went to my favorite restaurant, Schlemmer, where I always eat when I'm in town and ordered the same amazing salad I do every time, smothered in blue cheese and crisp bacon—just the way I like it. I then wound my way back to our hotel to debrief about what must have been an incredible day. I thought it might be interesting to pass by the US Embassy on my wander and as I approached it, adjacent as it is to the Hague's finest hotel, the Hotel des Indes, I found hundreds and hundreds of people gathered in front of the Embassy in an unorganized, impromptu sharing of grief for the innocent victims of the horrible attacks where planes became weapons. This event amazed me because, despite having left the US behind—politically, as a residence, and as my birthplace—once I arrived at this gathering, I felt an overwhelming need to be there and share in the collective despair over the needless deaths in New York, Washington DC, and rural Pennsylvania, not just for America—but for all of humanity.

After all, though Americans were surely the majority of those killed on that horrible day, people from 60 other nationalities were also killed on September 11th, something all too often forgotten by those remembering these events. I couldn't bring myself to sing the patriotic songs some of the Americans and a handful of the Dutchies there did, but I sure did feel the sadness and horror that these attacks brought about. Knowing what I knew of geopolitics and the often-reactionary responses the US would surely engage in, I worried about the shape of the world to come, the violence the US would unleash to get its revenge and the instability that would surely follow.

I often have colleagues, friends, and acquaintances in the places that the US and its allies such as Israel invade, attack, and then occupy. I have friends in the cities the US and its ally's bomb. I know actual people just about everywhere where the US commits its misdeeds. I know they are not alone in doing these things, and that other big powers also engage in horrible acts, but the US was where I was born and raised, and within this status, my position was clear. Lead by example. Lead by acting with restraint and reliance on principles and laws and not with unfettered destruction. Above all, act in accordance with international law and strengthen this system of peace rather than constantly undermining it, for when you do, it will always come back and bite you sooner rather than later. They supported Saddam Hussein against Iran in the war between those two nations in the 1980s. They supported Noriega in Panama until they didn't and then invaded to get rid of him in 1989. They helped create the Mujahidin in Afghanistan to fight the USSR and look where that got them. Every time it seemed, the creatures they created came back to bite them.

Life Lesson No. 58: A victim is a victim is a victim no matter who they are or where they are from.

By the time the UN began operations in Iraq after the latest US invasion in 2003, I had already decided I would likely never work again in a place where the US had used military force—especially when it was based on proven falsehoods and driven by oil, money, power, and support for controversial allies. Shortly after UN High Commissioner for Human Rights—that's right, Sergio Vieira de Mello —very hesitantly agreed to a request from his close friend, UN Secretary-General Kofi Annan to run the UN office in Baghdad, Sergio's office contacted me to see if I could help sort out the daunting maze of problems besetting the housing, land, and property sectors, as I had done in a growing list of places. I agreed and drafted a plan to establish an Iraqi Housing, Land, and Property Directorate. If implemented, it could help resolve millions of HLP disputes, some from Saddam Hussein's misdeeds, others from the Iran-Iraq war, and more resulting from the US invasion. This was far from an easy task even in the best of times, but having worked in so many conflict-ridden places, I felt like I had a pretty good grasp of these matters. One key difference, of course, was my reluctance to go to Iraq for the project. Although the work had little to do with the US occupiers and was entirely a UN initiative, I'd had enough of US invasions and agreed to work only if I could do the legal analysis and institutional design remotely.

I finished the paper in late July 2003 and submitted it to Sergio. His office spent a few weeks urging me to break my no-travel pledge and come to Baghdad to discuss the plans with Sergio and his immediate staff, make my pitch, and bring it to life. Whether in an email or by phone I kept saying no but did start reconsidering my stance and was increasingly inclined to go, albeit briefly. In the end, despite the enticing prospect of working with good friends at the UN HQ in the Canal Hotel, my internal warning lights went on—*Beware Lion Hounds*—and once that happened, nothing could pull me away from my normal life, which I then shared between Bangkok and Geneva.

I was so close to dying—again. The last time I received a direct communiqué from Baghdad, it was from Sergio's long-time aide, Egyptian Nadia Younes, whom I mentioned earlier. She thankfully liked my paper and plans, emphasizing the time I spent highlighting the linkages between security issues and broader HLP concerns. In the exchange we discussed the agenda for the high-level meeting planned for the next morning on my paper to discuss how to implement its proposals; a gathering that I presumed would be similar to the meeting in Kosovo where the UN formally decided to accept my recommendations.

I received this email less than a day before Nadia and 22 others, including, Sergio, my friend Arthur Helton and others were brutally murdered, and countless others injured, in a huge terrorist bomb attack on the UN HQ by what turned out to be the very same organization that claimed credit for 9/11. A number of movies have been made and books written about this horrible act of terrorism and I urge anyone reading this book to explore those to understand these events more deeply, as well as learning just how incredible a man Sergio was during his too brief time in this life. I was in Bangkok when the bomb exploded and watched CNN from my apartment for hours not knowing who was alive and who was killed.

Life Lesson No. 59: Beware lion hounds.

Two of my close friends, Andrew Clapham and Mona Rishmawi, were in the building and I had no idea whether they had survived or not. I immediately wrote a very emotional poem for them imploring powers beyond ourselves to save them. What else could I do at that stage? After anxiously watching every bit of film on the bombing for hours and hours, I finally caught a glimpse of a dust-covered Andrew wiping blood from Mona's face with a small tissue, too small for the job at hand. But they were alive. I let out massive tears of relief running out to my lush balcony looking at the river and then the sky thanking those powers beyond ourselves whoever or whatever they may or may not be. Andrew's father had been caught up in an IRA bombing decades earlier, so it wasn't the first time the Clapham family had experienced such a thing. Mona's family, being Palestinian, lived through the Nakba and the ethnic cleansing that created Israel in 1948, suffering like all Palestinians from the loss of their country, billions upon billions of dollars in uncompensated land and property thefts, and daily brutality from the neo-*apartheid* regime so solidly in place in Tel Aviv. Andrew is now recognized as one of the world's best international lawyers and Mona became a Director at the UN and continues to hold high-ranking positions, so quite the power couple. I always see them whenever I'm in Geneva.

A few years back, we had dinner at my hotel, the Hotel Eden, where I often stay due to its proximity to the UN, UNHCR, and various NGOs. Most importantly, it's near the Botanical Gardens, Lake Geneva, and best of all, the UN Beach, where I've spent more than my fair share of time over the years—despite it being meant for permanent UN staff, which I certainly never was; consultant, happily; staff member, no way. We were in the very empty restaurant with only one other table occupied. A middle-aged woman sat alone at the table, someone none of us knew. After reviewing the small menu, she pulled out a book to read while waiting for her meal, and lo and behold, believe it or not, it was one of Andrew's many books! Again, what are the odds? I mean his books are great, but they are hardly pleasure reading. Knowing that this poor woman must be extremely bored if she was reading *Human Rights: A Very Short Introduction* over a lonely dinner, the prankster within me knew I just had to do something. I got up, both Andrew and Mona imploring me not to do anything embarrassing. I shrugged off their concerns; I guess they had not yet realized that nothing embarrassed me anymore, and went up to the woman who I had never seen nor met before and simply said, as you do, "Do you believe in magic?"

Life Lesson No. 60: Don't just seize the day, seize the moment.

She clearly suspected I was making a move on her and tried to ignore me but because the place was so empty, she simply couldn't. So, I then said "This is a great book, isn't it? Have you ever thought about what it would be like if you were to read a book, and rub the author's name on the cover with your fingers, like Aladdin's Lamp? What if you could close your eyes and suddenly the author would appear right in front of you. You could then ask them anything you wanted about the book, their life, or anything else. Wouldn't that be amazing if we lived in such a world?" I waited for her response, and as was not uncommon during my interludes with strangers, she was both dumbfounded *and* intrigued with a shocked look on her face wordlessly saying, "What in the hell are you talking about?" I charmed her quickly enough and put her at ease, though, and made sure she knew I wasn't actually as weird as my words, so I repeated them and said, "Let's try it. Just close your eyes and rub your forefinger over the name of the author and let's see what happens. Just keep your eyes closed until I tell you to open them. You can trust me, I promise."

Amazingly a small smirk begins to appear, and she starts rubbing Andrew's name. I then motion quickly for Andrew to come over quietly, putting my forefinger on my lips to make sure he made no noise, and stand next to me. The magician within me then tells the woman to open her eyes and I say: "Voilà, life is amazing, magic happens, please meet the author of your book, professor and international lawyer extraordinaire Andrew Clapham! You did that. You made it happen!" Her calm demeanor crumbled, and she is visibly flabbergasted, didn't see *that* coming and clearly can't believe it. We're now laughing and smiling, and she then had a great talk with a man who must have surely become her favorite author, at least I hope so. I tried this again once on my own, closing my eyes and rubbing the name of my favorite novelist Tom Robbins, then opened my eyes and suddenly found myself dancing the Jitterbug, a whiff of beets and perfume in the air, my beloved Pan, Alobar and Kudra not far away....magic happens, but alas, so does tragedy.

Life Lesson No. 61: Sometimes you can trust people who say, "Trust Me." Most of the time, however, you should not.

This wonderful interlude happened years after the Baghdad bombing but those events will never quite leave their minds, no question about that. Sergio's fiancé Carolina stayed briefly with Mona and Andrew in their Geneva flat after the Iraqi heartbreak, the same apartment where I sometimes stayed when I was in town. There are so many dimensions of tragedy associated with Sergio's untimely and early death at the age of 55, many which are not part of the usual consideration of these events. Most importantly, there is no doubt in my mind that the world would have been very different if Sergio had lived, as his chances of becoming UN Secretary-General were far from small. With him leading the UN, the organization might have achieved something approaching its true potential. Hundreds of us who knew him were personally devastated by his loss and honored his life in various ways. Several years ago, when I was last in Geneva, I went to the Cemetery of Kings where he is buried, and found Sergio's white stone grave, alone in an empty area of this elite resting place for the famous. I stood before him, bowed three times, thanked him and shed another tear for yet another human rights hero who died way too early. On the day Sergio died, 19 August 2003, I wrote the very private poem for Andrew and Mona I mentioned earlier, not knowing if they were alive or dead, and emailed it to them. I wrote one for Sergio, too, though he never saw it.

Burma - Tragedy of a Lost Country That Never Was

Over the years I have spent many months of my working life in Myanmar, which I will call Burma, and decades working to address the brutal denial of housing, land, and property rights across this lost country that never was. Most of the time I was based in this steamy country's biggest city, Yangon, and from there would travel far and wide to assorted other destinations in a country once known as the rice bowl of Asia, but no longer. Formerly known by its colonial name, Rangoon, this humid, aging, and sometimes seedy town was once a sleepy backwater where old Asia seemed shabbily preserved. It was in dire need of renovation after decades of ruthless military rule by the much-feared *Tatmadaw*, as the armed forces call themselves. In just a few short years, it quickly transformed into a traffic-laden, construction site-filled, bustling town after the so-called "political reform process" began quite unexpectedly in 2011.

We all know what has happened since then. After a decade of gradual opening up, with increased access to the Internet and the digital world, the arrival of mass tourism for the first time, new buildings, and even a stock exchange, Yangon and many parts of the country began to enter the modern era. Then, after just a single decade of relative freedom, the dominant military staged another illegal coup in early 2021, brutally cutting short these improvements, killing thousands and imprisoning tens of thousands for supporting democracy. This effectively ended all the many tentacles of development and modernization that had sprang forth like wildflowers once the reform process commenced, imperfectly, but growing, nonetheless.

Indeed, the coup, arrests, frequent counter-demonstrations, a global outcry, and the horrible and needless deaths carried out with impunity by the military dominate the news of the unraveling of what had been a promising young democracy. Meanwhile, these thousands upon thousands of now-terminated reform efforts—in every crack and crevice of society—are stifled at best, and most likely over for good—unless the *Tatmadaw* returns to the barracks once and for all.

As neither a citizen nor a permanent resident, I can only comment so much based on my legal reform work undertaken there and my many eyewitness accounts. However, my lengthy experience as a caring world citizen inside Burma attests to the goodwill of millions of locals and many thousands of humanitarians who worked hard to help this extraordinary country set out on a path assisting it to reach its true potential. Sadly, these efforts have now been dashed so that a feared military—the very army meant to protect the population—can return to its old ways of complete control and killing without regard for justice, stealing land, raping, pillaging, and destroying the environment for resources like ruby, jade, teak, and rare earth minerals. All these despicable behaviors have been thoroughly and accurately documented and known worldwide. The UN human rights chief, for instance, correctly called the situation in Burma nothing less than a "multi-dimensional human rights catastrophe",[12] and it is almost impossible for even the most optimistic among us to imagine it getting better any time soon. The fighting between the military and the now-armed opposition has grown so fierce in recent months that it would not be possible to characterize the situation as anything less than a national civil war. It's a grim scenario in which millions upon millions of innocent civilians will suffer.

I didn't expect the coup to take place when it happened, but clearly the military was dissatisfied with its 25% guaranteed seat allocation in Parliament. The requirement that any constitutional amendment needed 75% of the votes to pass ensured the military's total control. If need be, they could block any vote with their voting bloc. They had no need for more power; they already had it! But they were particularly perturbed at their embarrassing second electoral wipe-out in a row by the National League for Democracy (NLD) in the 2020 elections, and thus for an already humiliated institution, respected by few but feared by all, this was a breaking point, and so the ruthless killing began yet again. Many believe the decision to start the "political reform process" in 2011 had less to do with promoting democracy and well-being and more with ending sanctions and giving the military access to the modern weapons they were desperate to acquire. Reportedly, the state of their weaponry embarrassed many in the military, especially when they compared their stocks to those of neighboring countries, and they

---

[12]https://news.un.org/en/story/2021/07/1095392.

believed that they could regain some respect by accessing global military markets. If you look closely at the military vehicles and guns being used right now against the civilian opponents of the coup, they sure do look bright and shiny and new. Most of these are now provided by one of the military's few allies, Russia.

Life Lesson No. 62: Be wary when autocrats befriend each other, especially when they kiss and hug.

During one of my stints inside Burma, for several months I worked intensively on land rights and mine action, which involves the removal of land mines from "contaminated land." I collaborated with Norwegian People's Aid and my long-time human rights colleague, New York attorney Andy Scherer, the long-time former head of New York Legal Services. Andy and I had worked together in various places, including Thailand, Latvia, Canada, New York itself, and several times in Burma. We were joined by a great Burmese-American named Geoff Myint, who had a particular fondness for the town of Bogalay.

If you want to understand the depths to which the military and their equally dubious cronies will go to make money and steal, consider this. Whenever a vehicle belonging to a mine action organization—selfless, empathy-driven groups working to clear land of illegal weapons so people can reclaim it—is out doing a scouting mission on mined land that will shortly be cleared and made safe, it will be tailed by cars with no license plates, darkened windows, and all the other accouterments. These cars, with disturbing and greedy occupants, follow slowly, stopping whenever the mine action vehicles do, never speaking with the de-miners nor making any eye contact even, just taking notes and GIS coordinates. Their objective is to figure out which land will be cleared first so that once it is made safe at no cost to them, they can grab it before the legitimate owners register and reclaim it. Needless to say, the army and their business cronies saw any land suspected of holding any potential valuable resource—especially rubies, emeralds, oil, gas, or rare Earth minerals—as a potential mother lode. They would casually and very systematically disregard the poor farmers who actually owned the land without even thinking twice, with a dismissive attitude that: "They're just poor farmers anyway; who cares about them?" Money talks, making a living off the land walks, in sad and authoritarian Burma.

I have so many stories from my time in Burma, but I'll focus on just a few that might help those unfamiliar with the country understand it a little better. I'd worked on human rights issues in Burma pretty much since the early start of my human rights working life, but only visited there for the first time when I moved to Bangkok just an hour's flight away. This was in 2004, still seven years before the so-called reform process began and the military was still very much in control. There were strong international economic sanctions in place against the government and it was still controversial to even visit the country at all, especially for the purposes of tourism. As we were both human rights activists, Kirsten and I decided to go and meet with her colleagues from UNHCR and a host of others working against all odds to bring justice to the people of Burma. We stayed in the best non-military-owned hotel and were among the few guests in what felt like a nearly deserted city, especially compared with Bangkok and other crowded and hectic cities in Asia.

At the time, Yangon had few cars—and certainly no motorbikes, which are ubiquitous in so many Asian cities, especially places like Hanoi, Phnom Penh and Mumbai. Yangon made yet another odd decision: banning them after a military family member died in an accident involving a motorbike years earlier. This had about as much logic as the brilliant decision by the former dictator Ne Win who decided overnight, after consulting his fortune teller, to change the denominations of all currency notes from 10 to 9, and to invalidate all existing notes forthwith. As a result—surprise, surprise—the economy tanked further, the people lost even more faith in the local currency, the kyat, which had already hit record lows, and Ne Win cemented his legacy as yet another incompetent egomaniac who, like so many who find themselves in power, drove his country into the ground. Imagine waking up in a country where the vast majority of people have no bank accounts, so hold any savings they may have either in the form of land or a home, and if they have no gold or jewelry, will hold the rest in hard-earned cash. You wake up with 2000 *kyat* comprised of twenty 100 *kyat* bills, none of which are valid anymore. What was issued following this idiotic decision were 90 *kyat* notes, 9 *kyat* notes, and so on, all denominations of 9. I mean seriously.

Throughout this first trip to the hidden land of Burma, we mostly had access to UN vehicles and traversed the country extensively in the relative safety of the famous white SUVs. When we didn't have this luxury, we used local taxis, and after four or five rides, we became great friends with one particular driver. I won't mention his name because being associated with foreigners now can lead to arrest, punishment—or worse. That's just how bad Burma has become in recent years since the 2021 coup. During that first trip, some 17 years before the last coup, things were incredibly repressive, dark, and depressing and this amazing driver, let's call him Win (again, *not* his real name), let us know in so many words that he hated the military, like so many do, and that his hope rested in the NLD and Aung San Suu Kyi (ASSK). During this time, Suu Kyi stayed under house arrest in her faded mansion on the shores of one of Yangon's famous lakes. She was still seen globally, at the time, as a human rights icon, before the horrendous mistakes she made after coming to power in 2015, especially her unforgivable failure to speak out against the ethnic cleansing of the Rohingya. Not long before the Rohingya atrocity, her legal advisor was murdered at point-blank range in broad daylight in front of Yangon airport, a brutal act that she failed to address in public or condemn for weeks. In 2004, though, she had almost deity-like status because she was the daughter of the country's founder, General Aung San.

One key tourist stop in Yangon is Aung San's home, where ASSK was brought up. We thought it was worth a visit for the beautiful colonial-style architecture alone. When we were there, as always, we were the only foreigners and had to sign in before entering as you always did during those days any time you'd visit a temple, museum or other such destination. Every time I signed in, I did so as Nacho Libre, so little does he know, but good ole Nacho has been to quite a few places in lovely Yangon. The lonely and far from overworked tour guide in the house was nice enough, but when I asked where ASSK was these days, pretending I didn't know, he smiled and said, "She is currently a guest of the government at a wonderful home in another part of Rangoon." We looked around the house, imagining what it would be like to live in such a place. Little did I know that so many of my UN friends would actually have this experience while living in Yangon years later in homes that were even grander than this one. Great houses, but the stories of killer scorpions and vicious pythons in the garden tempered my admiration of these pads, especially when I'd be visiting and they'd say to me "You're courageous to walk around without shoes on." "Why?" I'd naively ask.

Win, the taxi driver, his teeth totally stained with the remnants of red beetle nut which he must have chewed since his earliest days, waited outside of the famous house of Aung San, perfectly parked for our easy access in the pouring monsoon rain. Off we went to our next destination, which would be the utterly bizarre Drugs Elimination Museum which I will attempt to describe shortly. On the way there, he says in very broken English "You want go Daw Suu house see?" We interpreted this as: Do you want to go see Aung San Suu Kyi's house? We were totally interested in seeing where she was being held against her will but knew this could be dangerous so we said no, but he insisted. "No, it OK, I go many times see by drive look, it OK, it OK." We ask, "Are you 100% sure it is safe for you to drive us there and just drive by?" Again, he assures us that it is safe and that he's done it many, many times. I mean all we were doing is driving down University Avenue on our way to somewhere else, but in a place like Burma this was considered heresy. He then says "Please, Sir, please, Madam, I want you see my leader, my hope for Burma people." We give in and say, "OK just drive by and tell us when to look", not knowing at the time that you can't see much of the house from the road.

And then, within a split second our mellow day turned vicious, and just as we turned into University Avenue soldiers were everywhere; the very young, very unprofessional, very heavily armed soldiers of the dreaded *Tatmadaw* surrounded the car and were very clearly unhappy with our presence there. Literally within seconds, we were stuck alone in a gauntlet comprised of dozens of the types of soldiers you do not want to mess with. These guys were 18 or 19 years old, clearly trigger-happy and in need of respect as they received none anywhere else apparently, and ready to scare the shit out of us, but especially dear and wonderful Win whose predictive qualities paled in comparison to his driving skills in the rickety little machine he called his taxi.

I have worked with my fair share of soldiers over the years and Kirsten has worked with and had to deal with far worse armed men than me, so at least of the two of us I was likely the more scared one, but both of us were truly afraid for Win. Two of the skinny boy soldiers pulled him violently out of the driver's seat and marched him over to their commanding officer, who made him kneel on the parched pavement in the oppressive 35°C weather and beg for forgiveness for trying to take two foreigners to see Aung San Suu Kyi's house. This was devastating to see; our beautiful new friend who was so kind, so gentle, so loving in every way, reduced by these hateful people to a groveling mess afraid for everything including his life.

Life Lesson No. 63: Far too many national heroes disappoint in the end.

It reminded me too much of scenes from the Viet Nam war era where it took very little for a pro-US soldier to shoot someone in the head at point blank range for doing nothing wrong. The soldiers were standing outside of both of our backseat doors on either side of the car and when we tried to get out to intervene, they immediately slammed them shut in our faces and yelled "No Move!" We simply couldn't do anything else, so I pulled out a huge, rudimentary map of Rangoon and pretended to discuss with Kirsten where to go next, very obviously pointing to tourist spots like the Shwedagon Temple whenever the soldiers guarding our car looked in. We hoped to convince them we were just tourists with our driver, which we were, not revolutionaries secretly meeting with ASSK to plan the dictatorship's overthrow.

Meanwhile, Win had his palms together in the traditional *wai*, Buddhist-style greeting which is the utmost sign of respect and used increasingly throughout the world, especially during the no-touch phase of history we lived through during the worst days of COVID. But in his case, he was begging, both for forgiveness but especially for them not to take his taxi license away which, he told us later, they were threatening to do, making it impossible for him to work and earn the meager income he did. These motherfuckers shoved him to the ground, so his face was planted firmly on the hot gravel, then took his taxi permit and ripped it up right in front of us, spat on the ground and walked away. It seemed the confrontation was over. The paranoid soldiers likely figured it wasn't worth doing more in front of foreigners—who would most definitely tell the world what had happened. I think even these guys knew how bad their reputation was and how much they were universally hated and figured it wasn't worth the hassle, thankfully.

Win stumbled back to the car with that horrible look of terror and fear etched across his face, terrified but relieved to be alive. He told us this had happened to him before, but never as badly as this and that because they destroyed his taxi license, he wouldn't be able to drive a cab for another six months at least. We were glad he was more or less OK physically, but devastated for him on the financial front, so a couple of days later when we left and went back to Bangkok, we gave him the equivalent of three years' salary and hoped he would spend it wisely. What more could we do? We wrote back and forth with Win for years but, alas, eventually lost touch. He was a reminder that anyone can be friends with anyone, anywhere, anytime.

I was reluctant to go back to Burma after that trip unless some serious changes were on the cards and lo and behold some years later it seemed things were changing, and for the better. The book I put together with Zeke Simperingham, *Housing, Land and Property Rights in Burma: The Current Legal Framework* in 2009 now sat on the bookcases of all the NGOs and UN agencies in Yangon, as well as a growing number of embassies and elsewhere, really putting HLP rights onto the map. The book even popped up at Rangoon's best bookstore and in the airport duty-free section right next to *Lonely Planet Burma*. People continued to be amazed at why we prepared a 1250-page book during the deepest and darkest days of the dictatorship. What did we know that no one else knew about the political changes to come they would keep asking, and we had to disappoint them as our guess was just as good as anyone's about the country's political future. If I had to guess at the time, I would not have wagered that the reforms would have begun when they did in 2011. I started hearing stories about the looming changes but didn't really believe them. So, I checked in with my good pal Richard Horsey who is one of the world's leading Burma experts and analysts, and from what I hear, the best non-Burmese Burmese speaker around, smart lad that he is, and he confirmed that the changes were indeed real. It was, by all means, not guaranteed to all work out, but the country was definitely slowly beginning to open up—and reform was in the air. And with that, having by now worked in so many countries that had undergone similarly deep and structural political change, I returned to Burma in 2012 and spent a big chunk of time there on and off until 2017.

Life Lesson No. 64: Sometimes what seem to be eccentric human rights projects bear extraordinary fruits.

As is so common when a country undergoes the beginnings of structural political change, from conflict to post-conflict, from autocracy to democracy or from military dictatorship to something more promising as so fleetingly occurred in Burma, the hardcore capitalists from around the world swarm to the place like salivating vultures ready to pounce on what they call "pent up demand", wanting desperately to flood the local market with their wares. I was on many flights into Yangon sitting next to these types who were almost palpably whimpering like a dog before a walk, so anxious to get out there and start making their millions. You could view these rather gaudy displays on every flight in, all around the airport and then all across Yangon and elsewhere as these rich dude wannabees ran around like headless chickens so obsessed with all those dollars to begin rolling in. Some of them even wore full traditional Burmese clothing figuring this would give them preferential treatment by the authorities, and these people we began to call NAGLs—*Not A Good Look*—always steering well clear when we ran across them. I'd seen these types all across Eastern Europe and the former Soviet Union, in post-apartheid South Africa, in Sri Lanka and so many other places where these generally uninspiring salesmen went looking for their commercial Shangri-la.

During the early days of the reforms Yangon had few restaurants that were worth going to, but one had been around forever, Sharky's. I believe it is named after the owner, and the crowd there was often an odd mix of NGO and UN workers like me, Zeke, Andy and others, a whole bunch of NAGLs, some tourists, and an equal number of military friends and cronies, sitting there behind their mirrored shades, arrogance and slime oozing from every pore and dripping onto their repulsive and garish gold chains as their cars with blackened windows idled outside waiting for their return after dining on Sharky's excellent burgers, fries, salads and pizzas. I am not even sure if the national dish *mohinga* is on the menu there. Once the reforms went on and became more entrenched and seemingly real, a whole spate of new restaurants opened up all across Yangon including some truly great ones which served the world's best Shan potatoes bar none. They were so good, in fact, that I actually looked forward to visiting as I planned my next trip. This, too, happens in all those political reform places, and even if the politics doesn't often change as deeply as one might wish, the culinary delights usually did improve greatly.

Life Lesson No. 65: Don't be a NAGL

My first post-reforms visit in 2012 came at the request of one of the main presidential advisors, tasked by President Thein Sein to work with me on various HLP issues. I prepared a series of background papers for him and we met often to discuss the precise things he could do, many of which he did succeed with. However, his job was made far more difficult because of not only the heavily outdated HLP legal code, but in particular three new HLP laws that were quickly approved by the parliament in 2012. The new foreign investment law had several provisions directly affecting key HLP matters, but the *Farmland Law* and the *Virgin, Fallow, and Vacant Land Law* were more significant. Although these laws had a few positive features, they were clearly designed to ultimately benefit the military and their cronies. I believe these laws were drafted long before the reform process began and formed part and parcel of the plan orchestrated behind the scenes by the true power—former dictator Than Shwe, now securely hidden in his walled fortress in the new capital of Naypyidaw. The military knew full well how important the HLP sector was in the country and what a horrid source of human rights violations it had been in the previous decades. They did not want to give up any of their ill-gotten gains nor give meaningful HLP rights to the poor majority in the country. So, in effect, there was nothing democratic or equitable about these laws whatsoever; they were simply new laws made to look progressive, but which in fact imbedded so much of what was already so wrong about the HLP sector in the country.

Life Lesson No. 66: When spying make sure the newspaper is right side up

I never had democratic hopes for the military and painfully rather quickly lost faith that the NLD would live up to expectations. The most hope I had for the people of Burma came from a single meeting with a political figure I respected deeply—NLD co-founder and former political prisoner, Win Tin. We met in his incredibly modest home, with no need or wish for all the showy trappings that so many others in positions of power wish to have in Burma. In him I saw the type of person I thought should be governing this country. A kind, gentle, genuinely interested, democratically-minded, human rights respecting wise man, unfortunately slowly pushed aside by age, infirmity and most of all by the political conservatism professed by both the NLD and the military, he was one of the few people I think could have really brought this country closer to its true potential.

During many trips to the country, I was often tailed in the gloomy streets of Rangoon by some of the world's spookiest spies. These flunkies, and this is an understatement, were always so obvious that I was almost embarrassed for them. Andy and I once met with some of the country's leading land rights activists in a very public meeting place—a restaurant on the top floor of one of the few high-rise buildings in town. Nearby, two shabbily-dressed eerie spies sat at the only other occupied table in the room, pretending—very badly—to have a conversation, making it obvious they were tailing our activist friends and observing us. With literally millions of acres of land illegally grabbed by the military over the decades I guess their bosses were starting to get nervous. At one point they disappeared and I just knew they would be in the bathroom together, so I quickly went into the men's room to tacitly let them know we knew what they were up to and they jumped 10 feet when they saw me enter, shaking in their boots that they had been busted for their amateurish ways by a lowly human rights activist. I went back to the table and let everyone know our two friends on the neighboring table were most certainly some seriously incompetent spies and that maybe we should part ways. We pay the bill, make plans to meet again to discuss strategies to assist their restitution campaign, and lo and behold who is there right by the exit as obvious as could be but the spies. I tell Andy to go left, I would go right, and the others could disperse so there was no way they could keep following all of us. They tried to follow Andy and me, but we shook them, and off we went into the Yangon night.

A friend of mine, who worked in Burma on human trafficking issues—of which there is no shortage—was an avid runner. Every time she went for an early morning jog before the heat set in, some poor guy *in a suit and tie* would try to keep up with her as she twisted through narrow alleys and dirt lanes. I heard another great spy story where the one being spied on was staying at the most famous and expensive hotel in Yangon, the famous Strand. He tried to blend in, having tea in the lobby, while his spy read the *International Herald Tribune* upside down, instantly revealing his cover to the activist he was instructed by his superiors to follow.

Indeed, so much that the *Tatmadaw* dreams up is just so utterly ridiculous, it's a wonder they have been able to maintain power for as long as they have. They don't seem to mind the isolation and sanctions, content to keep milking as much money as they can from illicit drug production and distribution, clear-cutting virgin forests, and digging minerals and gems—from wherever they find them—in the most environmentally damaging way. They generally destroy and disfigure the land and the people of this otherwise amazing country for a few bucks to spend on some of the world's ugliest real estate and gaudy riches. The sheer architectural hideousness of the general's homes in Yangon and elsewhere astonishes me, replete with fake Roman pillars, oversized balconies—seemingly built for eventual waving Mussolini imitation moments—and thicker, sharper, and higher coils of barbed wire than I have seen anywhere. These thugs may be content in their isolation, but they are excessively paranoid of losing it all. And to think I always thought Buddhism was about non-attachment, simplicity, compassion, and oneness....

There is so much more I could say about Burma and my thousands upon thousands of interactions with the people there. I could recap the political horrors foisted upon the people of the country throughout its years as a British colony and since its independence in 1948, with new tragedies *again* shafting the 60 million souls of this artificial country, especially since the latest military dictatorship began in 2021. But you can read about these things in countless books and reports that Burma watchers and NGOs have been churning out for decades. In fact, my friend José and I published a book on our work on HLP rights in

Burma a couple of years ago called *Before a Democracy Died*.[13]

However, one thing you probably won't read about, but which encapsulates much of Burma at a political level, is the astounding Drugs Elimination Museum in Yangon. It's so odd, so unique, and so unbelievable that you must experience it to believe such a place even exists. I haven't been there for a few years now—having shown it to a whole range of foreign friends who were working for justice in Yangon—but when it was open, had you visited, chances are high that you would have been the only guest. This cavernous, Costco or Walmart-sized multi-floored building, hotter inside than outside, is quite easily the weirdest museum ever conceived. One must wonder which geniuses were behind this utterly absurd attempt to portray Burma, one of the world's most prolific drug producers, as the *best* at eliminating drugs—using this museum as proof. Gaslighting in its finest manifestation. Given that Burma is widely known to be the world's second largest opium producer, with nearly 60,000 hectares under cultivation, second only to Afghanistan's 225,000 hectares dedicated to this cash earner, perhaps a museum called the Drug Facilitator Museum might have been a better name.

This echo-filled, pongy, and pungent museum has floor after floor of very poorly constructed amateurish, life-sized mannequins depicting the Burmese military's supposed relentless struggle against drugs. The hope is that viewers will believe these ridiculous re-enactments, rather than the truth—that the *Tatmadaw*, its cronies, and various ethnic armies make millions from permitting and actively promoting the cultivation and manufacturing of illegal drugs of many varieties. There are too many of these faked displays to describe here, but a couple of my favorites showed a whole alley way of Western junkies with needles dangling out of their arms and faces like demons unconvincingly seeking to show both that it's only Westerners who use these drugs. And make sure you don't miss the massive scene of soldiers lighting huge bales of what is presumed to be heroin on fire to show their commitment to eradication.

---

[13]Scott Leckie and José Maria Arraiz, *Before a Democracy Died: Housing, Land and Property Rights in Myanmar*, Palgrave/MacMillan, 2023.

It is as if they entrusted a group of third graders to put the display together, which must be so embarrassing to any of the few self-respecting soldiers who remain truly concerned with protecting their fellow country men and women. Most, I suppose, guilelessly believe they've pulled yet another fast one over on the world. They must really believe the world is stupid. They delude themselves into thinking that visitors to this strange place will somehow be convinced of their sincerity. However, the only thing this museum conjures up in any reasonable person is that this pathetic attempt at public deception reflects not the military's weakness—but its contempt for everything but itself. Citizens and foreigners alike realize the military can do almost anything they want with little chance of them ever paying a price for any of their evil deeds they've gotten away with for so many decades. It is so sad knowing what this country could be and seeing just how deeply rotten to the core it is in ways so entrenched that only the most massive overhaul will yield the conditions for the true democracy that everyone in this country deserves. Sadly, that day does not seem like it will be arriving any day soon.

Life Lesson No. 67: If a government builds a museum in honor of itself, be skeptical (and wear a mask; it is likely to smell)

I made so many trips to Burma that it's hard to keep track of them or distinguish precisely which event happened on which trip. However, what I do know for certain is that each journey was dedicated to the same ends for my colleagues and me: getting housing, land, and property rights taken seriously once and for all. We made substantial progress in this quest and produced a whole series of publications, how-to-manuals, speeches, articles, lectures, meetings and all the rest that resulted in all of our ideas reaching ever-higher levels on the political agenda in the country. Detailed proposals for a national restitution law and commission that I put together with the talented Spaniard José Maria Arraiza of the Norwegian Refugee Council were finally getting a hearing and being taken seriously. Eager to review the scale of land crimes, I wrote a book on land grabbing in Myanmar in 2019 called *Land Grabbing as an Internationally Wrongful Act: A Legal Roadmap for Ending Land Grabbing and*

Housing, Land and Property Rights Abuses, Crimes and Impunity in Myanmar.

Another paper on land expropriation that I wrote for the International Finance Corporation, the one and only time I ever worked for them, was widely read and cited but quickly became highly controversial because of the ugly truths it exposed. The IFC must have faced a lot of backlash for that paper because they tried to censor it when I put it online. This caused a small uproar from the people of Burma, including some of the millions victimized by these processes. The IFC eventually reversed their decision, and I believe the report remains online to this day. Another report I co-wrote with Shaun Butta for Displacement Solutions and a local partner organization in Yangon called EcoDev urged the government to establish a *National Climate Land Bank*. It gained attention from national MPs and even some ministers. And the list goes on, but where these will all lead now is far more likely to be nowhere than somewhere, at least as long as the military continues its stranglehold on things.

Life Lesson No. 68: Don't ask permission. If it is the right thing to do, just do it.

Even before their February 2021 coup, though, the bureaucracy in Myanmar and the deep control of the military and the government over so many aspects of society were positively suffocating. I met a law professor and the dean of Yangon Law School during a meeting with commissioners from the Myanmar National Human Rights Commission, two of whom became good friends as time rolled on. We met them at the university to discuss how we could assist the underdeveloped law school. I felt like I was in the film *Raiders of the Lost Ark* in an old, decrepit, and unkempt, dark, dusty, and dingy building that did not in any way resemble any of the numerous law schools I had taught at or otherwise visited. It was crumbling and barely making it. It felt like I was beamed back into the 1800s, in fact. The "library" was a small room of books haphazardly stacked up on each other, everything totally covered in thick dust as if no one had entered the room in years and each pile marked by a hand-written sign as to what topics were included in each unseemly stack. Seeing this, I desperately wanted to help, so I proposed that a team of lawyers and I teach four full-time law courses at the school in the coming months, and that we would cover 100% of the costs. We would ensure that these courses would be totally free to the law school and the students, something that would have cost hundreds of thousands of dollars at the law schools where I teach in Australia these days. I was happy to take full responsibility for designing the courses and finding the funds to make it happen. I took the dean and another law professor out to a nice traditional Burmese dinner and we made a plan. Right at the end of the meal though, the dean suddenly said: "This is wonderful, but of course, we will need approval from the Minister of Education." Uh oh, I thought, I didn't see that coming. So, we completed all the paperwork, submitted the request to the minister, and took care of all the other necessary formalities, and you can probably guess the end of this story.... Yep, ole Scott and his smart legal team never ended up teaching any of those courses at the Yangon Law School because the Minister simply never gave his permission. Burma is that kind of place, even in the comparatively good times, let alone now during the return of the interminable night.

Life Lesson No. 69: Great ideas, even if fully paid for, don't always eventuate.

Now, in 2026, I mourn for the present and future of my countless close friends in this country—Shan, Burmese, Karen, Mon, Rohingya, Karenni, Chin, and so many other beautiful fellow human beings. These wonderful people could remake this country into something truly extraordinary—if only given the chance. But herein lies the rub, and a seriously bad rub it is. For as much as I love Burma and its many peoples, how many times in Yangon did I have to hear tear-inducing lines like: "Up until today, I had no idea my colleagues were racist, and in an instant, I knew they all were just that." Or: "How they can hate a people so much with whom they have had virtually no contact, astounds me!" Or: "How is it possible that in a land where nationalist Buddhists claim to be protecting the world against the loss of this compassionate religion, can they wantonly hate all Muslims and be ready to kill at a moment's notice?" One might expect this from the highly nationalistic military, but not from ordinary people, let alone NGOs and others who often turned out to be far more nationalistic and shamelessly racist than I could have ever imagined. I've seen it myself way too many times to deny its existence, as much as I wish it weren't so, including from people I would have never thought could possibly hold such views. But so it is here.

Life Lesson No. 70: Nationalism and Buddhism should be incompatible…

It was these—and many more irreconcilable contradictions that pervade Burma at all levels of society—that led me, after years of deep involvement in the country, to reluctantly step away. This decision came not long after the ethnic cleansing of nearly a million civilians and the military's rampant killing of the Rohingya in the west, supported by the NLD government. Watching NLD leader Aung San Suu Kyi try in person in The Hague to justify what most of the world saw as genocide in front of the International Court of Justice made me nauseous. Seeing a fellow international legal expert next to her doing the same thing made it even worse. Needless to say, none of the hundreds of thousands ethnically cleansed into Bangladesh have returned since their expulsion in 2017. After hearing justification after justification from people in Yangon, claiming these were not Myanmar citizens but Bengalis, along with all of the other racist rationales trotted out to justify genocide, I reached my breaking point.

Despite the progress made on the HLP front, I could no longer justify committing any more time to these issues in Myanmar. My turning point was the Rohingya genocide, but what with the military coup four years later, the chances that I will ever set foot in what in so many ways is a country I deeply love, feels exceedingly low.

When the *Tatmadaw* becomes an accountable, transparent, civilian-led and rule of law-based military, and when true democracy comes to a country so deserving of it and when nowhere else is calling me, I will return, so it might just be a while, sadly. This again breaks my heart for the millions of kind souls who still call this place home. After visiting the country numerous times to work on housing, land, and property rights issues—including proposals for a new restitution law and justice mechanism to restore the rights of millions whose homes and lands had been stolen by the military and their cronies—I called it quits. I had grown too tired of realizing that the country's problems were far deeper than I initially assumed and that true, meaningful change wasn't going to happen as quickly as I had hoped. So, my days in Burma are over and done which I very much wish wasn't the case, but alas so it is.

Life Lesson No. 71: Sometimes starting over is the only logical option.

At least I have the freedom to decide whether or not to return to a country which has so much beauty, so much wasted potential, so many good people and other things you will find nowhere else on the planet, but for my friends, for the democratically inclined and for those who cannot leave or refuse to do so, the choices available to them now seem to decline by the day. I will miss my incredible driver who drove me thousands of kilometers all throughout the country, always there on time and waiting patiently. I'll miss those wonderful nights drinking gin and tonics and single malt and playing outdoor snooker until the wee hours. I'll have to be content with what might be the largest *longyi* (wrap around cloth) collection in Australia for a non-Myanmar national. I won't be adding more to it, as I did on each visit when I spent many afternoons shopping for the finest longyis, always bringing home at least a dozen, sometimes more. I'll miss the markets where I bought as much as I could to boost the meager savings of the poor market stallholders. I'll have to cook carefully now that I can no longer buy the hand-carved wooden spoons that I picked up on every trip. And the handmade ink stamps that were made for me on every trip on a busy street corner with logos of my various NGOs and projects, and for my daughter's latest obsession, will have to serve me for longer than usual.

And so it is that my time in the country that never was, is effectively over and done. It breaks my heart to see how the country is being driven so terrifyingly into the ground, yet again. I hope I nudged things at least a little bit in the right direction and that one day the people I was trying to help will get at least a taste of the justice that is so long overdue. And perhaps the new National Unity Government that appears to be unifying a whole range of once totally disparate groups may well win the day. But the suffering to be endured between now and then is too devastating to even contemplate. All I can do now is to offer blessings to you my Burma friends, blessings to you all; you deserve so much better.

Life Lesson No. 72: One day...

Chapter 5

Gaia

It is worse, much worse, than you think.
—David Wallace-Wells[14]

The links between human rights, natural disasters, and climate change have occupied my attention for 30 years thus far, long ago far too aware of the sadly obvious future that awaits us in the already unpleasant present by prioritizing the need for governments everywhere to take the rights of people affected by climate change seriously. Having seen these effects already take tragically tangible form in places as diverse as Australia, Tuvalu, Bangladesh, Burma, the Maldives, Kiribati, Fiji, the Solomon Islands, the Netherlands, Thailand and beyond, it was obvious to me long ago that the real fight, the fight against climate change, is upon us now and for the long road ahead. Back in 2009, I had the following to say in a speech I gave to the annual meeting of the Climate Action Network Australia (CANA) in Melbourne:

---

[14]David Wallace-Wells, *The Uninhabitable Earth: Life After Warming*, Tim Duggan Books, 2019.

I'd like to take you on a journey to two very different futures. First, let's go to a future built on the foundations of three decades of political intransigence, delay, and simple disregard for those who were forced from their homes and lands because of climate change. The year is 2039. Those of us lucky enough to still be alive will have endured far more than ongoing economic malaise, receding hairlines and the loss of friends and loved ones along the way. Life in 2039 is rocky at best; strewn with boulder-like challenges far greater than the soothsayers of 2009 could have ever imagined. The past three decades have been witness to incredible turmoil, change and consternation, but also something the first of what have been three African American Presidents talked so much about—hope. For hope is what all of us here saw on the faces of our friends and neighbours from Tuvalu— Kiribati—Vanuatu—the Carteret Islands in PNG—and everywhere else in the so often ignored Pacific—way back in 2009 when the notion of climate change, displacement, loss of land and loss of nations began to seem an ever more real prospect to so many throughout the small island nations to our north and east. Thirty years ago, some of those active within the climate change movement and a small handful of Governments spoke forcefully about the links between human rights and climate change and how those forced to flee their homes and lands must not be treated as helpless or unworthy victims who should be left to fend for themselves. These voices, though, did not win the day in Copenhagen in 2009, and what could have been a series of rights-based initiatives in support of forced climate migrants throughout Asia and the Pacific became instead chaotic, Darwinian free-for-alls, pitting the well-connected and the wealthy against the poor and middle-class majority. Although fewer people were displaced globally by 2039 than some of the more dramatic predictions made in 2009, nevertheless millions in Asia and the Pacific have had to flee their former homes and lands due to a combination of climate-induced consequences. Some who had the resources and wherewithal to flee early lost only a portion of their assets and in some instances were even provided with interesting – albeit inequitable – forms of compensation. Australia, New Zealand, Singapore, Hong Kong and a handful of other wealthy countries offered resettlement places for early leavers through new forms of business migration visas which often involved investment promises of a million dollars or more. And these same Governments often spoke of their immense generosity and humanitarian spirit in addressing the displacement caused by climate change at international gatherings. For the tens of millions unable to afford the paid visa schemes, however, life was anything but easy. Millions ended up homeless, landless, and jobless, and the slums around many of the region's great cities exploded as masses of new urban poor migrants sought to find a place in the city. Insecurity in areas partially vacated by forced climate migrants became steadily worse, leading to a series of violent conflicts. Long dormant land disputes in areas less heavily affected by rising seas, inundation and drought re-emerged causing further instability. Many went hungry as famine swept across formerly fertile areas. And people died - in droves - as disease, deprivation and despair cut short the lives of millions across the region. Such is the world of climate displacement in 2039.

And now, I'd like to take you to a point three decades from today - to a very different reality - where for three decades forced climate migrants have been treated as human rights laws say they should be - as beneficiaries of human rights. Looking back now thirty years later, everyone agrees that 2009 was THE year that made the next 30 years what they were to become for so many of the world's forced climate migrants. In 2009 choices were made, and decisions approved by politicians and power holders that went on to shape the human rights realities of those forced to flee their homes and lands. For in 2009, in the face of horrific financial turmoil and the worst economic threats in a century, in a twist of fate that still baffles the minds of the world's more pessimistic pundits, the world came together in remarkable fashion in Copenhagen and declared that human rights would—from here on in—guide climate policy the world over, both at home and overseas. Led by the Maldives, Kiribati, Tuvalu, and assorted others, and joined by a chorus of millions of global citizens in the lead-up to Copenhagen who pushed for forced climate migrants to be treated as holders of human rights, Governments actually listened and agreed to give those forced to flee their homes and lands that most Australian of things - a fair go. By 2011 detailed internal relocation strategies and regional and international resettlement plans had been drawn up and approved in all of the world's countries most under threat. Huge tracts of land were set aside for forced climate migrants as land banking schemes took hold in dozens of countries as the vital nature of planning was finally embraced.

The awarding of the Noble Peace Prize to Forced Climate Migrant Organizer Extraordinaire, Ms. Ursula Rakova and her organization Tulele Peisa from the Carteret Islands in Papua New Guinea in 2014 spurred a series of actions from Australia to Fiji, the US, Canada, Europe and across Asia to set plans in motion to ensure that there would be land, homes, and jobs for the world's climate displaced. In 2016, in an extraordinary act of island-to-island solidarity, both the Philippines and Indonesia each offered 50 uninhabited islands to Pacific Island Nations for use in re-establishing the nations, cultures and heritage of many of the rapidly submerging small island States. Australia and New Zealand developed intensive education and skills training programmes to assist the many new migrants that began to call these nations home. By 2021 a series of new legal rules and proposals had been developed which led to pragmatic deals being struck between almost entirely submerged nations and other nations willing to offer land and resettlement places for the islander populations. Some of these deals offered full exploitation rights of the Exclusive Economic Zones of Sinking States in exchange for a portion of the proceeds and migration slots.

Today, in 2039 most of Tuvalu is gone as are large portions of the landmass of Kiribati, Vanuatu, the Maldives, and a range of other small island nations. Coastal erosion, encroaching sea levels, inundation and perpetual tidal surges have led to mass displacement in Bangladesh, Viet Nam, and China. And while terribly sad and painful, the human rights measures put into place in 2009 and beyond were largely responsible for ensuring that at least the housing, land, and property rights of the vast majority of these forced climate migrants were protected. Displacement continues and what was once only a possibility has become a reality. But human resilience combined with approaches to these challenges where human rights are front and centre has made a bad situation far less horrible than it would have been had we ignored rights and placed expediency and fear ahead of human rights and climate justice.

Friends, we hold our common climate future in our collective grip.

We can choose – indeed, we will choose – the path of rights or we can choose the path of neglect, disinterest, and greed. Back to the present of 2009, it remains up to us to ensure that as bad as the consequences of climate change turn out to be, the rights of all to a decent place to live in peace, security and dignity will win the day.

Back to the present of 2026, approaching two decades later now, just how much of what I foresaw has come true and how much turned out to be wishful thinking? Well, as is always in the case of climate change, the news is not good. Sea levels are rising now faster than predicted, much faster. More people are now threatened with climate displacement than could have ever been imagined even ten years ago. Weather and climatic changes are even more unpredictable, violent, and frequent than was first postulated decades ago. Fires are breaking out everywhere, at all times of year, often in places not familiar with wildfires, and at a scale totally unprecedented. CO2 levels in the atmosphere just go up year after year, now surpassing 429 parts per million, far above anything close to safe levels. It seems increasingly likely that the 1995 movie *Waterworld*, one of the most expensive films ever made, was surprisingly prescient. Kevin Costner somehow glimpsed a future where, not too many generations from now, humans will have to redraw world maps to reflect the massive changes to coastlines. Just imagine that.

Life Lesson No. 73: Most predictions about climate change were wrong. As David Wallace-Wells warns us, it is generally much worse than expected.

And then imagine this: All of this, *yes all of this*, is the fault, the responsibility, and the result of the short-sighted stupidity of *us*, the human race; *we* brought about the Anthropocene, and *we* caused climate change. The countless appalling backward steps taken by the current US government in their climate denial frenzy has worsened things further than many of us could have even fathomed. Our economic system and our seemingly insatiable desire for more and then more and then just a bit more, is quite literally killing us. It's as if our species is a little bit too similar to that obese man in Monty

Python's film *The Meaning of Life* who is so gluttonous, so utterly devoid of any self-control or restriction, that he begs for just one more morsel of food after having gorged himself for as long as physically possible, and then suddenly explodes, killing himself and displaying one of the most disgusting cinematic visions a film viewer could ever see, literally eating himself to death, just as us humans are burning and drilling and chopping and digging and consuming and extracting ourselves into an almost willful collective death spiral.

Life Lesson No. 74: Climate denialism should be made a criminal offense.

Indeed, other than perhaps ensuring that nuclear weapons are eradicated and never used, we have no more important issue to deal with than climate change. We have already surpassed the 1.5°C threshold above historical averages. If we go beyond that level, let alone reach the now more likely 2.0°C or 3.0°C over long-term climate trends, *billions* of people will be in serious trouble—we'll be effectively cooked. The Inter-Governmental Panel on Climate Change (IPCC) now calls it *Code Red*. Not all of us, but literally billions of people will *not be able* to continue living where they live now, including huge parts of India, Australia, the United States, Sub-Saharan Africa, China and so many other places. The *2015 Paris Climate Agreement* was critical in setting the 1.5°C goal, but with global CO2 levels rising every year since, I'm not greatly optimistic. Learning recently that the richest 1% of humanity is now responsible for over 70% of CO2 emissions—and showing no signs of changing their behavior—adds to my list of concerns. This is appalling and if you personally want to do something to tackle climate change put your attention to the excessive CO2 secretions of the world's richest and you will not be wasting your time.

But all this work and the efforts of so many to get these issues onto the international agenda still has a long, long way to go as every prediction about climate change has been proven wrong, with the reality of climate change being and becoming far worse than originally thought. Think about your own government wherever you live and their attention to the massive problem of people being forced from their homes because of the effects of climate change, and ask yourself the following: Does my government have a climate displacement policy at all? Does my government have a specific official or office responsible for assisting climate displaced people? Does my government have land set aside for distribution to people made landless or homeless because of climate change? Does my government have a specific line in its national budget dedicated to helping climate displaced people? And the list goes on. I would wager that anyone who asks these questions will find it impossible to give affirmative answers to each of the five queries posed, so yes, we have a long way to go before climate justice takes hold. In the meantime, underlying these challenges, climate justice of all types seems lacking just about everywhere despite the efforts of so many.

I've tried, in my latest rendition of the war of the flea, to lend a hand to this struggle in a number of ways. In addition to teaching the world's first law school course on human rights and climate change every year for almost two decades now and writing books and reports, producing feature films and the like, I've worked for over 15 years with climate activists in Bangladesh, Fiji, the Solomon Islands, Panama, Kiribati, Tuvalu and elsewhere, as well as helping develop an international framework on how governments should protect their citizens' rights against the scourges of climate change, called the *Peninsula Principles on Climate Displacement Within States*. The people of Bangladesh were instrumental in inspiring those of us who drafted these Principles to ensure that they would be as effective as possible.

Bangladesh - Where to Begin To Fix Climate Displacement?

We've all heard of Bangladesh and seen images of the devastating and horrific severe flooding and storms that form such a routine part of life in this remarkable country of 170 million souls all squeezed into a territory just half the size of the Australian State of Victoria where I currently live. If Victoria, which has a small population of nearly seven million people, were as densely populated as Bangladesh, this state would have an unimaginable population of 340 million, something utterly impossible to imagine. I'm sure we all have pictures in our mind's eyes of the flooded roads of Dhaka and elsewhere that seem to strike each and every year, the slums and the massive challenges that face the wonderful people of this country. I've been there. I've seen it and can assure you it's all true.

Even before this largely, but by all means not entirely, flat country was so hard hit by COVID, the latest floods and a successful student-led revolution ousting the previous government, Bangladesh only received a tiny trickle of tourists—320,000 tourists in 2019, for instance—ranking it 166th in global tourism arrivals. These numbers are unlikely to increase anytime soon. One time, when I was in Bangladesh on a climate change work trip, it seemed that any time we would stop for food or head to our next meeting we saw the same faded and tattered 1970s-style posters on the walls of many of the places we visited, universally extolling the message of *Visit Bangladesh Now Before the Tourists Come*. Alas, I fear they may have been a bit premature in making that hopeful prediction. With climate change already devouring so many portions of the coastlines and riverbanks, tourist numbers may never increase. Climate activists, UN officials, and a handful of diehard cricket fans may come, but tourists probably will choose nearby Nepal or Thailand while they can, leaving Bangladesh to deal with climate change all on its own. And this is a great shame, for the people and the hopes they hold for their nation are things that should be seen first-hand for they will inspire even the most reluctant or pessimistic traveller.

In 2011, a group of us ventured forth across Bangladesh, visiting a whole host of places already grappling with the effects of climate change, during what turned out to be the coldest winter ever in a country not known for cold weather. It was actually excruciatingly freezing and none of us on the team of this Displacement Solutions mission were particularly prepared for this, especially me. We expected 30°C or higher and harsh humidity, but we got 4°C and extremely thick, never-lifting fog instead. We were on countless small boats, medium-sized boats, and sometimes huge ferries on even huger rivers with zero visibility through the freezing fog, but the mighty captains left port anyhow and we made it to the other side every time, even though it often seemed unlikely that we would. The cold seeped into my bones like it never had before even having lived in many very cold countries; I could not seem to get warm no matter what I did. It never seemed to cease no matter where we went, a sensation I hope to never feel again. It's one thing to try to get comfortable when it's too hot. But it's another thing altogether when all you want is warmth and no matter what you do, for days on end it remains elusive.

During short flights between places like Dhaka, Dacope, and Jessore, we spent a lot of time in vans traversing the country. As the team leader, as always I brought a huge bag of awesome food and drinks—dried mango, nuts, energy bars, water, tea—as well as copious quantities of wet wipes for our constantly dirty hands. We visited community after community, conversing with thousands of people living in brutal conditions on the frontlines of climate carnage. It was hard to imagine not just a few hours but decades of life on the edge of human existence, something none of us on the team hailing from privileged countries like Australia, Switzerland, and Holland could ever really do. We might romanticize it in a certain way, but there is no denying that a life like this would be ruthless in interminable ways, even if those suffering through it are somehow able to transcend the roughest edges of these realities. When your kid gets sick and you can't reach or afford a doctor, life is sheer misery, no matter who you are and no one should have to endure this—ever!

Sometimes when things go wrong, it turns out to be a blessing. This was certainly the case in Bangladesh, where our first local NGO allies turned out to be deceptive charlatans, which we thankfully realized before they did too much damage. In rejecting them, we found Young Power in Social Action (YPSA) and have worked closely with them ever since, for 15 years now. Founded more than 30 years ago and still headed by the extremely hard-working Arifur Rahman, YPSA has offices all across Bangladesh with thousands of incredibly dedicated staff. Together we have worked on the *Bangladesh Housing, Land, and Property Initiative* for more than a decade now, which itself is coordinated by my dear friend, the highly skilled and always jolly Mohammed Shahjahan. I love meeting and talking with these guys and others, with us using the honorific *bhai* for each other as we plan the next steps of how best to address some of the displacement crises facing the country. Arif-bhai and Shahjahan-bhai, two extraordinary gentlemen, so dedicated to the people of their country, and fighting daily for justice for the millions of people on the edge who are barely making it. Hey, Nobel Committee, ignore Trump's desperate and whiny pleas, and instead give next year's Peace Prize to actual deserving recipients like YPSA, Arif and Shahjahan, OK?

Life Lesson No. 75: YPSA deserves the Nobel Peace Prize.

We traversed countless and often crumbling dikes which are ubiquitous in Bangladesh, sometimes walking for kilometers down these narrow walls of protection against the rising seas, some of which had thousands of people squeezed onto them after escaping the vicious Cyclone Alia in 2009 that killed thousands and displaced millions more. Years later, thousands of families still lived in makeshift shelters atop two-meter-wide dykes, endlessly waiting to return to land that may no longer exist.

These people and the others we met with throughout a country in which at least 30 million, if not 50-60 million people or even more, are likely to be permanently displaced by the effects of climate change inspired me to try to do something, anything, for the rest of my life to lend a hand. Beyond other ongoing work there, the best I could come up with so far was designing what came to be called the *One House, One Family* at a time project, or OHOF, which became the world's first program specifically designed to provide new, permanent, and free homes for some of the most climate vulnerable families in the country. I would give anything to be able to have the money needed to adequately house everyone in Bangladesh, and the world for that matter, but alas I fall somewhat short, no matter what I do. Under the able field-level guidance of YPSA, OHOF builds permanent new homes for frontline victims of climate change in Bangladesh. To date we have been able to build 18 high quality climate safe homes, giving lifelong housing to more than 100 fellow humans, who will be able to live there rent-free for the rest of their lives. I raise the funds internationally, mainly from friends and family with a little extra to spare. At $7,100 per house—including land, doors, windows, a tube well for water, and administrative costs—it's one of the best social investments and acts of compassion anyone can make. We are hoping to build another 16 houses next year, and who knows after that. If you want to be a part of this, just find us online and be in touch. I can assure you that 100% of the funds we raise go directly to YPSA to build homes and manage the program. We gladly implement OHOF without any reimbursement, and it's a true honor to be able to do so. I'm sure if we all built homes for people we will never meet, grew food for people in need and even just greeted each other to shake hands, we'd have a better world.

Life Lesson No. 76: If you want to do something to confront climate change, <u>do something!</u>

Among the countless things I've learned from working in Bangladesh and other climate-affected countries is that without strong, dedicated, sustained, and deeply interventionary measures by the state —both in policy and law—millions will lose everything as the scourges of climate change worsen. Without clear institutional and governmental support designed specifically to assist climate displaced persons, families and communities, millions across the world will fall through the already gaping holes in protection which will only surely grow as global warming heats up.

I can't wait to return to Bangladesh and hope to do so sooner than later. However, during my last visit—surprise, surprise—I had yet another medical emergency. Due to the unseasonably cold weather, I picked up a very unusual cold that felt different than all other ailments I have sadly experienced so frequently throughout life, something to be expected in a place where night-time temperatures hit freezing while we slept in buildings meant for 30°C heat or more. On the plane back home, just as we started our descent into Melbourne about an hour from landing, I started getting a slight pain in my left ear which I thought was just the normal equalizing of the pressure often associated with reducing elevation, something I have obviously dealt with hundreds upon hundreds of times. What started as discomfort quickly turned into excruciating pain, like someone had inserted a knitting needle into my ear and was pounding away on it to get it to pierce my skull. Horrendous. No matter what I did to reduce the pain, it kept getting worse. By the time we landed, I could barely walk or suppress my moans of agony. When I did finally stand up, I somehow made it through the terminal but as I approached the passport control booth, I was heavily tilted over to the left, barely able to get my passport into the hands of the concerned looking official. Because I was so unwell, instead of going home we checked into the hotel across from the Tullamarine main arrivals hall and immediately called a doctor who came pretty quickly and said I needed to get to the hospital. By now, not only was there excruciating pain but my hearing was completely gone in my left ear. I found an amazingly talented German doctor from good ole Berlin who now lived in Melbourne and he got me into the surgical theatre as quickly as he could. With incredibly sure-handed microscopic surgical skills, this talented doctor repaired my devastated inner ear. After months of recovery, medication, and rest, my hearing returned, and within a year, everything was back to normal. Thanks again, Dr. T.

The adage "Beware Lion Hounds" popped into my mind again on my first flight after my ear had healed. Dr. T gave me a six-step plan to implement prior to every flight, which I have followed religiously ever since. Luckily for me, that knitting needle pain has remained far from my cherished ears. By now, you've likely noticed that despite my best efforts at prevention, my body often fails to keep up with my mind's desires, especially in places where I haven't developed immunity to resist the trillions of local bugs, bacteria, and viruses in all of the places I have been lucky enough to visit—but where I've often become seriously ill. I'll try to transcend these memories and return to the country where I faced the illness that nearly floored me for good. But if not, I know that through Arif-bhai, Shahjahan-bhai, and OHOF, my very real and personal links to Bangladesh will never wane.

Japan - Playboy Calls in Kobe: the Great Hanshin Earthquake

A couple of months after the Great Hanshin Earthquake in Japan in 1995, centered near Kobe, the UN called and asked me to arrange a mission to Japan to work with local NGOs and assess the human rights implications of the disaster. I instantly said yes and set about raising the needed funds, which came in quickly. The devastating Kobe quake killed more than 6,000 people, injured more than 40,000 and displaced 300,000, doing more than USD 200 billion in damage in the process. The scale of the death and destruction was shocking, particularly in a country so modern, so advanced, and so well organized.

Since then, I have been in Japan several times and love going to this place that has become one of my favorites over the years. Compared to so many other places, while there may be a level of frenetic energy and plastic fakery in Japan distinct from all other regions of the planet, there is also an underlying calm, a wellspring of respect and a commitment to culture that somehow lingers on strongly in the midst of so much modernism and advanced development. Nowhere else in the world simultaneously strikes you with such an inimitable combination of cutting-edge society and strict social norms and behaviors, which I wish were globally abundant. Long before COVID came along, for instance, if you are sick in Japan, it is *you* who wears a mask to protect others, not the other way around. When you meet someone for the first time, and often afterwards, you bow to show your respect, just as they bow to you to show the same. The entire staff of just about every dining establishment collectively greets you with a welcoming and boisterous "Irasshaimase!" as you enter no matter where you are or who you are, and there's nothing quite like sitting at a real sushi bar with only six seats for half a dozen lucky diners at a time, watching the masters at work—who have trained to perfection for decades—as they prepare cut after cut of the finest fish on the planet. The *sake* is beautiful, too. I asked one of these masters once if there was anything that he thought he could still improve after all those decades of finely slicing fish for the waiting customers, and he immediately replied "Yes, I have still yet to make the perfect batch of rice, 40 years and counting."

On the other hand, three years after this Earthquake mission in 1998, after flying in from Bangkok following a few weeks of work with Bhutanese refugees in isolated eastern Nepal—100,000 of whom were forced out of the Buddhist Kingdom in the 1980s—paranoid border officials at Kansai Airport in Osaka brought me deeply into the never-ending hallways towards the dreaded "private rooms" at airport security where they held me for hours while my friends waited in the arrivals hall. At the passport counter the official said to me after looking through my passport, "Sir, you have been to some very dangerous countries, did you bring any *danger* with you to Japan?" At first, I had no idea what he was talking about. Then he pulled out a large, one-square-meter laminated poster displaying all kinds of mouth-wateringly delicious-looking drugs and asked if I had brought any *danger* with me from those *dangerous* countries. Now, I may sometimes be partial towards a bit of mind-altering exploration, and as humans have been doing this for thousands of years, it can't be all bad. But smuggling and dealing are not my thing, especially not in Japan, which lags behind much of the world in addressing drugs reasonably and with balance, as many countries now do through tolerance policies, decriminalization, rescheduling, or outright legalization. Of course, I said no I had no *danger* with me and awaited the always bliss-inducing sound of the official stamp being pounded into my almost full passport. Instead, bowing the whole time, I heard him say, "Please come with me, Sir, for further inspection." Damn!

Not only would my poor NGO friends now be worried, but there was *every possibility* that I could have unintentionally and inadvertently travelled with something I shouldn't have in some long-forgotten matchbox in my toilet kit. When I started thinking about this, I knew that I would never consciously bring any contraband with me to a place like Japan, but at the same time the chances that I *accidentally* had illicit substances on me was very far from zero. If I did have something, I certainly didn't know it. As Austin Powers might say, "That's not mine." I immediately went into deep acceptance mode and waited for my luggage and the searcher to come completely violate my privacy based on no evidence whatsoever other than where I had been, and rifle through everything. Whenever real danger looks possible, whenever the next close shave is upon me, I seem to slip into a state of deep acceptance figuring that that is a better place to be if things go pear-shaped than letting my emotions loose and freaking out. So, the very polite and professional, white-gloved Japanese cop goes very systematically, like a well-oiled machine, through my suitcase, full of dirty clothes, books, papers and the rest and finally reaches the grey toiletries bag I had been using for years on end on hundreds of trips, the stains and ancient toothpaste on the outside and inside of the bag bearing testament. For so many years I travelled so much, so unexpectedly and so often with just a day or two warning that even though I am rather good about keeping things clean, I think I quite literally never, ever cleaned out my bag of toiletries.

The crisp-uniformed officers are taking their jobs extremely seriously and going through everything in my toilet bag with military efficiency. Opening up deodorant containers, unscrewing the top of the toothpaste tube, smelling the cologne bottles and then slowly but surely opening up and exploring what must have been more than 40 boxes of matches I had in there collected every now and then on various jaunts to places which still gave boxes of matches away, any one or more of which could have contained certain forbidden things. Even a small amount of *danger* in Japan would have probably put me in more than a little jeopardy, so I was in very deep acceptance mode and was sure they would find something. Much to my utter amazement they didn't, all the matchboxes were somehow clean and I was a lucky, lucky boy that day, that's for sure. They bowed, I bowed back, and off I went into the land of the rising sun.

Life Lesson No. 77: Always check your toilet kit before flying….Some of you may also wish to clean your credit cards….

A few years earlier, I had put together a stellar team of some of the world's best housing and disaster experts and we all arrived within a day of each other from all corners of the globe. The truly dedicated Enrique Ortiz from Mexico City, Aromar Revi came in from Delhi, Leilani Farha from Toronto, and me from Utrecht. It was a real oneness world team ready to see how we could help. We were met at the airport by local progressive human rights lawyer Katsuyuki Kumano and his team. Within minutes I knew Kumano-san and I would be lifelong friends and over the years this kind and caring man has, indeed, become one of my best friends anywhere on this planet. Being a human rights-inclined lawyer in Japan guaranteed this sympathetic and gentle man a challenging life in this highly conformist nation, not only because the system is about as stacked against such a person as can be imagined, but also because of the limited income available for this particular type of legal work. Kumano-san's commitment to alleviate human suffering is so huge and so admirable. It again makes me wonder what kind of world we live in where selfless human rights legal heroes like him are expected to receive modest salaries, while those using the law to entrench privilege and economic inequality and facilitate environmental destruction make so much more.

He lives in a beautiful but modest house on the outskirts of Osaka that he shares with his family and an incredible book collection attesting to his insatiable drive to always learn more. There is not a drop of materialist excess, and it is also that which makes it so appealing. The most recent time I was in Japan, a few years ago, I treated my friend to several days of Japan's finest offerings, including a stay in one of the coolest traditional *ryokans* in Tokyo, dining at one of the city's many Michelin three-star restaurants, Ishikawa (Tokyo has the most such stars of any city in the world), and a few nights at the famous Park Hyatt Hotel, where the excellent movie *Lost in Translation* was filmed. We walked for miles and miles every day all around the amazing streets of Tokyo, one of the very few cities of the world I can say I truly love.

At one point, we were in the most beautiful park one could imagine, and I made a little film of Kumano-san. We had a question-and-answer session, partly in Japanese, where I asked him how to say McDonald's in Japanese because I had heard locals mentioning a place I always avoid. Despite the good food in Japan, McDonald's remains popular there. I say "Konichiwa Kumano-San" and he replies "Konichiwa Leckie-San", and then in English I ask him if he can teach me how to say McDonalds in Japanese. Then he says, "Yes, it is Makudonarudo." I try to pronounce it, get it wrong and ask him again, all on film so my then McDonalds-loving daughter can see it when I get home. I try again and get it wrong and then he says "Ma-ku-do-na-ru-do", OK, now I get it. Luckily, we never had to eat at Makudonarudo during that first Earthquake mission back in 1995 but given the feverish pace of every day's countless meetings and constant travel, we resigned ourselves to more than one meal at the inimitable Lawson's, outlets of which pervade every neighborhood in Kobe, Osaka, Tokyo and beyond.

But when we were crisscrossing the entire Hyogo Prefecture where Kobe and most of the destruction from the earthquake was located the last thing we were concerned about was fast food. This was fast-fact-finding, and we found more than a few facts the authorities were not particularly happy about. For instance, in what was one of the world's first examinations of the specific human rights implications of natural disasters, we found that the official bodies in charge of urban planning had been given the choice of approving a government policy to be based on three possible options for preparing for future earthquakes: (1) High-level threat; (2) Mid-level threat; or (3) Low-level threats. Though the experts had almost universally urged them to plan on the basis of a high-level threat in the not-too-distant future, they instead chose the mid-level risk and planned accordingly. This included far less stringent building requirements, at an obviously cheaper price than those required under the high-risk scenario. As a result of this decision and other factors, thousands of people needlessly died deaths that could have been prevented had they done what the experts suggested.

We also discovered what can only be deemed as the discriminatory manner by which tenants were treated during the post-Earthquake recovery process. Owners were automatically guaranteed the right to return to their homes and found reconstruction grants not all that difficult to access. Tenants, however, faced an entirely different reality and were not given any assurance that they could return to their former homes or even neighborhoods. Indeed, many of the areas that had high levels of rental accommodation were subsequently bulldozed and turned into shopping malls and other developments, leaving thousands of these renters homeless over the long term.

As a result of these and other unfair and short-sighted policies, tenants and the elderly were the primary residents of the many temporary housing sites we visited across the region. By global standards these places were excellent, of that there can be no doubt. They had bamboo *tatami* mats on the floor, electricity, clean running water, air conditioning and so on. Yes, they were crowded at times, and no one really wanted to stay in these hastily constructed dwellings. However, they beat the post-earthquake shacks I had visited in the Dominican Republic, the horrendous conditions I encountered some years later in Bangladesh, and most definitely the post-tsunami homes I subsequently saw in Sri Lanka, the Maldives, and Thailand a decade later after the Boxing Day Tsunami. Be that as it may, the people were not happy and just wanted to be treated as equals to owners, and why shouldn't they have been?

Life Lesson No. 78: Bow often

We met with numerous public officials in all sorts of local, prefecture and national ministries and expressed our concerns in as clear a way as we could. I had met thousands of government officials worldwide by then and was very used to it, not intimidated in the least, particularly in a democratic country like Japan where you could speak freely without fear of harassment or arrest. But what was somehow shocking at these meetings was just how incredibly formal the regimented officials were every single time. They always sat in a row, wearing identical suits, were almost universally male, and after the perfunctory bows, would sit there holding their pencils, ready to write down everything we said. This was the side of Japan that bemused me so much and all I could think of was that these guys really needed to relax a bit, poor fellows. I knew they couldn't chill for fear of losing their jobs and risking membership in the sad, infamous *hikikomori* club, those who refuse to leave their rooms for *years* to avoid the social stigma and shame in Japan associated with job loss or unemployment. Almost 1.5 million Japanese practice *hikikomori* at any given time, and this voluntary isolation affects millions more, as their families and friends struggle to help them overcome it.

During this and subsequent trips, I gave speeches and lectures outlining our growing human rights concerns about the treatment of the victims of the Great Hanshin Earthquake, even years later. This was before the much worse horrors of the 2011 tsunami and Fukushima nuclear disaster in the north of Honshu near Sendai. We hope our work on the Kobe Earthquake helped improve how the displaced were treated after that disaster, the consequences of which continued to unfold years later. Displacement Solutions was awarded one of the Sasakawa Awards for Disaster Risk Reduction for our work on climate change and displacement that were given out in Sendai in 2015, so the links surely remained.

During that first mission we were on TV and the radio all the time, as well as in newspapers and magazines, with journalists following us wherever we would go. I was a speaker on a whole range of public panels, did many interviews in newsrooms and all the rest, all of which were exhausting but went smoothly, with favorable coverage of our criticisms. The only real controversial media story came about when Kumano-san asked me and Leilani if we would be willing to appear in *Playboy* magazine, the Japanese version of which was apparently one of the most widely read periodicals in the country, but they would say that wouldn't they? Anyway, having been shown a few *Playboys* when I was a kid at summer camp—like an eye-popping goldmine to a curious lad! —I wasn't really all that sure I wanted to be in one, even in Japan. Leilani, though, as an ardent feminist was dead-set against it and made this very clear. Kumano-san and a whole range of other NGO folks we were working with, including many women, universally said we really should do a story in *Playboy* because it was so popular and politically influential. So, we both finally agreed and now I can proudly say that I have posed for and had my picture in *Playboy* magazine, luckily for the avid readers of this well-liked journal fully-clothed.

We produced what became quite an influential report on the earthquake and its aftermath of negative human rights consequences called *Still Waiting*. We distributed it widely at the UN and beyond, and received huge media attention again, both in Japan and internationally. We raised funds to bring Kumano-san and others all the way to Geneva to testify about the ongoing problems facing earthquake victims, resulting in powerful UN decisions and findings that were widely used in Japan to improve the treatment of those who continued to struggle years later with the loss of their homes.

At the tail end of his visit, we took Kumano-san up to the French Alps high above Chamonix after we'd finished our intensive two weeks of work at the UN in Geneva and in an incredibly moving moment, we took a cable car up to the top of a mountain and Kumano-san huffing and puffing walked off by himself, which was unusual. I didn't know why he did this but let him go bliss out in this beautiful part of the world. After he hadn't returned after 10 minutes, we went to look for him and found him taking pictures of a photograph of his deceased mother that he had placed on the ground, leaning it against some high-altitude mountain wildflowers making sure she finally got her dream to travel to the Alps. What a magical moment, tears all over all of our faces. You are such a beautiful man, Kumano-san, and it is such an honor to call you a dear, dear friend.

Maldives - Islands Scraped Clean: The Boxing Day Tsunami

Most people will never be lucky enough to visit the Maldives and get to know some of the wonderful 400,000 people who call this country home. For those with the good fortune to be able to travel there, the vast majority of visitors go straight from the airport to the resorts located on the outer islands, never actually setting foot in the capital, Malé, or visiting any other of the three-hundred-plus islands in this amazing country, many of which are off-limits to foreigners. I was privileged to be able to do both on the several working visits I made to the Maldives following the horrible Boxing Day Tsunami of 2004 that killed more than 225,000 people across nine different countries. Having lived in Bangkok and frequently visiting Asia, lucky for me there are direct flights on Bangkok Airways from Bangkok to the Maldives. I had been to the Maldives before, but only to exquisite tourist islands under serious threat of permanent inundation due to human-caused climate change. When you transcend the hugely unsustainable nature of these resorts where virtually everything consumed has to be imported from overseas, when you suspend judgment about so many things and just focus on the pristine water, the whale sharks, the real sharks, the huge schools of barracudas, the sometimes still intact reefs, the incredible indigo colors of the sea and the utter luxury of the rooms and villas, there is no doubting that this really is one of the most amazing places on Earth. But no matter how nice it might be, there is something disconcerting about eating shaved Parmesan cheese from Italy, lamb cutlets from New Zealand, thinly sliced *jamón* from Spain and honeydew melon from Australia somewhere in the middle of the Indian Ocean in an over-water villa. Enter reality, though, by visiting the capital, Malé, and you will see how most Maldivians live. There you will hear their own unique stories of the types of things which exist everywhere and gain a more balanced picture of a country with great things happening, but which is also a nation beset with severe problems largely unknown to the rest of the world.

A day or two after the horrible events of 26 December 2004 took place all across the Indian Ocean, the UN asked me to come immediately to both Sri Lanka and the Maldives to work on housing, land, and property issues in the tsunami's aftermath. I quickly agreed and off I flew to Colombo where I looked into a whole host of issues after travelling along the entire southern coastline where so much aquatic butchery was very much still visible. I spoke to hundreds of people in the areas hardest hit that we visited and one man really sticks in my mind. This poor gentleman had lost 14 members of his family including his wife, parents and all of his children, several brothers and sisters, as well as losing his home and everything he owned. To see a man in so much emotional pain, completely and utterly devoid of any reason to live and so shattered by this unexpected tragedy was devastating. How could he, or anyone, ever come back to normal after enduring such misery? Multiply his suffering with millions upon millions of others across the region and you begin to get a sense of the sheer scale of carnage that wave unleashed the day after Christmas that year.

By far the worst effects of the tsunami took place in the Indonesian region of Aceh where some 167,000 people instantly perished as the wave took out entire cities within minutes. I was asked by the UN to go to work in Aceh, too, but I was too busy on other projects and happily gave that task to another HLP expert who did a superb job. The tsunami deeply affected many other countries as well, but surprisingly, the Maldives got off comparatively lightly despite their status as very low-lying islands with nowhere to run to, losing just 100 souls to the vicious waves. Nevertheless, more than a dozen islands were virtually wiped off the map, effectively scraped clean of anything that would continue to allow ongoing human habitation.

Most of the time I was working with the UN's human rights office (OHCHR), the UN's Office for the Coordination of Humanitarian Affairs (OCHA) and also enjoyed the pleasure of working with the Maldives National Human Rights Commission. During one such trip with the well-groomed and debonair Mark Cutts of OCHA just a month or so after the tsunami hit, we travelled far and wide and visited eight islands, including Malé, Thaa Madifushi, Vilufushi, Buruni, Kudahuvadhoo, Hulhumalé, Ugoofaaro and Hulhudhuffaaru, some of the more than 86 islands that suffered damage and home to many of the 12,000 people whom the tsunami displaced. We travelled day in and day out, staying in Malé at night and then heading to various islands by floatplane, barefoot pilots and all, all day long.

Sometimes when the small planes were full of other UN officials going out with us to check on the damage and the shape of the people, I'd sit up front next to the pilot and get a bird's eye view of what must be one of the best jobs in the world, flying low between some of the world's most beautiful islands, landing wherever you wanted and just taking it all in. Great pilots they were, too, as landing on water isn't always as easy or smooth as you might think if you've never done it before. Those planes allowed us to get around many islands that would have taken days to reach by boat, including several islands that were normally off-limits to foreigners, which we were fortunate to visit. One of these islands suffered a small portion of damage, but most of it was intact. Strolling down the pristine white sand "roads," past small, perfect houses made with dead coral that had washed up on the nearby beaches, swaying palms, and the smell of barbecuing tuna in the air, with no cars or motorized vehicles, made me want to stay forever. There wasn't a resort for miles and miles, and this true Maldivian place, untainted as it was, should remind us all that while we are all simultaneously the same, our unique cultures need to be protected and preserved rather than forgotten in the interests of global monocultures designed only to bring in more profit and keep capitalism going for another year.

The contrast between this incredible island and the capital island of Malé cannot be overemphasized. Malé is quite literally the most crowded place on Earth. I bet you didn't know that and asked yourself, "How can the capital of the Maldives, in the middle of the ocean as it is, be the most crowded place on Earth?" Well, if you were one of the few foreigners who do go there during their sojourns to the Maldives, you'll get it right away. Somehow, 212,000 people fit snuggly into eight square kilometers of precious land and you definitely feel it. In fact, it feels even smaller than that. I would run the perimeter of the island every morning before it got too hot and even then, during the quieter part of the day, I could never run more than 10 strides before having to dodge another person walking along the edge of this sardine can of a capital city. It's so crowded, in fact, that we heard from locals that some people had to sleep in three eight-hour shifts, three people using the same bed every eight hours. And the overcrowding has consequences. We were repeatedly told that Malé apparently had one of the world's worst heroin problems, with ever-growing numbers turning to mind-numbing opiates to forget about some of the rougher edges of life there. For some strange reason, people offer me drugs wherever I go, especially in cities. Nowhere has given me more chances to score some H than in Malé, though it's a drug I've never tried, nor ever will....except in dire hospital settings....

And yet, I love Malé and always feel at home there, especially enjoying the little basic cafes that dot the place and sell the world's finest tuna samosas, which I could eat all day, every day—so fine. Malé is the way it is due to a mix of economic opportunities compared to outlying islands, in particular those without tourist resorts, the looming threats of climate change already very much in view, and the normal urban temptations for young people wanting to join the global economy and partake in the Instagram lifestyles they see online.

Plus, in a world of rising sea levels and other climate threats, it's safer. Malé has a type of seawall comprised of huge manmade concrete shapes resembling the metal pieces of the kids' game of Jacks around it and very few other places have any protection whatsoever against rising seas or another tsunami. The government established a Safer Islands Program some years ago (carefully not using the word 'safe' in a world where sea level rise is happening at a terrifying rate) designed to relocate people to seven reinforced islands better able to withstand rising seas, but this well-intentioned program has many detractors, and reluctance to leave one's traditional home is totally understandable.

A new town near the international airport island called Hulumalé was built to handle some of the overflow of Malé, but it will take more than this to solve the country's problems. These days a Dutch firm has been hired to build an entirely new floating city near the capital to help in the battle against climate change and rising seas. Indeed, they will have to tackle the unsustainable economic foundations of all of the country's resort islands, as wonderful as they are, as well as figuring out how to deal better with the brutal rubbish crisis in the country which, beyond ocean pollution, includes considerable chunks of many islands permanently ruined to make room for toxic rubbish tips. There is even one entire island that takes all of Malé's waste, which must surely be one of the ugliest places on our once pristine Earth. Always the yin with the unavoidable yang, wherever you are.

Chapter 6

"Peace"

While I have always been rather reluctant to work directly in active war zones whenever I could avoid it, Rhodesian ridgeback howls never far off, I diligently worked in quite a few countries entering periods of peace or entirely new political realities after the overthrow of authoritarian regimes and the end of conflict. Of the more than 80 countries I've worked in thus far, a significant number of these were countries that were finding their way in what *was* an increasingly democratizing world.

This was particularly true in countries where I worked on HLP restitution issues, like Latvia in 1999, where our team found housing conditions far more dire than we had anticipated, especially during a freezing Baltic winter. I worked several times in often war-torn Serbia on a range of themes, mostly focusing on discrimination against the Roma. During one trip, I helped produce a film called *Vuka Vrcevica* about the brutal conditions in which the Roma of Belgrade tend to live in the horrendous garbage dumps of the capital. If the viewer had not been told this was in Europe, you would have never thought that such poor conditions could exist in the world's wealthiest continent. Whenever the camera appeared, residents held up bunches of five or six huge, *cat-sized* dead rats they'd killed the night before, while the badass and restless young men I was with imitated Snoop, Tupac, and Biggie, rapping in Serbian all day long. They jokingly called the deep, faeces-laden mud we waded through "chocolate," tyring anything to make it sound far better than it smelled.

Around the same time, I undertook a rather adventurous trip with the Organization for Security and Cooperation in Europe (OSCE) in Albania when Albania used to be like it was and not how it is now, to explore the possibility of returning properties taken without compensation by Enver Hoxha during his 41-year dictatorial rule from 1944-1985. I recall a meeting with several MPs discussing these things who seemed extremely impressive until the point where I suggested they needed to improve their tax collection capacities, something none of them were very happy about. As bad as conditions were in these and the countless other slums I had worked in, these countries were largely at peace—at least compared to a few short years before. Another one of these types of places where I devoted a good deal of time was in the former Soviet Republic of Georgia, where peace most distinctly became "peace."

Republic of Georgia - Not So Fine Wine for Breakfast

One of my most memorable conflict-related journeys took me to Tbilisi, the capital of the Republic of Georgia on my first visit to the Caucasus region which is known as a place of maximum viciousness when war breaks out there, as it all too frequently has. Things were not going well in Georgia when I started working there in 1998, but many adventures awaited so I happily agreed to work for UNHCR after an eventful dinner in Geneva. At that dinner, where I synchronistically met UN officials who needed a legal expert on HLP rights to help resolve thousands of restitution claims by IDPs across the country, I jumped at the chance and started my preparations.

Life Lesson No. 79: Be open but draw the line at gullibility.

During that same meal, which I remember all too well, a lovely Sri Lankan couple who later became close friends, pulled off one of the best pranks against me ever, executed with expert-level spontaneous precision. I had mentioned that I was still recovering from a horrible case of the chicken pox that I had picked up in a rudimentary medical clinic in Phnom Penh, Cambodia visiting an ill friend there some weeks before. At this point, their eyes light up a bit and as if rehearsed, though it simply could not have been, they almost in unison say,

"Has it happened yet? You know, the thing that happens to people in their 30s when they get chicken pox for the first time?"

I reply, "The thing? Which thing?", my insides already starting to feel the nerves of getting some new disease even while I had just recovered from this ugly disorder, especially when you get it when your youthful years have passed you by.

"You know, *the* thing, where you get the swelling and all that", they add.

"Which thing? I have no idea what you're talking about."

"How long has it been since the last pox disappeared?"

"About a month or so", and then they both shake their heads.

"Oh that's why, because it usually takes six to eight weeks before it really starts getting big."

Now I'm starting to get seriously uncomfortable and anxious and say much louder than normal "What? What the hell is going to happen to me?"

Then the husband of the couple puts his hands out and forms them into the size of a basketball and says, "Well, if what happened to my friend Sivanka is anything to go by, it will get about this big, the size of a basketball or if you're lucky a football."

"What is going to get that big, just tell me, I can handle it," I pleaded.

"Man, your scrotum is going to swell massively in about a week or two. It'll only last for a few days probably, but I'd advise you to get some extra-large pants that you can wear during those days", all said with a totally serious face, his lovely wife nodding in agreement with a concerned look.

"What? I have never heard of that before, are you sure?", totally believing them. It was at that point that they and everyone else burst out laughing having pulled a very fast one over my gullible self.

I was so relieved it was just a prank because during one of my first visits to India, and etched on my mind forever, I witnessed one of the worst sights I've ever seen. A man lay nearly dead, face down on the pavement with a massive extension at the crossroads of his legs and torso. It took me a moment to realize it was his scrotum, which, without medical care, had expanded well beyond the size of a basketball—a tragic and unimaginable situation, far from a laughing matter. This was one the most brutal images of the millions of brutal images of a human rights life that sticks in my mind and I pray that guy somehow got some medical care, though I sadly doubt it. That same day in Old Delhi, I saw another horrendous sight: a girl, no more than three years old—crying and wailing uncontrollably—desperately trying to pull her tremendously sick mother across an extremely busy and polluted road by her hair. The mother tried so hard to walk but couldn't, while countless drivers and rickshaws passed by as if this were normal in a land of caste and karma. So utterly brutal and another bit of proof if any is needed that Buddha's adage that all beings suffer was all too true.

A decade later in the Republic of Georgia, I luckily saw no images like those, but I witnessed other horrors that so often emerge when wars based on nothing other than ethnic difference brings out the absolute worst in our fellow human beings. As I always do when visiting areas of ongoing ethnic conflict, I again wore my *All One People* badge, as I did later in Kosovo and so many other places tainted by an excess of hate. But, yet again, not once during my time in the Republic of Georgia and South Ossetia did any local resident look on my badge with even the slightest degree of recognition. "What do you mean with that message?" was the usual refrain. I would explain what I consider to be one of the very few universal truths as slowly and clearly as possible but was always met with stares of disbelief that I could be so naïve to believe such a stupid thing. Clearly here, and in fact, everywhere, I'd have my work cut out for me.

It seemed like the Georgians didn't trust the Russians, the Russians didn't trust the Georgians, the South Ossetians distrusted the Georgians and felt close to the Russians, the Russians backed the South Ossetians, the Abkhazians wanted their own state, and Russia supported this. The result was a very violent war, first from 1989 to 1992 and then again in 2008. The consequences included tens of thousands of people being displaced from their homes, the issue I was to work on. As I write this in 2026, despite the efforts of so many well-intentioned people, none of these conflicts have been justly or satisfactorily concluded. With Russia illegally invading Ukraine and perpetuating war, these unresolved, albeit currently dormant conflicts in nearby Georgia could reignite at any time in this land of division and suspicion.

I entered Beware-Lion-Hounds mode before going to Georgia, partly because a UNHCR official all my friends knew had been kidnapped in nearby North Ossetia a few months earlier, then apparently held hostage in a dank and freezing cave for a year in brutal conditions before they eventually freed him. This put me ill at ease—but not enough to stay away. So off I went up to London to catch what turned out to be an odd British Midland flight from Heathrow to Tbilisi, a plane full of mineworkers going to Kyrgyzstan, all of whom were quite boisterous passengers, shall we say. After an hour of two, one of them asked me what I was doing in Georgia and I told them about my work to get people's homes back to them after having been displaced, and he and his friends who were listening in to this strange tale, all looked at me with confused looks, one of them saying "Oh, that's unusual work, mate."

Before hopping on to what was a very old plane, I met up at Heathrow with Ezra, an old Israeli friend of mine who calls London home (and who drinks his own urine every day) for a quick, urine-free catch up. Once, while spending a few nights at his house in St. John's Wood several years prior, one morning I stumbled into his kitchen after a very intoxicating evening the night before. I noticed he was making some fresh hummus which immediately pleased me. On the left side of the counter were two glasses of yellow liquid. I asked if that was the water in which the chickpeas had been soaked just as he was about to add some to his mixture. I remarked that there was quite a lot of it left over pointing at the other container. "Oh no, that's my urine, I always drink it every morning." As much as I love hummus, I declined his breakfast offers that hazy morning. Shortly after the hummus man and I said our goodbyes, I bought a £20 shirt for the woman behind me in line at the duty-free store as one of those random acts of kindness that I love doing, but this time also a bit of a superstitious attempt at doing such a good deed that I would not be kidnapped. It blew her away that I paid for her new shirt and I just said, as I always do, "Just do it for someone else one day soon and ask them to do the same for someone else." I hope she did.

Life Lesson No. 80: Commit as many random acts of kindness as often as you can. You will feel good if you do.

I arrived in Tbilisi at 3 a.m. at a darkened, scary, icy, heavily militarized airport desperately in need of renovation that I had never visited before. I couldn't decipher the beautiful squiggly language written everywhere. It was made even more strange in that I was one of only three people who actually got off the very full plane at this freezing, (-)10°C, very depressing place. All the other passengers continued on their way to Bishkek. It was definitely one of those life moments where you ask yourself: "Why am I standing in this place, at this hour, all alone and not very happy? How did I get here and why? Did I actually agree to this?" Just a few short hours ago I was sipping coffee and eating *pain au chocolat* in the warmth of my Geneva apartment and then hanging out with the urine drinker in London, and now this....

Luckily, in stark contrast to most of my many human rights trips, the government wanted me in Georgia, so I made it through passport control without too many hassles. I walked through the totally empty, faded arrivals hall and out into the open air, where five or six cagey-looking men approached me, asking if I needed a ride. I was used to such approaches, and they normally weren't a big deal. But in this unstable, extremely poor region, in below freezing conditions at 3 a.m. —in what looked like a city-wide power cut— I was in anything but bliss mode.

Life Lesson No. 81: Always check for your name at the airport arrivals hall. If you see it twice, take a taxi.

On top of that, my mind immediately remembered what happened to an Australian friend of mine not long before this when he took a job on a major building project in the Philippines. On his first trip out of

Australia, the poor guy was subjected to a humiliating and terrifying scam upon his arrival in Manila. He entered the arrivals hall and scanned the mass of humanity trying to figure out what to do. As is so common now, drivers hired for pickups at this notoriously unpleasant airport thrust hundreds of handmade signs with names toward his face. He finally saw his name on a sign and must have felt that wonderful sense of relief and relaxation I always feel when I see my name on a sign in those hot and steamy places often after 30 or more hours of travel. He said to the man, "Yes, that's me." The driver gestures to him to follow, carries his suitcase and they finally reach a car quite far from the terminal with someone already sitting in the passenger seat up front who the driver introduces as his brother. It's very late at night now and off they go into the wild and often rough streets of Metro Manila towards my friend's hotel. They drive and drive and drive and this could be normal in a city as big as Manila, but my pal was getting concerned after two hours in the car. When they started reaching rural areas with less people, and less light, he started asking questions of the driver to which he kept saying, "We are almost there, don't worry."

Well, he had every reason to worry. After three hours bumping along increasingly rough roads, the driver finally parked the car on the side of the road in complete darkness, pulled a gun out and told my friend to take off all of his clothes, leave his bags and get out of the car, which he did. The car raced off with all of his money, his wallet, his passport, his clothing, everything. There stood my friend on the side of some rural road, street dogs going crazy, in the middle of the night, naked and very afraid on his first trip ever outside of Australia.

He survived when kind farmers found him and lived to tell the tale. Because he shared this lovely story with me just weeks before, it was all I could think about on that cold, dreary night in Tbilisi's crumbling airport parking lot. It's one thing to be left naked and alone in the tropics, but another thing entirely when it's well under zero degrees outside, somewhere in the middle of the Caucasus. I keep shaking my head no to an array of rather suspicious guys, all dressed in cheap fake leather body length coats when finally, a rotund, very hairy, bearded guy comes up and says "UN, UN?" He didn't have a sign, but I looked him in the eyes and sensed he was likely a kind soul. Nonetheless, I asked to see some ID, which he reluctantly pulled from his pocket, scoffing as he showed it to me. It was such a worn-out UNHCR badge that it almost looked fake, but then I saw his battered white vehicle with "UN" on the side and knew it was cool. He turned out to be an amazing driver and took me far and wide across the country negotiating many a roadblock, bad roads and some less-than-ideal suspension problems in his car.

We reached my very rudimentary guesthouse. It had no TV or radio, no Internet, no water, no food, and usually no electricity due to ongoing power cuts. As such, a book and a bottle of duty-free whisky kept me company every night. The next day, on a freezing morning I found my way to UNHCR's offices and began trying to figure out the situation, assess the severity and potential reversibility of the problems, and determine how to fix the thousands of still unresolved restitution claims of people who wanted nothing other than to return home. I met with numerous local IDPs and refugees, NGOs, UNHCR staff, other international organizations like OSCE, judges and legal staff at the Constitutional Court, innumerable members of Parliament, government ministers, and others in the national Parliament building, which was in dire need of renovation. The grotesque state of the toilets remains memorable to this day. Some of these meetings were very early, and it seemed every MP was an amateur winemaker, as Georgia is a famous wine region. Offers of homemade hooch at 7 a.m. became standard, and who am I to refuse such offers when trying to get a new restitution law approved—even if the wine didn't always hold up to scrutiny?

One day, we left early for the unstable region of South Ossetia, which had unsuccessfully tried to assert its independence from Georgia, to meet officials and get their views on the restitution question. Somehow, I cut my hand badly on the corner of the metal sink in my guesthouse bathroom and needed medical care before heading into the wilds of Tskhinvali, the decaying, Wild West-like "capital" of the Russian-backed breakaway republic. On that intense journey, my excellent interpreter and I travelled far and wide, seeing the good news that a few people had returned to their homes—but mostly hearing stories of unresolved cases where people just wanted their homes back, even if other ethnic groups now lived in them. There were Russian troops all over the place in South Ossetia with their indicative striped shirts and they somehow looked harmless though I knew better as they observed us unarmed humanitarians dismissively.

We met with leaders of the self-declared Republic of South Ossetia in their headquarters, which seemed to be in an abandoned school. On the way, we passed countless destroyed buildings, cars without license plates—often driven by 12-year-old boys covered in dirt, expressionless faces masking a life of utter hopelessness—and depressing markets with few wares on offer beyond a few unappetizing food items on display. It reminded me of those World War II films of small European towns that were almost completely destroyed by the vicious combination of aerial bombardment and hand-to-hand fighting, both of which were so common during that horrible conflict. During one meeting with a leading politician, it dawned on me that the guy looked exactly like the actor who played Eddie in that great Jim Jarmusch movie *Stranger than Paradise*, masterfully played by Richard Edson, and I told him so. As the interpreter told him this, I noticed a small smile transform into a huge gleeful one and we were brothers after that. I told him he should go to Hollywood if the mean streets of Tskhinvali ever got too boring and it seemed like he actually gave it some consideration. We spent the rest of the day with the local UNHCR staff, who used an old Soviet-era house as their office. I had the best bowl of borscht of my life in that busy field office full of dedicated humanitarians.

I was glad when we made it back into the part of Georgia actually controlled by Georgians without being harassed or breaking down in places that truly felt like the middle of nowhere. We finished that adventurous day at one of the few decent restaurants in Tbilisi at the time, which had jail bars on the door, requiring diners to ring a bell, get checked through a hatch, and then be let in. It's changed a lot since then but Georgia was this kind of place at the time. The birthplace of Josef Stalin had some seriously unruly characters running around and organized crime was far from absent. I asked a local UN staff member if organized crime was a problem in Georgia—just to see what he would say—already knowing the obvious answer. He actually said, "Oh no, we have none of that here," one of the biggest fudges of the truth I heard during my time in Georgia, where I encountered a few, both serious and in jest.

One night, after most of the work was done and my report well underway, my UNHCR friend invited me to his house for dinner in Tbilisi's Old Town. At the time, it hadn't been renovated or gentrified —which I had assumed it would've been—so it felt like entering a movie set of crumbling old buildings, little to no commercial activity, and front doors covered in locks. As I left my guesthouse, now accustomed to the incredibly poor conditions in most of the capital's neighborhoods, with dirt roads and replete with decaying buildings that were once lovely, I spotted six or eight elderly women bundled up in the very cold and miserable conditions, sitting along the road with a few vegetables spread on dirty towels for sale. I felt so sorry for these grandmothers knowing that they had nothing, that the transition from communism to capitalism had certainly passed them by, leaving them in a tragic state of desperation. I approached one of the women and bought everything on her towel—four carrots, two beets, five potatoes, and a small bouquet of dying flowers—to bring as gifts to my friend that night and make soup for the meal. She was overjoyed, and, of course, I paid her 20 times what she expected to make from the sales if she even sold anything at all—knowing she likely hadn't on many days. I was happy to bring a smile to a face that probably hadn't smiled in a long time. In yet another synchronistic moment just after I paid the grateful Georgian grandmother, I looked left and spotted a fellow human rights activist I'd met in Latvia months before. We both had a "No way, how is this possible?" moment, then headed to my UN friend's house for a great night of many delights, including my soup. At the end of the evening, we went outside to get a taxi when a car with no sign, no nothing, stopped and asked where we were going. In the pre-Uber era, I asked my friend if it was a taxi, and he replied, "It is now." I made it back to the guesthouse safely but not before the driver used the words "fucking, fucking mother" about a hundred times, talking about politicians in his current country, politicians in his former country, all of the other cars on the road, and the world at large. Not a happy camper and who could blame him?

Life Lesson No. 82: Sometimes you just have to breathe deeply and accept.

Another night, on our way to a dinner meeting, we passed an Armenian priest blessing the sacred ground where an Armenian church had once stood before it was burned to the ground. It symbolized a small but important step toward peace and normality returning to the country—a sign that good things might just arrive after all. It's these little moments that one sees in countries undergoing deep transitions that mean so much, but which almost always go unseen or unannounced. It's like when people from one ethnic group begin straggling back to their original neighborhoods once it's safe after a war—or when refugees and IDPs move back into homes once taken by those who saw them as evil enemies. I sought to offer workable solutions to this issue in the Republic of Georgia.

Many of the more than 50,000 refugees and IDPs generated by the conflict lost their homes due to the dubious application of what is called an abandonment law. In Georgia, the *1983 Housing Code* contained a provision allowing authorities to strip anyone of their homes if left vacant for more than six months, even if they fled under *force majeure* circumstances simply to save their lives. Similar laws were widely used as convenient tools of ethnic cleansing during the despicable Bosnian War from 1991-1995, by Israelis against Palestinian homes since 1948, and in countless other places where stealing HLP assets was part of one ethnic group's strategy against another's. Although the Georgian government repeatedly recognized the right of return for all refugees and IDPs, it wasn't happening. This led to their request for UNHCR's assistance in resolving the issue, particularly regarding the Georgian-South Ossetian situation. And that's where I came in.

I identified the obstacles to return and securing property restitution rights in the country and proposed ideas on how to resolve them. Besides outright discrimination, the 1983 law clearly played a big role in the problem. The Georgian government had a series of obligations under international and national laws to promote safe and lasting return for the displaced, but a big push was needed to turn these rules into reality. As such, I recommended ensuring the primacy of the right to restitution, providing compensation when restitution was deemed materially impossible, and ensuring the reconstruction and rehabilitation of damaged housing. I emphasized protecting people against homelessness, enforcing housing rights, offering effective judicial remedies, and safeguarding the physical and economic security of the population. I drafted a housing and property restitution law for the government to consider and urged them to push for the issuance of a presidential decree on refugee and IDP return. I recommended establishing new housing and property claims commissions, modeled after the Commission on Real Property Claims in Bosnia. In a country where many couldn't return home due to misapplied laws—often decided in a manner contrary to the rights of those affected—we needed something new. This started a lengthy process, leading to restitution aims becoming a widely recognized principle from which to build a sustainable peace.

Life lesson No. 83: Give it back.

I headed back to Geneva after a while and was astonished at the airport that the passport official checking my Netherlands passport spoke to me in perfect Dutch, having lived there for a few years previously. I kept working on restitution issues in Georgia for many years after this visit and made fighting for restitution for refugees and IDPs everywhere a cornerstone of my work to this day. Stealing a refugee or IDP home or implanting one side's settlers into them is an awful and shameful act no matter who does it, and something widely condemned under international law but which still occurs far too frequently. As a global society, including those yet to be born, we need rules, laws, procedures, and, above all, the simple awareness that we must relegate these practices to the past, vestiges of a time when humanity embraced deluded perspectives, leading them to believe they were somehow superior to those whose homes they illegally occupied.

To those who wantonly steal homes, lands, and properties, and you know exactly who you are, I say this: Be bigger than that. Accept that what you have done is an offense and that what your ancestors have done is simply wrong. Admit that you and they have committed not just injustices but *crimes* that need to be remedied. Realize that you have the power within you to fix these crimes. You, Israeli citizen who now resides in a swank Palestinian home that was allocated to you by the Jewish Agency or on another piece of stolen Palestinian land, you have it within yourself to say no, do the right thing and return it to the real owners. You, Turkish Cypriot living in the home of a Greek Cypriot, you have the power within you to give that home back. You, Australian cattle farmer living on and working on what is clearly Aboriginal Land, you too have the power to restore it to its rightful owners. And even you, Chinese settler living in a Tibetan house in downtown Lhasa, you too, can realize that this is just not right and that this house, too, should be given back to the family to whom it belongs.

For everyone, everywhere who lives on stolen ground and stolen homes it is in your hands now to do the right thing, the thing that will actually make you feel good instead of guilty and fearful, the thing that will push us all just a little bit closer to the just and free world all of us deserve where respect and rights go hand-in-hand. As Midnight Oil so correctly sang "Let's Give It Back."

Sri Lanka - The Emerald Isle at a Time of Division

Sri Lanka surprised me in so many ways and it still does. The seemingly never-ending series of political crises and conflicts belies the incredible physical and cultural beauty of this unique island where I have now been many times. The fragrant smells of the tea-laden hillsides, the incredible food, and their sometimes very good national cricket team, especially when Muralitharan was bowling, make this place one of a kind. In 2026 the country is improving now, but when I worked there things were very different than they are today. During the vicious ethnic war—seemingly missing a rather key point of Buddhism—instead of a unified place grounded in the spirit of interdependence, in recent decades it has all too often been more like an emerald isle of division, a land where people far too often highlight differences rather than accentuating shared attributes. It is a land where these sad discords led to a ruthless and vicious war that lasted from 1983 - 2009, only ending in a final killing frenzy, the costs of which are still being counted today. The legacies of the brutal fighting between the Sinhalese majority and the Tamil and Muslim minorities remain, including a propensity for messy politics and a tendency to sometimes vote for so-called strong men who claim they will hold the country together at any cost. We can only hope that the progressive government elected in late 2024 will work its magic in a country very much in need of it.

Of course, I knew of these and other long-standing divisions within the country, but I wasn't prepared for their depth. As someone inclined toward Buddhism, it distressed me to see yet another majority-Buddhist country harboring such animosity toward its Hindu, Muslim, and other fellow countrymen and women, and vice-versa, too. Additionally, the treatment I copped several times from government officials, including one unimaginably racist, nationalistic, and arrogant asshole—who had somehow climbed up the ranks and with whom I had to meet on several occasions —was unexpectedly far worse than anything anyone had subjected me to in the many countries where I have worked, with the exception of Israel, but more on that below.

I'm not precisely sure why so many Buddhist countries have turned out this way, but the numbers are sizable. If one looks at the comparatively small number of Buddhist majority countries throughout the world, if there is any democracy at all, let alone a vibrant form of democracy, just about every majority-Buddhist country effectively misses this form of government. Sri Lanka is definitely doing better than most. The Tibetan government in-exile considers Tibet to be occupied by China, so no democracy there, although the exile government based in India is a model of progressive democracy. Cambodia remains a longstanding autocracy. Thailand, even if it holds regular elections, lives all too often under military rule. One-party states control Laos and Vietnam, and Burma reverted to military dictatorship in 2021 after its fledgling efforts to partially democratize. The list goes on.

Even tiny, unique Bhutan—though known for wonderful things—such as its use of gross national happiness (GNH) instead of gross domestic product (GDP) to measure progress, and its many still intact Buddhist traditions which are stronger than any other sovereign nation-state, treated ethnic Nepali nationals terribly. In the mid-1980s, Bhutan summarily stripped them of any possibility of citizenship and forced them into seven massive refugee camps in eastern Nepal, where they languished for over 20 years. I visited many camps in places like Jhapa and other areas, and while they were decent by refugee camp standards in poorer regions of the world, the isolated people there lived miserably, wanting only to return to their homes and lands in Bhutan, where their families had lived for generations. Long after these camps had been closed and once the refugees there were given resettlement options in a range of Western countries, I helped some Bhutanese refugees establish the Bhutanese Refugee Restitution Organization (BRRO) to try to get at least some compensation for the more than 100,000 people who were summarily forced out, but to date none of these refugee has been provided with any justice at all in their former country, as far as I am aware.

Life Lesson No. 84: A bit of joy and a bit of sorrow.

On my way back from the camps, I'll never forget the hassle I encountered just before boarding a Buddha Airways flight from Biratnagar, Nepal back to Kathmandu. As the only Westerner on the flight, the guard had stared into my eyes and asked, "You have smoke?"—clearly implying drugs. I smiled and so did he, for he knew I would have none, and we were suddenly soul brothers on the same page of life. He let me board and I gazed longingly at Mount Everest through the right-hand window of the small plane the entire way back to the capital. On that same trip, one night I ate *Thali* at a traditional outdoor spot in Kathmandu, sipping an amazing ambrosia-like lemon elixir. Feeling chatty, I asked the waiter, "What is the meaning of life?" Without hesitation, he gave the best answer I've ever heard to this question—which I often pose to unsuspecting fellow world citizens—"A bit of joy and a bit of sorrow, this is the meaning of life." I'll take that answer any day. He got a big tip that fine evening.

These ethnic Nepali refugees, long established in Bhutan—farming the land and living out their lives—eventually gave up the struggle to return to their legitimate homes and found safety in countries like the US, Australia, and Finland after struggling for two decades to return to their ancestral homes. Though they received asylum and were accorded official refugee status, all they truly wanted was to return home. They were treated as victims of their ethnicity or religion, treated as the "other" rather than as fellow beings. Buddhists should know better. A Bhutanese family I know received refugee status in Australia. Though they love it now, the day they arrived—in the middle of one of the hottest summers on record—landing at the beautiful Adelaide airport, the stifling outside temperature hit 47°C and the air was infused with acrid smoke from the annual summer bushfires. It was massively hotter than anything they had ever felt even in Bhutan or eastern Nepal, where the heat is always on the oppressive side. "Should we have stayed in Jhapa, perhaps?", they must have thought on entering the fiery cauldron that otherwise amazing Adelaide so often is.

Sri Lanka, too, generated more than its fair share of refugees over the years, with the vast majority of these being from the Tamil community that makes up around 12% of the population, as well as a large number of Muslim IDPs who were displaced during the early years of the war. The brutal conflict between the government and the Tamil Tigers or LTTE lasted a full 26 years with over 100,000 killed and up to 800,000 displaced at the height of the fighting. The war began in earnest after roving mobs went into Tamil neighborhoods and killed more than one thousand citizens at will, which in turn led to Tamil demands for their own separate homeland to be called Tamil Eelam. As the army resisted losing control over territory, they engaged in constant and bitter fighting in the north and east, where the Tamils are concentrated.

Frequent bombings and disruptions attributed to the LTTE occurred throughout the country, including in the capital, Colombo. In a brazen attack in 2001, the LTTE destroyed a large number of military jets and planes belonging to the national airline Air Lanka that were parked on the airport tarmac. Almost half of the national airlines' planes were destroyed that day, imagine that. This war was incredibly serious. Every time I flew Air Lanka, I thought about such possibilities.

The UN first called me to this otherwise lovely island to work on returning refugee and IDP housing and land to their rightful owners, as part of the Norwegian-led peace negotiations, which were ongoing and seemingly making some progress. You have to feel for those kindly Norwegians, trying so hard to bring people together in places like Israel/Palestine, Sri Lanka, and Burma, only to watch their good-faith efforts fall apart again and again after so much time, energy, good will and commitment to building peace. The parties involved simply can't find ways forward without massive shows of force and physical violence by the more powerful side. It wasn't Palestinians who ruined the Oslo Peace Accords which were not all that far from creating a two-state solution, it was the Israelis. And it wasn't just the Tamils (or the even smaller but often discriminated Muslim minority) who wrecked this peace process in Sri Lanka, but the government and military at the time that figured they could avoid compromise by wiping out their opposition with extreme military force. The war only ended after a widely criticized massive assault across LTTE-controlled areas, killing tens of thousands, mostly civilians, and defeating the LTTE as a fighting force forevermore.

But in 2003 it was a completely different story and a just peace looked and felt possible, even likely. There was much less fighting than usual, far fewer bombs and people from all sides were actually talking, so it all looked rather positive. I worked for a few months with a man called Justice Sriskandarajah, a wonderfully gentle Sri Lankan Supreme Court lawyer and High Court judge, to develop restitution proposals for a new law and a restitution commission. We formulated provisions for a peace agreement that then seemed almost inevitable. Indeed, it truly felt like we were on the cusp of a new and positive dawn of peace. Justice Sri-gi as I called my new friend and I had some great times together. As one of the few Tamil judges, he took pride in showing me his spartan chambers at the Supreme Court. Over several months, we travelled across Colombo, repeatedly meeting with people from all communities to push the restitution process forward. (I secretly tried on his judicial wig during one visit when he wasn't looking.)

Unlike many other officials I met in the country, Sri-ji was beyond reproach and appeared to be totally honest, above board and utterly uncorrupted by his high social status. He went to extreme lengths to absolutely record every meeting, meal, and activity to ensure he had proof of never taking a bribe, payout, or unlawful gift. I took him out to dinner once and he insisted on paying his portion of the bill. This was most definitely not my plan, yet I understood after his explanation and spent the difference the next night on some seriously good fish curry elsewhere near the very fancy Galle Face Hotel overlooking the Indian Ocean and its warm waters.

One meeting I remember particularly well was held with several representatives of the Muslim community who had borne the brunt of much of the fighting and subsequent displacement, particularly during the early phases of the conflict. Though large in number, it felt like the Muslim IDPs were often ignored in the peace process, and yet their organizational skills in making their very reasonable demands for justice were impressive. They presented the Justice and me with around 10 immaculately prepared binders, spanning a full meter, detailing the precise housing, land, and property claims of every single displaced Muslim family, totaling some 100,000 people. It was incredible to receive this amount of detailed information, which I presume the displaced Tamils and Sinhalese also had, though probably not as well organized, since we certainly weren't presented with such. This detailed information meant that, if there was political will, restitution would be infinitely easier from a documentation perspective than a process relying solely on personal testimony and witness statements to prove where people lived before displacement by the more dominant group. What was lacking, naturally, as it so often is in settings ripe for restitution, was the political impetus and the basic humanity needed to make it happen.

Life Lesson No. 85: At least Norway tried…

Remarkably, a similar situation exists for Palestinian refugees today, all nine million or more of them for which Israel is wholly legally responsible under international law and countless treaties it itself has ratified. Unknown to most people, even those involved in seeking a just solution to this conflict, a UN warehouse in New York City contains the entire original records of the housing, land, and property records of historic Palestine as of 1948. In recent years these records were digitalized and would provide more than sufficient evidence for a future housing, land, and property restitution programme that could once and for all resolve the millions of restitution claims held by Palestinians but not yet settled. More than 90% of historic Palestine which includes Israel, the West Bank and Gaza were legally owned by Palestinian families at the time of the establishment of the State of Israel, and these documents prove it. This goldmine of documentary evidence would make restitution entirely practical, contrary to claims that it's impossible by Israel and its supporters. With political will to back it up, billions of dollars' worth of Palestinian property currently under Israeli control—with no intention whatsoever of giving it back—could easily be returned to its rightful owners.[15]

Given how many Israelis have rightfully benefited from restitution rights and compensation payments implemented across Europe for World War II crimes, the refusal to offer the same hand to those from whom they have stolen housing, land, and property remains tragic—even shocking—in its lack of humanity. The current genocide and wanton destruction and decimation being carried out daily by Israel against the Palestinians in Gaza and the West Bank are just the latest displays of criminal hatred by a nation state that just seems to go from bad to worse decade after decade.

Our restitution proposals as part of the Sri Lankan peace process were presented to the UN which in turn gave them to the Norwegian Peace Negotiators. They in turn presented them to their negotiating partners from the government and the Tamils. Alas, right around this time the entire peace negotiation process began falling apart, fighting erupted again and our plans were shelved. If I don't say so myself, an international expert and a leading judge in the country put these good, solid plans together, and they would have worked had they been given a chance to do so. We clarified the law, outlined best practices, and proposed workable and potentially very effective procedures. Sadly, justice did not prevail and now more than 20 years later, hundreds of thousands of people who should have gotten their properties back never did; at least not until now, maybe one day. And, alas, I just learned that dear old Sri-gi is no longer with us, so he will never get to see HLP justice arise in his country, after passing away at the young age of only 61.

The UN called me back to Sri Lanka immediately after the

---

[15]For a very comprehensive overview of these documents, please see: Michael R. Fischbach, *Records of Dispossession: Palestinian Refugee Property and the Arab-Israeli Conflict*, Colombia University Press, 2003.

horrendous 2004 Boxing Day Tsunami. I wrote earlier about my work in the Maldives after the killer wave so I won't explain too much about the specifics of the disaster, other than to say that the carnage unleashed in Sri Lanka was far, far worse than in the comparatively lucky Maldives. The tsunami killed more than 30,000 people along the southern and eastern coasts of this emerald isle and the ferocity of the unrelenting ocean was there for all to see along hundreds of kilometers of destroyed shoreline, much of which we witnessed and investigated. It was awful. At one place, a very full train had been broadsided by the tsunami and killed most on board. At another place, one of many we visited, the unrelenting waves decimated the ground and first floors of a massive beachside resort, killing scores of people in that resort alone. These stories unfolded all up and down the coast, in particular in the small villages and fisher folk communities located along the beautiful edges of this island who catch the fish that are responsible for some of the most delicious dishes known to humankind.

Brutally for them, it was not only the destruction of their villages that these communities had to deal with, but as is so common, the aftermath of "reconstruction" as well. Following the Civil War in the United States from 1865 onwards, "reconstruction" became synonymous with entrenching the same abhorrently racist views against people of color that caused the war in the first place, just without the legality of slavery to back them up. In a way, it was the same in Sri Lanka and so many other places, where authorities often use natural disasters as a shameless pretext to achieve objectives they could not during normal times.

In this case, these policy-making geniuses came up with a plan that came to be known as the *100-meter rule* which meant that no one could rebuild any structure including villages and homes that might have been within this 100m zone for generations. Consequently, they would need to find a new place to live, which isn't easy when the ocean just swallowed up what little you had, leaving you with nothing —other than your land. Then, even your land is legally reclassified as no longer yours. This happens all the time after disasters and while it could be justifiable in some humanitarian ways, it always raises serious human rights concerns.

We carried out a project in the Philippines with the International

Federation of Red Cross Red Crescent Societies (IFRC) after the Haiyan Typhoon disaster in 2013 where they tried out this exclusion zone idea but retracted it when my associate Zeke Simperingham of Displacement Solutions, who now works in a leadership position with the IFRC, discovered the lack of a legal basis for doing so. These scams were tried in all of the countries affected by the tsunami and so many other places after disaster struck, including in Nepal where we worked on these issues following the 2016 Earthquake there. It's common, but it's wrong and does nothing to prepare these countries for the next disaster down the road other than increase the landless population and all the requisite challenges that this inevitably poses. This allows authorities to free up valuable coastal land for potential development in cahoots with unscrupulous wheeler-dealer developers. These developers often exchange briefcases full of money—or even smaller stuffed brown envelopes—with officials in return for new and often fraudulent "title deeds," "contracts of sale," and permission to build the next resort on land that was never theirs in the first place. It's rampant, it's awful, it's a violation of people's rights and it stinks. Next time you're staying in a coastal resort if you ever do such things, ask yourself whose land you might be reclining on in your lounge chair next to the swim-up bar in the pool as you gaze across the azure sea and sip your Mai-Tai. You might be surprised what happens if you start asking around, I can assure you.

Chapter 7

Occupation and Settler Colonialism

As much as an advocate for world citizenship and the gradual erosion of borders as I may be, conversely, I abhor empires, family dynasties, colonialism, especially settler colonialism, and the even more dastardly deed of illegal occupation by one country against the will and wishes of another. We need to banish these criminal antics to the ash heap of history, never to be allowed to emerge again. I have seen the impacts of these crimes all across the world and have been fortunate to have worked closely with countless representatives of occupied peoples throughout the past decades—Tibetans, Palestinians, Kurds, Kosovars, Sahrawis, East Timorese, Iraqis, and many indigenous peoples who felt and feel equally occupied. They all shared one simple wish: to be treated as equals, not as oppressed, discriminated subordinates. None of the occupied peoples I have worked with claim ideological, religious or any other form of dominance or superiority over their occupiers (in stark contrast to those doing the occupying!), but all share the wish to be free; it is as simple as that.

It is difficult to put into words what occupation feels like to the occupied, so the best I can do is simply ask you to imagine how you would feel if an invading army decided to take over the place you call home. They set up a government, fire all of the local officials not loyal to the occupiers, ban the national army, and imprison officials of the national government, human rights activists, and others who refuse to bow to their will. They take control of the water supply, the food supply, and the energy supply. They impose brutal taxes and extort local businesses. The list goes on. What if this happened to you in your home, your street, your country? All that occupied peoples want is freedom from this. This is what the people of the occupied Netherlands felt during German occupation, what China felt like during its occupation by Japan. It is what Ukraine now feels like as it fights against Russian occupation and what Palestinians feel under the occupation, brutality and genocide being meted out against them by the State of Israel.

There can be no full emergence of a planet of free people, treated as equals under law until all occupations end, and until true sovereignty can be felt and exercised by all. For once humanity holds sovereignty as the norm, once at least a modicum of respect is apparent, at that moment bigger minds and bigger ideas can prevail (such as world citizenship), grounded neither in a hatred of the occupied nor the occupier, but based on the humanity we all share. You can witness the emergence of this awareness in countless ways in the real world. I have seen it manifest in too many ways to mention them all here. During peace talks or heavy political negotiations between opposing sides, those sparks of mutual recognition between sworn enemies can give hope even to the most ardent pessimist. Not everyone hates each other in the same way, to the same degree or in the same amount each minute of each day. Things change and they can evolve. The famous friendship that unexpectedly emerged between Irish Republican Martin McGuinness—and his lifelong enemy— Unionist Ian Paisley is perhaps the most well-known example. It forms much of the basis for the *Good Friday Agreement* that ended the Troubles in Northern Ireland all those years ago, even if it feels fragile at the moment.

Life Lesson No. 86: There is no them.

There are countless other examples I've seen first-hand—when Palestinians and Israelis laugh and wine and dine together (though today this seems almost impossible to imagine), when Tibetans and Chinese counterparts share a joke over momos and tsampa, or when an East Timorese and an Indonesian diplomat admire the same beautiful landscape with the same spark in their eyes. These are all bits of truth that can keep bringing us closer to what I hope is the goal of all of us, a world built on the foundations of world citizenship. But before this can occur, all occupied peoples must be free in order for all of us to be free. Or, put much more eloquently by Nelson Mandela, "For to be free is not merely to cast off one's chains, but to live in a way that respects and enhances the freedom of others." I couldn't agree more.

Tibet - Eye to Eye with a Bodhisattva

Everybody wants a happy life - and our individual happy life depends on a happy humanity. So we have to think about humanity, discover a sense of oneness of all seven billion human beings.[16]

— Dalai Lama

It's not often, but when I'm feeling down, hopeless about the state of the world, sad, or lonely, I sometimes look at my hands and think of all the millions of hands I have held, shaken or high-fived all over the world, and grasping the delicate and gentle touch of His Holiness the Dalai Lama's (HHDL) soft hands so many times clearly stands out the most. It has been a while since I held the HHDL's hands in mine, but I was lucky enough to spend a whole series of moments with him from 1990 to the early 2000s when I was particularly interested in all things Tibetan. Luckily for me, this included many beautiful moments with the Dalai Lama himself, just him and me, hands in hands, peering deeply into each other's eyes but more on that in a moment. Of course, I had read books by the Dalai Lama and heard rumours of his enlightened mind and even almost magical powers, but it was meeting my

---

[16]Dalai Lama XIV, Desmond Tutu and Douglas Abrams, *The Book of Joy: Lasting Happiness in a Changing World*, Avery, 2016.

girlfriend at the time that brought me directly into the Tibetan scene. She survived being shot twice in Lhasa, Tibet on International Human Rights Day in 1988 and you can read her whole story in her excellent 2023 book (in Dutch) called *De Rode Kogel* (The Red Bullet). The very first time I was in the same room with the Dalai Lama was in 1990 at an event in Amsterdam that friends from the Tibet Support Group had organized just over a year after her being shot twice, and right before my kidneys broke down and put me into the hospital for a lengthy and painful stay.

Now, in case you are wondering, I am not one of those "Dalai Lama is God" people, of which there are more than a few, but there is no doubting that this Nobel Peace Prize winning, compassionate and kind man belongs to a very special human category. Something incredible happens when he is around. The energy of the space changes, it softens, it becomes more vivid, more vibrant, special. There is something difficult to describe going on which is so positive, and it is certainly at least partially because of this that certain political interests seem so afraid of this gentle, calm and loving saffron-robed monk. I have seen this manifest many times, but beyond my own personal moments which I'll outline shortly, let me first tell you about one middle-aged British gentlemen, who was almost aggressively non-religious, non-spiritual, non-esoteric anything at all. He was a hardcore academic type, human rights activist and cool as can be, but mystically inclined, crystal energy believing or Kosmic consciousness embracing he most certainly was not - as far from it as possible. A battle hardened human rightser who would find showing soft emotions in public as desirable as a visit to a Middle Ages torture rack, visibly melted into bliss nodules of glee right before my very eyes after an embrace with HHDL. I wish I could accurately describe in words what happened, for it was a marvellous thing to see.

Life Lesson No. 87: Bliss nodules of glee for all.

A few years later, during the World Conference on Human Rights in Vienna, I approached one of the Dalai Lama's Tibetan assistants, a close friend. I asked him to guide His Holiness toward another friend, Charles, who was working on health rights issues, so the two could meet. Naturally, I hoped for a repeat of the kind of moment with the other man I just mentioned. Charles was the nicest guy, totally dedicated to human rights, but like the other guy I described, with not a visibly spiritual bone in this body, at least none I knew of. I thought it would be great if the two could meet, so Ngawang guides HHDL over to Charles, seemingly picking him out of a rapidly growing crowd. HHDL takes Charles' hands, looks deeply into his eyes and briefly embraces him. I watched as an initially reluctant, very tall Charles transformed before my eyes, his biggest smile morphing into a sense of calm—the likes of which I had never seen in him. It washed over him as he slowly, blissfully, and hesitantly walked away to ponder what had just happened to a man who thought he'd seen it all. Apparently, he hadn't. I looked all over for him the next day amongst the thousands of participants attending this major global gathering, and finally found him and asked about his moments with HHDL. In a manner totally not the Charles that I was used to, he teared up and was almost dumbfounded trying to explain in a coherent way something difficult to clarify in language alone and said: "It was unimaginable what I felt at that moment. I am 67 years old and have been all around the world a million times and nothing has ever come even close to whatever it was that I experienced in that moment. I guess it was true joy or something like that...." I sat there smiling very happily, so glad to have facilitated that, and to this day he still doesn't know that it was me that guided HHDL his way. I have no idea what to call it or even what it is precisely that happens in such moments, but I do know that I have never seen this anywhere else.

China, which gained control over Tibet in 1949, describes anyone who supports the right to self-determination for Tibet or who otherwise backs HHDL as either a member of the "Dalai Clique" or as a "Splittist", someone intent on splitting the motherland. As is well known, the one-party state of the People's Republic of China, headed by the Chinese Communist Party, accepts no dissent, particularly on issues relating to Tibet. While China has achieved extraordinary things since Deng Xiaoping famously said something to the effect of: "To be rich is glorious" in the 1980s, it has come at a considerable cost, and its stand on Tibet has only become more intransigent. Many years ago, what most Tibetans see as the occupation of their country, the Tibetan Government-in-Exile in a major concessionary act, dropped its official demands for full-scale independence and proposed transforming Tibet into a demilitarized Zone of Peace with a degree of regional autonomy in a classic embrace of Buddhism's middle way. Alas, this vision seems as far away today from becoming reality as it has ever been.

The occupation led to the Dalai Lama fleeing for his life in 1959 after he attempted for a decade to regain political control over this mountainous land. He and more than 150,000 Tibetans have remained in exile in India and elsewhere ever since. During that time, in a manner similar to what has occurred elsewhere, China has implanted millions of Han Chinese settlers into Tibet in its own version of settler colonialism. With each passing day Tibet's chances of renewed independence seem ever more distant, despite the incredible efforts of the Tibetan Government headed until recently by my old friend Lobsang Sangay. Although he had what must be one of the world's hardest jobs, Lobsang is lucky in that he gets to be with the Dalai Lama all the time.

I've only had that chance a few times, but of the millions of moments of an eventful life, these moments with HHDL are definitely some of the most precious. Besides arranging that little moment of bliss between the HHDL and Charles, I had a whole bunch of similar moments during those amazing summer days in Vienna at the 1993 World Conference on Human Rights. One time we were lined up waiting for HHDL to come into a room. I was standing with my pal José Ramos Horta, the current President of Timor Leste, who also knew the 14th Dalai Lama. As HHDL and his crew passed by, the crowd grew unruly and a little bit too large for comfort. Ngawang grabbed me and José, instantly turning us into two bodyguards for the Bodhisattva of our age. We surrounded him for the next 15 minutes, keeping him safe until he reached the room for his next speech. Ngawang and the other Tibetans gave me the Tibetan nickname of Tashi Drungtok, which he told me meant something like 'bright sparkly one', so I'll take that tag any day.

Another time HHDL was giving a talk outside the official venue in Vienna at a public park nearby. All of us went there and I stood back while a bunch of people tried to get their moment with him. After he finally hopped back in his car in the right-hand passenger seat in back, window down, I went up alone to the car, smiled and he reached his hands out, we held hands for a few moments, me yelling Pu' Rang-zen, Pu' Rang-zen, Free Tibet, Free Tibet, to which he replied "Rang-zen, Rang-zen, yes, yes, Tashi Drungtok." I was a happy lad that day, for sure. A year or two later at another event in Holland hosting him, they put me in charge of the green room where he would wait before going on stage, to both act as security as well as just to keep him company. He only came along briefly, but it was another one of those moments you remember forever.

My immersion into the Tibet scene continued to grow and for two full years, a luxury of time I haven't had again since, I spent each day writing, re-writing and editing and re-editing my own tiny contribution to the Tibetan cause, a 200-page book called *Destruction by Design: Housing Rights Violations in Tibet*, published in 1994. I hadn't looked back at this book for some time until recently, but when I did, I found that it has remarkably withstood the tests of time. On the negative side, however, I discovered exactly what I hoped would never happen. Real-life events revealed that every single one of my many predictions of future human rights violations came true, and sadly, China implemented all the moves and maneuvers that seemed imminent at the time of publication, much to the Tibetans' detriment. Niels Bohr famously said something like "Predictions are difficult to make, particularly about the future." Well, sadly, I bucked the trend on that one, alas.

We distributed thousands of copies of the thick and beautifully designed book to every government at the UN in Geneva, sending them by post all around the world to other strategic recipients and then brought a whole car full of boxes of the books, hundreds of copies, to a big international Tibet meeting held in rural Norway in 1994. We drove from Holland, through Germany, then Denmark to the northern tip of the country, then on an overnight ferry that was extremely rough, finally landing in wonderful Norway. The very prim and proper border guards, dressed immaculately and behaving in the most law-abiding manner possible, asked these clearly alternative-looking people in a car with Dutch number plates why we were visiting Norway. The Dutch plates likely signalled to them a car from what they probably saw as a pro-drug country travelling to a very anti-drug country, a group to which many of the Nordic States belong. The car was chock-full of more than

80 boxes of undeclared goods. We simply told them about the meeting we'd be attending and that we'd filled the boxes with non-commercial items. They said, "OK we have some dogs who wish to smell your car." Again, I had one of those moments of dread with my mind racing seeking to determine if I had forgotten to remove some long-lost piece of contraband in my luggage, and the dogs went a bit crazy leading us to have to open a couple of the boxes, but no funny business was found other than my books crammed into every free space in our aging, borrowed BMW. We distributed over a thousand books at that meeting of Tibetan support groups from across Europe. In subsequent years, seeing the book populating countless NGO bookshelves and noticing the actions Tibetans and their supporters took on housing, land, and property issues made the whole project worth it, even if China didn't seem to care much.

A few years passed and I continued to support my Tibetan friends (and my growing number of Chinese friends who supported Tibetan independence), always doing whatever I could in Geneva to help them out at the UN, but it had now been a few years since being in the same space of the Dalai Lama. So, when I heard that he was coming to Switzerland again, I immediately called Ngawang, who was now the head of the Tibet Office in Geneva and asked him if he could get me some tickets, which he promptly did. HHDL was to come to an event hosted by an organization called Moral Rearmament which was formed in the immediate aftermath of WWII. It offers an incredibly beautiful venue in the foothills of the Alps in Caux, Switzerland, accessible by a cogwheel train up a steep track. Once you arrive, the vista across the rest of the Alps and Lake Geneva below is well worth the trip. But views were the last thing on my mind; I wanted some serious good vibing with HHDL. As many times as I was able to share close proximity with him, I had a lingering feeling that I never took full enough advantage of these embracing moments and was committed to the whole hog on this occasion. This time I would make sure to stand eye to eye with the Bodhisattva of our times, hand in hand, and peer as deep as I could into the well springs of enlightenment and see what I could find there.

How would I make the most of this event, I wondered. I had two tickets but my wife couldn't make it so I had to take someone else. Who better to take than the most fervent pro-China supporter I knew in Geneva, a great American guy who worked for the coolest, albeit probably, least well-known UN agency called the UN Research Institute on Social Development (UNRISD). I loved going to meet with my friends at UNRISD because they were always so progressive, so internationalist, so oneness in orientation, just the types of people one would think would dominate UN staffing numbers, but who really stood out compared to so many run of the mill UN staffers.

For all its flaws and foibles, though, the UN is the best there is at the moment. It is *it*. The absurd and dangerous Board of Peace now being egotistically touted by Trump and a handful of others will never achieve its dubious aim of replacing the UN. If a movement or a cause is seeking either vindication, justice or even independence, the UN will be involved, for sure. And my incredibly good fortune to have assisted oppressed and occupied peoples even in a tiny way has always been at the top of my list of career highlights. I have conversed with many oppressed people struggling for freedom, discussing what they would do on independence day when their country was finally free, the hateful occupiers having departed, and the rightful owners back in charge. I recall one of the many times strolling through Geneva with Ramos Horta well before East Timor got its independence where we discussed this. He pretty much ended up doing what he said he would if and when they became free, but I'm sure getting shot and surviving, as did actually happen, was not on his agenda.

I discussed the dream of a post-*apartheid* South Africa with a woman who moved me to tears telling of the first time she publicly raised her fist in support of the ANC and freedom, singing for the first time the song which became the national anthem of the rainbow nation, *Nkosi Sikelel' iAfrika*. She told me what she did both on the day Mandela was freed from his 27 years in prison and on the day of South Africa's first non-racial free election. I have similarly conversed with Palestinians, Kosovars, Kurds, Syrians, Bougainvillians and Tibetans, one of whom says he will be standing on a hill near the Dalai Lama's Palace the *Potala*, cheering with hundreds of millions, maybe billions the world over that Tibet is at long last free. I'll see you there my friend, but even if I never do, know that sometimes even the worst of things such as being forced from your country can have at least a small silver lining. There is no doubt that the wisdom of Tibetan Buddhism and all that it entails is quite literally millions of times more well-known now throughout the world than it would have been had the leader of the Tibetan people been isolated in the *Potala* his entire life. This is a small consolation, but still important.

I ask my American UN friend to join me to come to the mountains and see the reincarnation of all previous 13 Dalai Lama's, figuring that after the amazing Charles-HHDL rendezvous, I should at least try to get him to re-evaluate China's hard-line stances on Tibet. He agreed to come, so I immediately called Ngawang and asked him to please make sure we could meet up well before HHDL came into the room so I could have a minute or two with him before he went on stage to achieve my two aims: 1. Turn my friend on to the Tibet scene; and 2. Peer deeper than ever before into HHDL's eyes and see what happens when I do. A day before the event was to take place, he calls me and says he couldn't make it but that his 19-year-old sister who had just arrived from South Carolina could come in his place. My mind raced and then I said "OK, just don't tell her what the event is, just say it's some special event and I will accompany her there and look after her on this adventure." He says OK and then I meet up with Tori at the train station in Geneva early the next day, we hop on the train and head towards Montreux where we'd get on the cog train.

Montreux, of course, is the town that hosts the famous annual Jazz Festival and where everyone's favorite band Deep Purple famously penned their iconic power chord-laden metal opus *Smoke on the Water*, after looking down at the fog layer covering Lac Leman. We went to the Jazz Festival a few times and while it had that stiff, somewhat sterile Switzerland vibe to it, particularly compared to festivals everywhere else, it was always fun. It was weird being the only person dancing of the thousands watching Laurie Anderson first, and then a whole set by Lou Reed, but I didn't care - I boogied even alone.

Even odder though was seeing Ratdog play there, Bob Weir's band following the end of the formal Grateful Dead after Jerry Garcia's untimely death in 1995, for what must have been the smallest number of fans for a show by Bobby or Ratdog ever. The event started with the great Buddy Guy who played an amazing set. Guitar rocker Chris Rea followed, who played his heart out. After both acts played all they would play, the massive room, which I'd estimate held over 3,000 people, cleared out almost entirely, leaving fewer than 100 of us Deadheads for the Ratdog show. Despite being billed as the top act, the organizers overlooked the fact that the Swiss hadn't yet embraced the Deadhead culture. This was both sad for the poor ole Swissies who largely went through life without the Dead experience, but at the same time utterly awesome as just a few dozen of us hardcore Deadheads, most of whom were Americans, got to rock out to a virtually private show for a night to remember.

Life Lesson No. 88: Deep Purple is probably not really everyone's favorite band.

We got to Montreux and I asked Tori if she knew yet where we were going. She still had no idea. Even as we boarded the cogwheel train with obvious Buddhists and Tibet supporters all around us, to the eyes of a young woman who had never left South Carolina, let alone the United States, now in Switzerland a day later, heading up a mountain to an event she knew nothing about, she still didn't get it. Even when we arrived at the venue and I asked again, she still said she didn't really know. I found Ngawang and we walked to the perfect spot near to the door where HHDL would enter the room and where he would guide him to Tori and me. I'm standing there as the small crowd begins filing into the beautiful, quite intimate room, nervous in anticipation both for what I was about to do and for Tori whose life would be turned on its head.

The Dalai Lama entered the room and Ngawang brings him straight to me, he takes my hands as I barely hear Ngawang remind him that I was Tashi Drungtok the author of *Destruction by Design*. When he heard that yet another sparkle shoots from his eyes, having written me the nicest letter of thanks for my book some years earlier, and which still hangs on my wall today. I then make my move, those soft and gentle hands grasping mine, and I go for it. I gazed as deeply and intensively as I possibly could right into both of the Dalai Lama's eyes, our faces just inches apart. I clearly noticed that he saw exactly what I was doing and then as if he was shifting into the highest possible gear, he goes for it, *totally*. He noticeably moves into Bodhisattva overdrive and then the merger begins. To the extent that I can even formulate concepts now, for

I am now in a place I had never before been, his eyes literally become pools of glittering nectar, rippling and liquefying right there, my own eyes now unable to control the countless streams of tears flowing down my face and then he goes deeper again and I climb into these pools within his eyes bathing myself and all of humanity, all of life now, life that ever was, life that would ever be, immersed in the healing elixir of whatever it was that that was.

We then had a mutual mind merge where oneness became fully tangible, fully real. It was as if not just our eyes and hands had merged, but our souls, our spirits, everything that is always already there, but which we almost universally fail to recognize, or see or even try to. It was there at that moment and it remains there to this day and, indeed, has always been there as long as there has been life and will be there for all of us to look forward to who have yet to see it, as long as there is life.

This was pure and eternal, selfless, compassionate oneness-infused love, free of any hate, free of any distinction or division, free of any delusions, just pure truth, eye to eye, one Saturday afternoon gazing into the HH Dalai Lama's eyes on a Swiss mountain top suddenly aware of the Bodhisattva before me. Just imagine what our planet could be like if more people were like this!

We finally let go of each other, for he had to move towards the stage, and I stood there quite literally shaking and almost unable to stand at which point I looked over to Tori who was standing there in total and utter awe, unable to move, just overwhelmed by what she just saw and then said to me in a strong American drawl, "Oh my Gawd, was that like the Dalai Lama or something?" "It sure was, Tori, it sure was", I whispered back as I wiped my tears away.

Palestine - Eye to Eye with Ethnic Cleansing, Apartheid, and Genocide

> *It seems to me a matter for simple common sense that we cannot ask to be given the political rule over Palestine where two-thirds of the population are not Jewish. What we can and should ask is a secured bi-national status in Palestine....*
>
> —Albert Einstein, 1946

There I was, eye to eye with a bodhisattva, and a few short years later, eye to eye with something entirely different: the gruesome consequences of generalized oppression as well as a military occupation inflicted by Israel onto the Palestinians, year after year, decade after decade dating all the way back to 1948. The situation today has never been worse and the daily images broadcast to the world of the decimation of Gaza and the rapidly worsening annexation of the West Bank by the fundamentalist fanatics now governing and supporting the State of Israel continues to shock the world. The war with Iran that Israel (backed by the United States just started days ago in March 2026), is just the latest crime of so many crimes these two allies continue to carry out contrary to all international rules. They commit these crimes despite the fact that Israel has voluntarily ratified the UN Charter and countless human rights and humanitarian law treaties creating legal obligations on its behalf to respect, protect and fulfill the rights of everyone under its jurisdiction, including the Palestinian populations it illegally occupies.

It is almost impossible to conceive of this now but not all that long ago, in 1993 the Israeli government and the Palestinian Liberation Organization (PLO) signed the Oslo Peace Accords which, among many other things, actually imagined a two-state solution of two peaceful neighbors living respectfully side by side as all other nations generally do. Oslo was far from perfect, particularly on the issue of the right to return and restitution of Palestinian homes, lands, and properties, but at least it envisaged a future where some semblance of mutual respect would be the cornerstone of a better way forward. Nowadays, Oslo lays in tatters and the complete and utter subjugation of the Palestinians by Israel is the order of the day. Every day, it seems, the news from the region somehow gets worse. Just today as I write this, it was reported, for instance, that Israel is responsible for the deaths of 81% of all journalists killed across the world in 2025. Also in today's news, reports emerged of a lawsuit by the family of the United Nations Special Rapporteur on the Occupied Palestinian Territories, Italian human rights expert, Francesca Albanese, against the Trump administration for issuing draconian economic and other sanctions against her for her unpaid work as Special Rapporteur.[17] These sanctions, which include an asset freeze, prohibitions against US persons transacting business with her and a travel ban to the United States, against an independent UN expert with diplomatic immunity who is just doing her job have been described by Amnesty International as a "disgraceful affront to international justice."[18] Also, in today's newspapers, additional items came out deploring the failure of the international community to deter escalating annexation and apartheid in the occupied West Bank.[19] This is one day in the 78 years (almost 30,000 days) since the establishment of Israel in historic Palestine commenced. A single day. And it is like this, day-in-day-out, month after month, year after year, decade after decade.

I guess just about everything that could be written on Palestine, the treatment of Palestinians by Israel and the attacks on Israelis by Palestinians has been written and more articles, books, reports, and films come out every single day, as I just noted. All I can originally offer, therefore, are my personal, real-life eyewitness experiences working on relevant human rights issues in the region and opinions gleaned from working with Palestinians and seeing and learning about the lives they endure across the West Bank, Gaza, inside Israel itself, and globally. Though the issue of refugee and IDP return and HLP restitution is not often on the top of stories about the area these days, it must be recalled that millions of Palestinians in the sad diaspora want nothing more than to return to the homes and lands from which they and their families have been systematically and very intentionally ethnically cleansed since 1948, during the founding of Israel. As international law clearly states, in more than 200 different texts, until these recognized rights are implemented, these restitution claims remain outstanding, unresolved, pending, and in need of attention and

---

[17]https://www.theguardian.com/world/2026/feb/26/francesca-albanese-un-lawsuit-trump-sanctions. See. Also: https://www.ohchr.org/en/statements/2025/08/us-sanctions-special-rapporteur-francesca-albanese-threaten-human-rights-system.

[18]https://www.amnesty.org/en/latest/news/2025/07/usa-sanctions-against-un-special-rapporteur-francesca-albanese-are-a-disgraceful-affront-to-international-justice/.

[19]https://www.aljazeera.com/news/2026/2/26/global-impunity-fuels-israels-illegal-push-to-annex-west-bank-amnesty.

resolution.[20]

It appears to be a matter of policy that notwithstanding what criticism is directed at Israeli practices, the government will seek to question the facts, deny responsibility, claim bias, seek distraction, shift blame onto the Palestinians or otherwise simply not address the assertions of wrongdoing. Whether the disproportionate killing in Gaza in response to the deplorable attacks by Hamas in October 2023 where, as of today, the horrible death ratio now stands at roughly 37:1; 37 Palestinian deaths for every Israeli death, the fact that 70% of those killed were women and children, that 80% of those killed in Gaza were non-combatant civilians or the worsening impacts of the occupation of the West Bank and the increasingly lawless behavior of the illegal settlers, Israel tends to reject all criticism out of hand rarely even committing to independently examine the merits of the critique. That the current Israeli government automatically disputes findings that conclude that it is responsible for genocidal acts, such as those allegations recently made by the UN Independent International Commission of Inquiry on the Occupied Palestinian Territory, including East Jerusalem.[21] Beyond the findings of this body, another case is now under consideration at the International Court of Justice brought by South Africa against Israel, also alleging genocide, named as the case concerning Application of the Convention on the Prevention and Punishment of the Crime of Genocide in the Gaza Strip (South Africa v. Israel).[22] Countless news reports, human rights findings and articles also place the genocide label onto the acts perpetrated by the State of Israel. Israel is, of course, not the first country to deny it is responsible for a genocide, but it is the most

---

[20]In my one of my own efforts to reveal the massive scale of recognition of the right to HLP restitution, I put together a book containing well over 200 treaties, laws, resolutions, and cases directing addressing the right to housing, land, and property restitution. See: Scott Leckie, *Housing, Land, and Property Restitution Rights of Refugees and Displaced Persons" Laws, Cases, and Materials*, Cambridge University Press, 2007.

[21]See, for instance, the Final Report of the UN Commission of Inquiry https://www.ohchr.org/en/press-releases/2025/09/israel-has-committed-genocide-gaza-strip-un-commission-finds.

[22]See: https://www.icj-cij.org/case/192 and https://www.hrlc.org.au/news/2024-2-1-icj-south-africa-v-israel-human-rights-law-centre-statement/.

recent government to do so. There are many within Israel who are willing to dispassionately examine allegations against the State by independent observers who believe in the protection and promotion of human rights, but they remain in a small and virtually silent minority, awaiting a new day when a new government with a new point of view seeking sustainable peace finally comes into being.

The facts and the history of the Israeli-Palestinian conflict are crystal clear to anyone who wants to find them. As an impartial human being who is not Jewish, Arab, Muslim, Christian, Israeli, or Palestinian, but a simple part of our shared humanity who cares about human suffering no matter the cause and who loves all people equally, like any self-respecting world citizen should, it is beyond dispute that so far there is only one winner in this tragic battle and as history has so sadly recounted over and over again, to the victor have thus far gone the stolen spoils. And yet, often when they are criticized by the UN or other impartial observers, threatened with boycotts, divestments or sanctions, or are facing yet another UN resolution demanding they atone for their crimes, Israel will all too frequently assert that such sentiments are biased against them, that the UN is biased against them, or that any criticism is at its core anti-Semitic. In even more extreme responses, some will simply assert that they and only they are the true owners of the Holy Land as outlined in religious texts dating back thousands of years and all the rest of their usual distractions from the real facts at hand. These refrains are tragic in so many ways. Above all else, they make the conditions needed for a negotiated peace settlement and any future where Israelis and Palestinians are treated as true equals completely impossible. And, as well, they undermine important efforts to tackle actual anti-Semitism which remains rife throughout the world, as the recent tragic massacre at Australia's famous Bondi beach so sadly reveals. Simply responding to every critique as if by its very nature it is intentionally anti-Semitic only leads people to doubt or downplay actual acts of anti-Semitism. It is so sad that a government that claims to represent such a proud people needs to resort to such untrue claims to seek to justify what it knows to be false.

I know, for certain, that the percentage of Israelis that truly believe such assertions falls far, far short of 100%. First of all, it is important to recall here that Israel is not, as much as they may wish people to believe, comprised of a population which is 100% Jewish. Rather, in 2026, Israel is 73% Jewish and 27% non-Jewish, and yet it insists on calling itself "the Jewish State" as if the 27% non-Jewish population and the Palestinians (who are generally not included in these figures unless they formally live within Israel itself) simply did not exist. Zooming out, at the global level less than half of the world's Jewish population actually reside in Israel; 55% of Jews do not.

I have befriended and spoken with thousands of Israelis and Palestinians over the years. I know and love many of them; they are fellow humans, many are world citizens at their core, if only they could take a break and delve deeply inside to feel their true nature. I personally know hundreds if not thousands of Jewish people who do not support the views of the present Israeli government and who wish for an entirely different reality in historic Palestine where humans are treated as humans first and foremost, and where a state built on the foundations of equality, human rights, and historical justice can come into being that somehow resolves this seemingly never-ending zero-sum-based conflict.

But reality all too often doesn't allow that and when such a tiny proportion of Israelis, and even fewer of the world's Jewish population have ever set foot in a Palestinian area or refugee camp to witness the brutality for which they are responsible, the carnage just continues. This omission just pushes things further and further from a peaceful resolution to this seemingly never-ending conflict to the point where today there seems to be a widespread sentiment within Israel that the Palestinians don't even exist, that they are essentially sub-human and are not worthy of human rights protections at all. The regime now led by an indicted war criminal will be viewed by history with great derision, of that there can be no question. Many will ask why so few within Israel did so little to stop him and his allies. So, too, will the students of tomorrow ponder why the international community equally did so little to stand up for the right of the original inhabitants of historic Palestine.

As a human rights expert all too familiar with the horrors the Jewish people suffered under the evil rule of the Nazis and how the Holocaust touched every single Jewish family and continues to do so, it pains me beyond measure to see how a religious group that has suffered so much at the hands of truly evil people and ideologies of hate over centuries, for 78 years have so callously facilitated the disintegration of Palestine and the millions of fellow humans who now suffer at their hands.

Just take a minute, go to the internet, and look at the comparative maps of historic Palestine in 1945, then 1948, then 1967, and finally, today.[23] Any fair observer can see that Israelis completely and utterly dominate everything in historic Palestine—day in, day out, 30,000 days and counting—while the Palestinian people suffer ever more in an epic battle they seem as far as ever from winning. And if you doubt that Israel as a State has been built on the back of ethnic cleansing, read Jewish Israeli author, yes Jewish Israeli author, Ilan Pappe's *The Ethnic Cleansing of Palestine*, which gives a scathing and truthful account of these horrors. An even more recent account of the horrors that have been carried out against the people of Gaza by Omar El Akkad entitled *One Day, Everyone Will Have Always Been Against This* is additional required reading.

Life Lesson No. 89: History can shape our worldviews, but all too often it can enslave us and make us behave very badly.

Indeed, if there is anywhere on Earth where a society organized on the obvious basis of our shared humanity is more desperately needed, it is within Israel and the territories it occupies and brutalizes. This is not to discount or deny any of the violence that has been committed by Palestinians or others against Israelis. Far from it. Billions of people across the world believe strongly that a non-violent future offers the only possible way of bringing a long-term solution to the seemingly never-ending crisis in the region. And I believe that, too.

However, it is a great understatement to say that we have a long, long, long way to go. We now face a reality that many within Israel and not a small number of its American supporters wish for nothing less than an ethnically pure Israel comprised exclusively of Jewish

---

[23]See these shocking images here: https://visualizingpalestine.org/visual/shrinking-palestine/

citizens. As outlandish as such a vision may be, let us consider for a moment what it would take to create such a reality and the scale of criminal activity that would be required to bring this outrageous vision into being. Indeed, such a vision could only ever be achieved as a result of mass ethnic cleansing, mass forced displacement, massive land and asset theft, bloody conflict and comprehensive genocide. If we were to imagine the opposite occurring where no Jews remained within the same area, something that no one with any credibility truly believes despite the rhetoric one may hear, this would be equally outrageous and unacceptable.

As hard as it may be to hear for people from all sides in this conflict, the *only* way forward is a shared one, even though this may be impossible for many to imagine now. Violence will not end through ever-worsening brutality and de-humanization. Peace, prosperity, human rights and democracy can only come about when people begin seeing each other and treating each other as equals, as fellow human beings with the same needs, the same wishes and the same hopes and dreams.

Be that as it may, I fully know and appreciate the road to reach such a reality will be long, arduous and not all that likely to occur as things now stand. But that does not mean that it is not the right thing to strive for. Indeed, in all the places I have travelled and worked across the world, in none have I encountered such deep, visceral hatred of fellow human beings as I constantly noted when I was in Israel. The out-and-out dehumanization so many Israelis are capable of when it comes to Palestinians is staggering beyond belief, and so painful to hear every time it is shamelessly uttered as I heard over and over again, each and every day. Most Israelis have little to no life experience with Palestinians and conveniently see all of them as a unified set of terrorists with only one quest in life, and it is this complete lack of interaction and exposure that serves only to deepen the rifts that much further.

On the other hand, I know many Israelis and Palestinians who live as humanists in their approach to the world, and who believe in a just and fair peaceful solution to the Israeli-Palestinian conflict. But on both sides of this intractable battle they remain far too few in number. One day perhaps, these residents of Israel and Palestine will be seen as the tiny vanguard today that grew into a movement that *finally* began to build a constituency for a unified country that could be called "Palesrael," as my late Jewish friend Joel Kovel described his vision of a shared and more beautiful future political reality there. Dismally, as is so often the case, Joel paid a terrible price for his compassion-driven views. Shortly after publishing *Overcoming Zionism: Creating a Single Democratic State in Israel/Palestine* in 2007, which drew heavily on our time together there, Joel was publicly fired from the university where he had taught for years. He told me that he had been labelled as a "traitor" and a "self-hating Jew" because of his progressive political visions, though officially, they fired him for some mundane administrative reason. Major efforts were also undertaken to essentially censor his book, but the publisher backed down in the end when violations of freedom of speech concerns were put forth. He wasn't the first and certainly won't be the last.

A few years after Joel ran as the Green Party candidate in the 2000 US Presidential election, I met up with him by chance in Woodstock in upstate New York, yet another one of my many homes away from home, usually staying in the very house that Carlos Santana and his band rented out during the famous 1969 concert, and who left graffiti behind on the back wall of one of the closets as a lasting legacy. Joel was so interested in my work with Palestinian refugees seeking to exercise their HLP restitution rights. These rights had been reaffirmed countless times under international law for decades in support of the rights of the then more than six million Palestinian refugees worldwide. Today, this number has almost doubled! After showing his interest, I said, "Well, come with us when we head to Israel and Palestine in a few months." He immediately said yes and several months later we met up in Bethlehem in the Occupied West Bank, Joel flying in from New York, me flying in from Bangkok and another human rights hero and film maker, Fionn Skiotis, flying in from Melbourne. During the trip we would meet with countless Israelis including human rights lawyers and NGOs working on promoting Palestinian restitution themes, UN officials, various overseas diplomats, Palestinian law groups, NGOs, activists and ordinary people all across this contested area where so much suffering has been meted out since 1948.

Since my earliest days of political and human rights engagement, I was aware of the Israeli occupation of the West Bank, Gaza Strip, Golan Heights, and other conquests from 1948 onwards. Given the importance of this issue, which remains probably *the* greatest threat to international peace and security, I couldn't ignore it. Although never officially acknowledged, it is widely believed that Israel has several hundred nuclear weapons. As the only country in the Middle East with this capacity for Armageddon, it holds significant influence over how geopolitics unfolds in the region. I have heard it said repeatedly, though I have no way of proving this, that their nuclear weapons are targeted not only at countries Israel sees as enemies but at countries they consider to be friends, as well. Just imagine that this is true. If it is, then imagine the political implications of these allegations. Again, I have no evidence of this, but one hears this all the time when the topic comes up in discussions about this sensitive topic. The disproportionate size and power of their military, the universal draft they maintain for both men and women, their huge annual expenditure on weapons, an unparalleled surveillance system as well as constant US support no matter what horrors they carry out, all contribute to a sense of near complete impunity and ruthless dominance. Israel's 1950 *Law of Return* puts the icing on the cake by giving every Jewish person in the world the right to "return" to Israel even if they have never been there while the Palestinians who have lived there for centuries were forced out and never allowed to exercise *their* right to return to their places of habitual residence. Go figure. As noted, 55% of the world's Jews have not taken advantage of this law and remain non-Israeli residents, a fact that surely must dismay the fundamentalist ideologues who seem to dominate Israeli government today.

These realities and more lay the foundations for the gradual, step-by-step, day-by-day, awful erosion of both Palestinian territory and any chance of a just settlement, for which Israel and their main financial backer is ultimately responsible. The collective cognitive dissonance of the vast majority of Israelis, somehow trying to mete out some form of displaced revenge subconsciously and surreptitiously for the criminal evils committed against Jews and others during the Nazi period by shifting active blame onto the Palestinians who are from - wait for it - Palestine, is just a devastatingly sad sight to see. In many respects it is as simple as this: No one will ever do to us what was done to us ever again, and if we have to occupy a country and decimate another people to ensure this, then so be it.

With hundreds of Jewish friends, I fully understand their lingering fears that the Holocaust could happen again, and I have seen multi-generational traumas played out before my very eyes, just recently having a moving chat with a young Jewish friend born in 1991, 46 years after the end of the Holocaust, who grapples daily with what happened to his grandparents during that horrible historical epoch. I have only the deepest compassion for him and countless others like him and all victims of anti-Semitism in whatever form it takes, but why must it play itself out within systems planned and designed to end in ethnic cleansing, *apartheid* and now genocide?

I know for certain that a better way in historic Palestine is absolutely possible and that it must be found. To bring this about will require massive changes in the collective mindset of all of those involved. But having had thousands of discussions with Israelis both inside Israel and out of the country, despite the vitriol and hatred I have had to endure, against all odds I somehow remain hopeful. So many Israelis I know, and even more non-Israeli Jews I know and am close friends with, absolutely hate what is going on in Israel and want nothing whatsoever to do with it. They find it shocking that they are linked to a country whose Prime Minister and former Defense Minister have been indicted for war crimes and crimes against humanity by the International Criminal Court. But they remain a small minority.

One of the saddest discoveries I made when visiting Israel and the remaining Palestinian territory is how few Israelis have ever met or befriended a Palestinian, let alone visited their towns and villages or spoken with the people they perpetually see as their enemy, despite their many similarities. And, sadly, this includes many of my Israeli and Jewish friends from whom I had expected more.

I know from experience that simply meeting people from other places, other religions, other cultures and other practices is by far the best, most rapid and easiest way for people to begin to understand, accept, like and then love people from backgrounds often very different from our own. Life becomes so much better when we know people from other places. With such an awareness that all of us can become friends with everyone else, the world stands a far better chance than if we continue down these destructive nationalistic and ethnically-based roads. Israelis and Palestinians share so much beyond their simple shared humanity. They often look similar, eat many of the same foods, and certainly share an immense love of hummus (as I do!). They share many religious stories and most certainly share the same land mass. A unified future must somehow be possible if enough people embrace this vision of a multi-ethnic tomorrow. Some even share the vision of unity and a better way forward—a cosmopolitan notion that a politics free from human rights violations, land theft, and terror is more possible than many realize.

Choosing a new way forward based on their shared humanity first does not mean at that Jews will lose their Israeliness or that Palestinians will lose their Palestinianess, just as Germans did not lose their Germanness by joining the European Union. Rather, by actively choosing to associate with a larger and more diverse entity, a layer of identity is *added* not taken away and the foundations of peace and prosperity are greatly expanded.

But often, just when you start thinking a solution to all these problems might actually be at hand, and a multi-ethnic, secular, social democracy just might be in the cards, a brick in the face tells you, no way man, not yet and maybe never. I remember one time when Fionn and I were in an Israeli taxi near Tel Aviv and the driver asked us if we had been to *Mini Israel*, a theme park attraction similar to *Madurodam* in Holland where artists constructed the whole of historic Palestine in miniature, which they had simply called Israel as if the millions of Palestinians living there simply didn't exist because the Israelis didn't want them to. We had heard about this odd establishment but pretended we hadn't and innocently asked if *Mini Israel* included the West Bank, and his immediate and suddenly aggressive reply was "West Bank? No such thing. Judea and Samaria, it's all Israel." You hear this type of thing all the time, showing the depth of self-deception and cognitive dissonance Israelis foist upon themselves to rationalize the crimes they know, deep down, they and all of Israel committed to create Israel as it is today. They know their government has built a country on stolen land and assets, decimating an entire nation of people in the process, and in moments of quiet honesty will postulate that they and only they have rights to every square meter of the territory once called Palestine. To make matters worse, the United States Ambassador to Israel, staunch pro-Israel right wing fundamentalist Christian Mike Huckabee, publicly asserted in an interview in February 2026 that Israel could claim a biblical right to territory that covers most of the Middle East, saying that it "would be fine if they took it all."[24] Needless to say, these views were strongly condemned by many countries but the simple fact that the US government representative felt confident enough to assert such an extremist view says tomes about where we are today.

This is despite the fact that US popular support for Israel has never been lower and corresponding support for the Palestinians has never been stronger.[25] In fact, in the most recent poll more Americans sympathized with the Palestinians than Israel, a dramatic shift after decades of support. This will have dramatic consequences and may be the beginning of an opening for a far better and more equitable future, or so we can hope.

Despite claiming to be a democracy, and in fact, proclaiming that they are the only democracy in the Middle East, Israel continues to detain more than 10,000 Palestinian political prisoners.[26] Add to this the tens of thousands (if not many more) of Palestinian homes that have been wantonly destroyed by Israel over the years, the theft of billions upon billions of dollars of housing, land, and property assets and the outright killing of more than 73,000 Gazans since late 2023 (80% of whom were civilians; Reminder: wilful killing of civilians is a war crime under international humanitarian law), and one begins to understand the scale of Israeli crimes against the Palestinians. One recent study indicates that the actual total of dead may be as high as 126,000, with many more than that severely injured.[27] Is this really the behaviour of a democracy? Just sit with that number for a moment.

---

[24] See, for instance, https://www.abc.net.au/news/2026-02-23/arab-muslim-nations-condemn-us-ambassador-comments/106374092.

[25] See, for instance, https://news.gallup.com/poll/702440/israelis-no-longer-ahead-americans-middle-east-sympathies.aspx.

[26] See: https://www.btselem.org/statistics/detainees_and_prisoners.

[27] https://www.mpg.de/25778228/1125-defo-gaza-study-reveals-unprecedented-losses-of-life-and-life-expectancy-154642-x.

Imagine all those lives that went unlived. The pain and anguish suffered by the surviving family members and friends. The utter misery foisted upon so many people, again, most of whom were civilians, women and children. Every single one of those deaths a tragedy. Every Israeli death equally a tragedy. Democracy should never allow such a reality to emerge.

On top of this, though condemned repeatedly as violations of international law in so many different ways, with never-ending US support Israelis continue to build illegal Jewish settlements as a means of taking over ever more land throughout Palestinian territories. These settlements and the increasingly violent and fundamentalist settlers that live there are graphic signs of how far Israelis will go to take over everything they can. There are now more than 880,000 such settlers, each and every one contributing to making a just peace in the region out of reach.

On a more positive front, few things move me more than when people have an a-ha or *satori* moment, recognizing the erroneousness of their ways and seeking forgiveness, knowing there's no going back from that understanding that one's ways were so very wrong. I have seen it in the eyes of many of my Israeli friends as they, often with great difficulty and discomfort, first reluctantly, and then with true contrition, realize that what has been done in their name was just not right. This is by all means not exclusive to Israelis, but it is something that needs to occur far more often if we are to have a planet worth living on. This is true across the world, but nowhere more so than within the colonial-settler societies, all of which have committed various historic crimes, including what many would label as genocide, as they invaded, occupied, stolen and settled land, and decimated the original inhabitants. These societies include the United States, Canada, Australia, New Zealand, Brazil, China, the UK, Israel and others. Because all of these powerful countries share the dubious distinction of being colonial-settler nations, they seem to be rather reluctant to sternly criticize one another for such crimes for fear of being criticized themselves for the very same practices. "If we stole land, how can we criticize them for stealing land?" or so the thinking must go in the minds of these deluded dominators.

Yes, there have been some small strides forward in recognizing such crimes and beginning to atone and do something about them, though these remain small, piecemeal, and often rather pitiful when compared to the scale of the crimes committed. Native Americans, First Nations peoples in Canada, Aboriginal and Torres Strait Islanders in Australia, Māori in New Zealand, indigenous peoples across Brazil and the Palestinians and other occupied populations all know the consequences of colonial occupation and domination. It is long past time to redress these crimes, return stolen land, pay compensation, and facilitate self-determination.

In Australia, public events pay respects to the traditional Aboriginal and Torres Strait Islander traditional owners of the land, which surely helps draw attention to these important facts. The state of Victoria recently concluded a formal treaty between the government and all Aboriginal peoples residing in the state, setting the stage for ever improving relations and justice-based solutions for resolving past crimes. Might we imagine something similar one day in the Holy Land? For decades, such a treaty was seen as nothing more than an impossible dream, surely never to come to fruition, but in the end, justice prevailed, and it did come into being. In fact, discussions are now well underway on how to create a nationwide treaty modelled on the Victorian experience.

Beyond this important treaty, a Stolen Generations Reparations Package is now in place in Victoria. It provides eligible applicants (members of the Stolen Generation who were forcibly removed from their families as children as part of a broader assimilation policy of earlier Australian governments, estimated to be more than 25,000 children) a payment of A$ 100,000 (+/-USD 70,000), a personal apology from the State, access to healing and reconnection to Country programs. Even a decade ago, let alone since Australia became a Federation in 1901 or the original invasion of the country by the British in 1788, such a program would have been deemed impossible, and even absurd. But things changed and now this good faith effort at atonement and justice is real and solidly in place. It is not everything, but it is something and surely a major step in the right direction.[28] It shows what is possible when people organize, when people show

---

[28]For an overview of this program, see: www.vic.gov.au/stolen-generations-reparations.

respect, and when the dominant power (the guilty ones), realize that a shared sense of justice is what builds a better society for decades to come.

Similarly, for almost a century, few would have believed that the evil *apartheid* regime in South Africa would give way, largely peacefully, to a democratic, post-racial South Africa as occurred in the early 1990s. A truth and reconciliation commission was formed to address past crimes as a way to move forward and the new 1996 South African Constitution, considered one of the world's best such laws, was approved as a means of building a state truly based on the will of all of the people, not just one single race.

The independence of Timor Leste, a country that suffered the loss of one-third of its population while under occupation by Indonesia, seemed impossible until it suddenly didn't, almost without warning. The fall of the Berlin Wall and the Iron Curtain, and then the Soviet Union itself, were each deemed impossible scenarios until they were not. The United Nations started out with 50 original members. Thanks to its work managing much of the decolonization process, UN membership today stands at 193 nation states, 143 more than in 1945 when the UN was founded. Things change for the better. Oppressed peoples do achieve freedom and independence. Territories devoid of any human rights protections transform into human rights protected zones and the list goes on.

Could a similar scenario one day come about concerning the decades-long Israeli treatment of Palestinians, now widely seen as built on ethnic cleansing, and a form of both the international crimes of *apartheid* and now, even genocide? This was what happened to the heinous racist regime that ruled South Africa for almost the entire 20th century before the white minority was forced to accept that 13% of society should not rule over 87% with laws based on racial discrimination and other disgusting hatred-laden views. Much of this occurred because of the personalities involved, in particular Nelson Mandela but also FW de Klerk of the ruling *apartheid* regime who saw the writing on the wall and agreed to begin the process that would inevitably end the evil of the racist system that had been in place for so long. Who might the individuals be in Israel and Palestine today who can play similar roles? Is there an Israeli FW de Klerk? Is there a

Palestinian Nelson Mandela? If they are there, and I know them to be, they are alive today and the sooner they initiate the new era of equality and justice, the better.

In the context of Israel, too, perspectives are slowly changing. In 2021, in fact, the very cautious and far from radical Human Rights Watch (HRW) issued a major report entitled: *A Threshold Crossed: Israeli Authorities and the Crimes of Apartheid and Persecution* that everyone reading this book is encouraged to read.[29] Three years later, in 2024, HRW outlined acts of genocide, noting that "Israeli authorities have deliberately inflicted conditions of life calculated to bring about the destruction of part of the population in Gaza by intentionally depriving Palestinian civilians there of adequate access to water, most likely resulting in thousands of deaths."[30] Sadly, things have only gone from bad to worse and today in early 2026, one is far more likely to hear continued allegations of genocide, even from Israeli human rights groups. Israel denies the genocide claims and ruthlessly attacks anyone who makes these claims but such attacks do not erase what has happened in recent years.

Life Lesson No. 90: Far more people believe in the potential of Palesrael than we might assume.

What if, instead of waiting for more bad news, more hatred, more crimes, more killing, more dehumanization, more land thefts, more house demolitions, more annexation, more discrimination and crimes, millions of us were to push for a totally different vision for the region where a unified one state solution, Palesrael, were to become a secular, cosmopolitan, egalitarian, social democracy just like the rest of Europe, a region that so many Israelis claim to wish so much to emulate? What if, finally small 't' tribe was to become bit 'T' Tribe? This may seem utterly absurd or impossible today much like the cases just outlined may have seemed well before a semblance of justice prevailed. But is it really impossible to imagine this? In such a vision,

---

[29]https://www.hrw.org/report/2021/04/27/threshold-crossed/israeli-authorities-and-crimes-apartheid-and-persecution.

[30]https://www.hrw.org/news/2024/12/19/israels-crime-extermination-acts-genocide-gaza.

as things evolve, there will surely still be Palestinian, Jewish, mixed, atheist, agnostic, Christian, Muslim, Orthodox and Armenian neighborhoods and cities just as there are in any cosmopolitan society. But in addition there will be an embrace of true equality, non-discrimination, one person-one vote elections, transparency in public matters, investment throughout the land, and the peace, security, and prosperity that so many people ultimately want. Israelis will remain Israelis and Palestinians will remain Palestinian but living as equals under a shared flag. This would be a cosmopolitan, democratic, rule of law governed Palesrael—just imagine the possibilities.

What if Israel and Palestine were to come together like East and West Germany did after all those years of separation? What if these two entities were to merge together after decades, even centuries of animosity, much like the countries of Europe have done in the form of the European Union? Is this really the impossible dream it may seem today? Some living within the borders of historic Palestine today believe in this vision. This is the future they want. They may not be the majority yet but who is to say they will not one day be greater in number than the fundamentalist ideologues and fanatics of today? How many are there today? Dozens, hundreds, thousands, tens of thousands? Maybe even more than that? Hundreds of thousands, maybe even the silent millions? It's hard to say but I can assure it is very far from zero.

And yet, I fully understand that tragically we are still so far from this better reality emerging. The largest and heaviest book I own, which was given to me by its extraordinary author, is simply called *Atlas of Palestine 1948*.[31] This huge book, measuring 50cms by 30cms, contains hundreds of pages of detailed maps revealing the scale of land theft and ethnic cleansing meted out against the Palestinians that has built the modern state of Israel. Hundreds of colored pages show in meticulous detail and prepared with an eye towards accuracy and precision, just how much has changed on the ground since the establishment of the state of Israel. One chart reminds us, for instance, that in the immediate run up to 1948, Palestinian Arabs owned more than 23 million donums of land and Jews owned slightly less than 1.5

---

[31]Salman H. Abu-Sitta, *Atlas of Palestine 1948*, Palestine Land Society, London, 2004.

million donums. Another 1.5 million or so was classified as public or State land. A donum is 1000 sq meters or approximately one-quarter of an acre. Overall, thus, out of approximately 26 million donums of land, Palestinians owned more than 90% of the land within the borders of historic Palestine. The original property records confirming this ownership of these lands are kept under lock and key in a UN building in New York City and were entirely digitalized some years ago. This is the land that would be subject to any eventual HLP restitution program should such a program ever be put into place as they have been in so many countries over the past several decades. The facts are there for all to see and the ongoing injustice is staggering beyond belief.

It is within this context, that the intransigence and pure hatred of so many of those in power in Israel and those who support them, daunts and depresses me too much. I cannot psychologically bear the next phone call from a friend whose house has been demolished by the Israeli military or whose family has been attacked by settlers yet again. I cannot handle hearing more stories of dispossession, of family graves being desecrated, of olive groves being destroyed, or of State-driven terror being wantonly meted out against innocent people who just want to live a peaceful life where they have lived for hundreds of years. The wall to climb for justice in Palestine is so high, and alas, seems to be higher and more unreachable every day. It is heartbreaking to know so deeply just how horrible the occupation remains. I have worked on the Palestinian refugee issue for many years, working with incredible groups like Badil, which works tirelessly for Palestinian refugees, as well as preparing thick and detailed official briefing papers on HLP restitution rights for the Palestinian Negotiations Support Unit following the Oslo Peace Accords when peace actually looked within reach. I also engaged for a time with the impressive Israeli group Zochrot in the early 2000s, an amazing group of concerned Israelis that actively supported the right to housing, land, and property restitution for Palestinian refugees. Such groups and people *do* exist. This must not be forgotten.

As a person who bases his views on international law, human rights principles, our shared humanity, basic morality, ethics, and justice above all else, I too, still proudly and without hesitation support the right of return and HLP restitution rights for all Palestinian refugees who wish to return to and reclaim their original homes. This right has been recognized at the UN and elsewhere over and over and over again. But I have to admit that any hope I may have had that Palestine would soon be like South Africa or East Timor turned out to be, is clearly on the wane. Maybe the ideas of an author such as Ali Abunimah in his important 2006 book *One Country: A Bold Proposal to End the Israeli-Palestinian Impasse* will one day take hold, but for the moment things certainly do not look this way. Far from it, sadly. Recently, I watched a short film on Netflix called *The Present*, which —aside from the brutality of what Israel is doing today in Gaza and the West Bank, not to mention Iran, Lebanon, Yemen and all the other countries it bombs these days—reminded me again of the petty, unnecessary, and bitter indignities Palestinians endure daily, how they are searched, harassed, and humiliated by gun-toting Israeli soldiers, as well as treated universally with suspicion, even the babies and small children.

I painfully witnessed this countless times, and even as a citizen of two countries that generally have a soft spot for Israel, I had to personally endure it repeatedly when entering or leaving the West Bank or even just crossing from one town to another—let alone at what are called 'flying checkpoints' that could appear wherever Israeli soldiers decided to harass Palestinians. At such crossings, we ourselves were always aggressively hassled by the soldiers who seemed to have nothing better to do than try to degrade us for simply being there, not to mention what they routinely did to the Palestinians who stood in lines with us. We only had to endure this for a period of days but the people on whose land this takes place have had to endure these indignities for decades and decades, and it only gets worse as the years pass. I just heard on the news today, in mid-February 2026, that the director and family of the Oscar winning film *No Other Land*, Hamdan Ballal, was brutally targeted and attacked by Israeli settlers in his West Bank village Susiya. The violence just gets worse with each passing week almost 80 years after the establishment of the State of Israel.

I have seen this with my own eyes on countless occasions. Once, while examining the deleterious effects of Israel's ever-hardening takeover of the Palestinian town of Hebron, I watched thuggish teenage settler fanatics not more than 13 or 14 years old try repeatedly to hit us in the head with huge rocks, bricks, and bottles as they targeted us with a barrage of projectiles trying for a direct hit. We took cover and then watched as they illegally broke into dozens of closed Palestinian stores with crowbars as Israeli soldiers stood by without intervening, laughing as they allowed yet another crime to take place. Another time, on our way to a refugee camp in Nablus to strategize with refugee leaders there on an acceptable restitution system for Palestinian refugees—victims of Israel's *Plan Dalet* and other acts of ethnic cleansing—hyped up, trigger-happy Israeli soldiers harassed us as much as they could and get away with it. The original Zionists, of course, remarkably based their actions on the phrase, "For a people without a land, a land without people," ignoring the millions of Palestinians already living there and owning more than 90% of the property and figuring out how to get rid of them. These delusions have only worsened over time. Most readers will be surprised to learn that numerous proposals were made to establish a Jewish state prior to Israel being established in historic Palestine in a series of different locations across the world. These included part of the British colony of Uganda, a small part of New York state in the United States as well as an area near Sitka, Alaska, a province in the USSR, within various Italian colonies including East Africa and Libya, parts of Australia and many others.

During what will surely be my final visit to Israel, as visitors we were repeatedly treated like trash, subjected to countless barrages of bricks, stones and bottles, sworn at, spat upon, verbally abused, and generally mistreated more than I had ever been before anywhere else on the planet. Yes, let me say that again. Despite the millions of miles I have travelled, the scores of countries I have visited, the hundreds of slums where I have spent time, working in countries emerging from war and ethnic conflict trying to build peace and countless unruly places I have often found myself, never was I treated as badly as I was in Israel. I have worked in almost half of the world's countries and visited many more, many of which were undemocratic dictatorships immersed in war, hardship, and general malaise, but never have I been treated worse. Our American, Australian, and Dutch passports offered no protection whatsoever against this maltreatment.

Beyond the targeted harassment by Israeli soldiers settlers and various fundamentalists that we faced throughout the West Bank and even within Israel itself, the worst we experienced occurred when we were *leaving* through Ben Gurion Airport. Just as I was checking in to leave, the officials pulled me aside, took all my things, forced me to send my personal briefcase that I always used as carry-on luggage on thousands of previous flights into the plane's hold, lengthily interrogated me with ridiculous questions, and then strip-searched me, subjecting me to the worst full body check ever, forcing me to stand and disrobe and get probed by a border officer wearing squeaky rubber gloves and a look of hatred on his face that I had rarely before ever felt. As I gazed as deeply as I could into his eyes, I saw such immense fear, such anxiety, such unresolved PTSD, such despair and as bad as his treatment of me was, I knew I was leaving this place forever, but he would be stuck here to harass and abuse travellers' day after day after they left this place for the last time. And whoever you were, whatever your name may have been, rest assured that while I hate your cruel deeds, I refuse to hate you. But in the end, if your goal was to reduce the likelihood of me ever returning, you succeeded.

Ever the optimist, however, I believe that a growing portion of the world recognizes that things really need to change in Israel but also that any meaningful change must come from within. As always, I believe that my vision of unity and acceptance is the only way forward. It may take time and seem ludicrous now to even propose it, but in time, it will come as it has in so many other places on Earth. Einstein said as much in 1946 in the opening quote to this section above. It bears remembering, too, that Einstein also famously postulated way back in 1915 that "Nationalism is an infantile disease. It is the measles of humanity." For those who do not realize it, Einstein was Jewish.

The population of historic Palestine (Gaza, Israel, West Bank, Golan Heights) is roughly half Palestinian and half Jewish. This is the reality no matter what either side may wish. Birth rates of both sides are roughly the same with the Israelis leading slightly. Most Jewish people in the world do not live in Israel. Most Palestinians do not live in Palestine but form one of the largest diasporas anywhere. Mutually finding a way to live together is the only possible way forward. Other countries have done this, so now it is time for this tiny slice of the world as well. As a famous Palestinian leader once told me "Scotty, we do not choose our families nor or neighbors. We just need to find a way to get along with them. We choose our friends."

Similarly, I will never forget a discussion with a gentle, elderly wood carver somewhere on the edges of a Palestinian refugee camp in the West Bank established in 1948 following their forced displacement from their homes and lands. I had never met this man before, but we connected immediately once we began talking to one another. He was covered in sawdust from the woodworking he was doing that day, in this case he was sculpting Jesus statues from wood which would one day be for sale in a tourist shop for visiting Christians to the birthplace of Christianity. I was traversing the West Bank making a film on restitution issues and focusing in particular on the idea of building a multi-ethnic democratic state as a basis for peace. I interviewed dozens of people, Palestinians and Israelis, all randomly chosen from people we happened to run into, and from my personal experience it quickly became crystal clear that Palestinians were far more likely to support the idea of a shared Palesrael. My new friend Mohammed the wood carver left a permanent mark in my memory because of his constant refrain of "Why not?"

"Mohammed, would you be happy to have Israeli neighbors?"

"Of course, why not?"

"Mohammed, would you be happy to share a meal with a Jewish family?"

"Of course, why not?"

"Mohammed, would you be happy if your daughter were to marry an Israeli?"

"Of course, why not?"

"Mohammed, would you be happy to live in a peaceful, multi-ethnic, cosmopolitan state comprised of equal citizens from all across historic Palestine, now under the control of Israel?"

"Of course, why not?"

Mohammed was far from alone. I came across similar replies all over the West Bank—Nablus, Bethlehem, Hebron, Qalqilya—and beyond. This was certainly not universal but far more widespread than most would imagine. It is the middle-way, accepting views such as those of Mohammed and the others with whom I spoke that could form the basis of a unified future. If leaders and political parties on all sides of this conflict were to emerge based on this view of the world, surely the results could not be worse than now.

I am friends with hundreds of Jewish people, Palestinians, Israelis, Arabs, Muslims, Christians and so many other groups that live in this region. I don't care what your religion is or your ethnic background. I care about what your values are. I care about your commitment to equality, human rights and non-violence. I care about your willingness to speak to the other side. I care about how you treat your fellow humans. Almost all of these friends—not all, but a solid 98% of them—would love nothing more than to live in a secular social democracy, a place where a shared and equal future for everyone was apparent, and where empathy guided the way. They are there. They accept that democracy means all people are treated as equals, where you win some and lose some, where good faith and good will guide an inclusive political process where working together and accepting each other will build a far better future than continued decades of hate, division, dehumanization, and cruelty. May their numbers grow.

And so, instead of a catastrophic future involving crimes too horrible to even contemplate, let us rather imagine a day not too dissimilar to what has already occurred in many countries across the world once true change takes effect, when the international news media unexpectedly announces that a recently elected new Israeli Prime Minister will shortly be arriving in the Knesset to make an unforeseen announcement. News stations and podcasters across the world change their planned programming and begin broadcasting as the top Israeli government official enters the room. She calls the chamber to order, makes sure the national and international media are present and ready, and then solemnly lays out her missive:

Good afternoon, everyone.

Today, as your new Prime Minister I have a message on behalf of the Israeli people for my Palestinian brothers and sisters, our neighbors, and our new friends, and that message is:

We are sorry.

We know the meaning of suffering and we apologize for the hatred, the theft, the destruction, the discrimination, the killings, the demolitions, the arbitrary detention, the humiliation, the torture, the dehumanization, and everything else we did but should have never done.

We are sorry. Please forgive us.

Eighty years of brutality end today. Let us join hands in solidarity with one another as equals and be citizens of our one shared nation. Let us start over and build again.

The days of zero-sum conflicts where one side wins and one side loses are finished. The days of win-win outcomes are upon us. There is no other way.

Let this be a nation where mutual respect, human rights, democracy, fair and just voting and continued prosperity for all form the foundations of this new homeland for all of us.

Together we are stronger.

We are now unified for a better future for all of us.

For now, and forever.

One day....

Chapter 8

Independence

Call me a dreamer of political realities that may seem even less than impossible (if there was such a thing), but sometimes dreams come true. And sometimes, countries that seemed lost forever, like Palestine or Tibet today, subsumed by larger neighbors or occupiers, re-emerge as new, free nations, finally able to exercise their legitimate rights to self-determination and sovereignty. When I first started living my unorthodox, rather eccentric human rights renegade life, one of my greatest dreams was to find a way to work for the independence of occupied peoples. With great good fortune, I was able to lend a small hand to a whole range of liberation movements, some of which actually won. Two of the most memorable were my times working with the people of Timor Leste and the island of Bougainville.

Timor Leste - Welcome to the Newest Country on Earth

One of the most extraordinary things about navigating the human rights chambers of the UN is the first time it dawns on you that you're actually surrounded by people and representatives from nearly every major political movement in the world, especially those involving occupation, war, and violence. These are the people you might have seen on the news the night before and, then a few days later they're suddenly your fast friends. Look left and you'll see the Western Saharans from *Polisario*, look right and you'll spot the Palestinians, look in front of you and there are the Tibetans, and then right next to you is a group of people from the brutal independence struggle of East Timor. There's José Ramos Horta, their leader, and there's José Guterres and all the other Timorese Josés ready for another round of fighting for recognition and justice. When I first met them they had been at it since 1975 when East Timor was brutally occupied by invading Indonesian soldiers who took advantage of Portugal's quick departure as their centuries as colonial overlord came to an end. The invasion and occupation by then non-democratic Indonesia, which the US and Australia knew about but shamefully failed to stop, resulted in the deaths of up to one-third of East Timor's population—amounting to more than 200,000 people. One-third of a nation's people killed. One of three. Horrible. Imagine the United States experiencing the killing of nearly 110 million people or Australia losing more than nine million and you begin to have some idea of the trauma the poor people of Timor Leste were forced to live through. And imagine again, that it was precisely these two countries—the United States and Australia— that green-lit the invasion and occupation of East Timor in 1975. Shame.

When I first met and befriended the entire Timorese crew, I had no idea how much time and energy I would eventually—and happily— devote to working with them, both at the UN to bring attention to their cause and later, after their independence in 1999, living in their newly independent country to work on land issues. José Ramos Horta received the Nobel Peace Prize together with Bishop Carlos Belo in 1996, and that gave a tremendous boost to the liberation movement. I was in my Geneva apartment with my pal Paul Kennedy, the host of Canada's best radio program, *Ideas* on CBC, when it was announced that José had won the Nobel. We both danced the jig and then I immediately called José to congratulate him, knowing this could be a potential game changer in the quest for independence. This turned out to be true. Just three short years later, after 24 brutal years of military occupation, unfathomable ruthlessness, and poverty for all, it finally came to a rather sudden end.

This was thanks to many concurrent factors, but none more so than the incredible opposition led by José and his political allies from Fretilin, combined with pressure on the ground from the guerrilla army of Frelimo, which included the first president, Xanana Gusmao. Right after the UN transitionally took over Timor, before gaining full independence, and shortly after I arrived, we travelled deep into the interior to visit some of the provincial towns of the island. Out of the blue, we came across a platoon of battle-hardened but happy Frelimo soldiers, initially suspicious after years of actively opposing the occupation—but glad that independence was near. I took one of my most cherished photos with them in black and white, posing with some heavily armed guerrillas who would soon become part of the new national army of a free, democratic, and unoccupied Timor Leste.

Longstanding dictator Suharto's death created unexpected political instability in Indonesia, and his replacement by a more reasonable leader, who recognized that the cost of illegal occupation was no longer worth it, led to a quick political turnaround, making independence look increasingly likely. When the occupiers finally did leave, though, this unleashed a wave of horrifying behavior by the departing Indonesians resulting in the mass destruction of just about every building, every bridge, every road, indeed, anything that could be destroyed was destroyed. Retreating troops hounded—and often killed or maimed—the Timorese. Fires roared across East Timor and José and his crew desperately sought outside intervention to stop the killing and destruction. Remarkably, in September 1999, Australia— surely feeling guilty for their horrible decisions in 1975 to back Indonesia's occupation—heard the call and brought in 5,000 soldiers, which quickly settled things down. But the damage was done, and it was widespread and deeply dark.

Between late-1999 and May 2002 when Timor Leste became a fully free, sovereign independent nation-state, recognized by the rest of the international community and a formal member of the UN, the UN Transitional Authority on East Timor (UNTAET) governed the fledgling country. It was under the auspices of UNTAET, headed by Sergio Vieira de Mello, that I first came to the country I knew so much about but had yet to visit in person. I lived in Geneva at the time, so reaching Timor took a very, very long time requiring a route that took me from Geneva to Zurich to Singapore to Brisbane to Darwin and finally, to the capital of East Timor, Dili. After five flights and over two full days, I was out of it physically but immediately perked up upon entering the partially burned terminal of tiny Dili airport, greeted by a hastily made sign reading, "Welcome to the World's Newest Country." This was truly an incredible moment arriving in a place which had shortly before been illegally occupied and then brutally destroyed by marauding soldiers on the rampage and now after a quarter-century was finally free. And most remarkable of all, my friends were going to govern the place. Impossible dreams can come true.

UNTAET called me in to work on housing, land, and property issues. Being an integral part of two of the few times the UN actually governed territories—UNMIK in Kosovo and UNTAET—was an honor, though the overall results were imperfect enough that no one has tried such initiatives again. At the time it seemed such arrangements were on the verge of becoming almost commonplace, and a sort of harbinger of things to come, but the challenges inherent in running a country are a lot different than providing aid and expertise, and the UN paid the price. Sergio faced increasingly strong opposition from the Timorese, and rightly so. And credit to him for courageously and correctly turning things around and putting the Timorese in charge and then spending the rest of his time there facilitating the emergence of the world's newest nation.

As the Indonesians had destroyed so much of the place, accommodation was at an absolute premium. We could find very few places to stay, given the fact that houses were needed for the thousands of international aid workers arriving to work for UNTAET in a place where large numbers of homes had been destroyed by the angry departing Indonesian troops. I looked far and wide for a place to stay and eventually all I could find was a sort of shipping container that formed part of a new set-up that resembled a mining or military base, replete with the incredible luxury of air-con in the housing unit, shared (though rather gooey) outdoor showers, and some of the worst food I have ever eaten.

I'm not sure what it was that I ate or drank that got me incredibly sick after three weeks of constant work and running all around the country, but again I was floored by some unnamed illness that brutalized me in every way possible. Uncontrollable fever and shaking, intestinal obliteration and all the rest. I was completely wiped out thinking I might die alone in a metal box, and physically unable to leave my container for days of utter health carnage. Prior to that, I had worked my tail off designing a restitution mechanism to settle thousands of unresolved housing, land, and property disputes, while trying to gain as much buy-in as possible from both the UN gang and the Timorese.

Much to my surprise, it was relatively easy to get the UN on board, though there was—as always—some internal opposition. This included a certain US official whose father's books influenced me greatly, but who himself exhibited the kind of American arrogance and self-righteousness that is so bad that few of them even notice—but I certainly did. It was certain Timorese citizens, however, who proved the most reluctant. There were a lot of vested interests doing the rounds, shall we say. Many people who probably shouldn't have been living where they did faced the real threat of having to relocate if a restitution project developed the capacity to return properties to their rightful owners.

In 1999, I met Sergio for the first time at the UN's headquarters in Dili. We arranged for a film crew that was filming us to interview him for a short film they agreed to make and were paid for—but never delivered. I had no idea he would walk this Earth for less than four more years. It was about a week or two after meeting him that I got sick. At a certain point the illness was so bad, and I was so worried, that I felt like I urgently needed a doctor. The only doctors available were found in the growing number of military field camps of tents housing UN peacekeepers sprinkled around Dili. Barely able to walk, hallucinating and delirious, I somehow made my way to the medical tent in the nearest military base that happened to be staffed by teams of dedicated Egyptian military doctors. They brought me in to figure out what was wrong. I told them my symptoms, they consulted in Arabic with each other, and then one of them asked "Are your stools foul-smelling stools?" I wasn't sure just how to answer this probing question with an answer so obvious that any reply seemed potentially wrong. They gave me antibiotics and other unidentifiable things. I took them all, and after a few days, I finally regained some internal balance and control, resumed work, and finished the report and proposals that I needed to write. Then I flew to Darwin, where I enjoyed the luxuries of the developed world like never before, downing a chicken satay pizza that tasted like the best thing I had ever eaten. I devoured it in just a few bites.

Life Lesson No. 91: Colonialism isn't over just yet.

Timor got its independence a couple of years later, which brought many a tear to my eyes as the struggle had finally been won. After working with so many different struggles for self-determination, it was extraordinary that at least one of them actually prevailed. Ramos Horta later became President and my pal José Guterres became Deputy Prime Minister. That was such a joy to see especially after knowing how they both suffered so much during the dreadful years of occupation. I went back in 2007, again for the UN on what turned out to be the first of numerous field missions by a Displacement Solutions team to human rights hotspots around the world relying on our Global Housing, Land, and Property Expert Registry. I was there with a great team to try to resolve a new wave of internal displacement, which had led to IDPs fleeing renewed fighting and instability and who were now living in public parks and other open spaces in Dili. We put together a very detailed and practical plan, grounded in HLP rights and designed to fix this situation and get some much-needed attention to the broader housing situation that remained deplorable.

Sadly, an international agency—known colloquially in many humanitarian circles (by everyone except its employees) as "the prostitute agency" for its repeated history of doing just about anything for money, even if unrelated to its mandate or expertise—won out, and our rights-based plan never saw the light of day. I have met scores of people that worked with this agency over the years and have to sadly say that with one or two notable exceptions, most were not impressive in any way other than this salivating obsession of more donor funds at any cost. In one particularly revolting moment, I almost hourly heard salacious stories throughout Dili from locals as well as UN officials about a staff member of this agency, spotted earlier in the week wearing only a bright orange thong Speedo, standing publicly on a beach popular with socially conservative Timorese, with his arms around two inexperienced aid worker women just out of college. Despite having absolutely no humanitarian experience, this painfully cringeworthy individual hired them to each run an IDP camp housing hundreds of desperate people. Awful. Anything for the bucks.

These rather grotesque cash-driven behaviors were nothing new to this awful agency, and by all means not isolated to Timor. I saw it all over the world, many times, as had so many of my humanitarian friends. One time, at a major global meeting on climate change in Geneva, where I had to give a couple of speeches not long ago, I sat with the NGOs at the back of the room, chit-chatting with the activists. The international head of the same agency walked down the aisle to our left, where we NGOs occupied about six rows of seats. This old, crusty, way-past-his-prime guy lifted his right leg as high as he could and intentionally ripped the biggest, smelliest, wettest, and most disgusting fart he was capable of mustering right next to the NGO row, from which a range of critical comments had come about his institution. He aimed it at us; it was clearly intentional. A woman from Argentina literally yelped in response to the loud and gurgly sound we all heard—and will never forget. He was just another creepy guy from an agency full of incompetent, low-level creeps which I can very proudly say I have never worked with and never will even if offers materialize.

Bougainville - The Victory Box

Bougainville, which is located right next to the Solomon Islands, but which legally forms part of Papua New Guinea these days, is an island nation with a population of 250,000 and the source point of the world's best cacao. The first time I learned of Bougainville I was running around the UN's hallways in Geneva. As I'm sure you have already done so yourself, when I first heard the word Bougainville, I thought it referred to delicate purple flowers, not a unique island culture struggling for self-determination.

The people of Bougainville first settled there more than 8,000 years ago. After thousands of years of their own history, French explorer Louis Antoine de Bougainville "discovered" the land in 1768. He promptly named this island, which again, had been lived on continuously for *thousands* of years, after himself, as such people so often loved to do during that historical epoch. It eventually became one of the very few German colonies in 1899 and then was occupied by Australia during the First World War. It was then invaded by Japan during WWII, fought over intensively and eventually returned to full Australian control at the conclusion of the war in 1945. In 1949 Bougainville was merged with the other Australian Territory of Papua which then became the shape of current day Papua New Guinea and which itself only achieved independence from Australia in 1975.

Bougainvillians were not particularly happy about this state of affairs and declared themselves the Republic of the North Solomons in September 1975 but failed to receive international recognition, a vital attribute of any effort to achieve statehood. It was then formally absorbed into PNG and became host to the Australian mining company Rio Tinto Zinc (RTZ) that set out to dig the world's biggest copper mine. This was meant to have help fund the post-independence economic development of PNG. Instead, in the eyes of many Bougainvillians, this actually led to massive environmental decimation combined with a total lack of respect for local landowners, leading to the emergence of an armed insurrection by the Bougainville Revolutionary Army (BRA) in 1988 against both RTZ and the PNG national government. It lasted a brutal ten years, resulting in over 15,000 deaths and the closure of the Panguna copper mine. The book and film *Mr. Pip* provide a good, albeit tragic, overview of what life was like on Bougainville during those horrible years, and it was not pretty.

The practices of both sides in this conflict left much to be desired, but there is no doubt that the excesses of the PNG side led eventually to the involvement of the United Nations in the territory. Having worked with the Bougainvillians for years at the UN, I heard more than my fair share of horror stories about what took place during the war—stories from BRA combatants, PNG forces, and especially innocent civilians, who were often caught between the two sides, especially the women. The frequent raping of village women was carried out all over the island, as was kidnapping, the burning of villages, destruction of crops, and generalized terror. I heard accounts of pick-up trucks loaded with soldiers capturing Bougainvillians alleged to be part of the BRA, tying them to ropes and then dragging them at high speeds across the rough roads of the island until they died after what must be one of the worst ways to be killed. I heard stories of the BRA sometimes capturing a PNG soldier, throwing him in the back of another pick-up, stripping him naked, forcibly masturbating him until ejaculation and then letting him go, his dignity and manhood in macho PNG destroyed forever after the commission of this crime. It was a bad scene across the board and went on and on and on, including a full-scale naval blockade around the island which lasted long enough for starvation to take hold, with people resorting to eating "barking cow", something very much not part of the typical diet of the islanders. I'll leave it to you to figure out what barking cow is. Yep, *barking cow....*

Life Lesson No. 92: I never laughed harder than when he told number 391.

In the middle of the war about which I had never heard a peep, living as I was in Europe at the time, an eccentric-looking white guy— who was surrounded by three or four of the blackest of Black people on the planet, the beautiful Bougainvillians—approached me. This guy quickly became one of my closest friends anywhere and remains so to this day. Mike Forster *aka* Foz or Spike or Tabuna was running around the UN for the first time in his life, clueless about what to do to activate the UN to help bring peace to Bougainville. After asking him a few questions, I said I'd help the Bougainvillians in any way I could, not knowing this island would figure so prominently in my working life for many years. Foz, whom I always called Spike, somehow owned a massive cacao plantation on Bougainville called Raua, around 7,000 acres in size, which produced some of the best raw materials for the world's finest chocolate—Bougainville cacao. Spike inherited the plantation from his parents and grew up as the only white Bougainvillian that he remains to this day. He was inducted into

Bougainville society as a chief and is called Tabuna, a title recognized by all in his island home. His upbringing was idyllic in many ways, but around college age, he grew restless and made his way to Stanford University in California, where he studied communications and worked on concert lighting for the famous shows of a new local band —called the Grateful Dead. I knew there was something about this guy I could relate to. He even smoked a joint or two with Jimi Hendrix at the famous Rainbow Bridge concert, so ole Spike has been around in a lot of circles that I jealously wish I could have been a part of, but I was just a bit too young, alas.

Spike was anything but an international lawyer or human rights activist. He was a farmer, a musician, an artist and a surfer, and OK, a stoner, too, but nothing wrong with that. The best joke teller I've ever known, the man had such a repertoire of jokes that he and a friend on Bougainville actually numbered every joke they knew, sometimes just saying "87" or "391", at which point both would crack up beyond control. Mike informed me of the rather extraordinary factoid that many young men on Bougainville, and probably a few more places than that, actually first "lose" their virginity to massive over-ripe papayas that had fallen many days earlier to the jungle floor, conquered by these teenage naughty boys after yet another day in the tropical heat by horny lads looking for some innocent action. The things you learn trying to help stop a war.

Mike is the embodiment of Sixties cool, and it is surely this coolness that leads me to unanimously award him now and forever the much-deserved award of the world's best UN lobbyist without question. Plus, he is an incredible artist and can paint like the best of them. I am proud to hang three or four of this multi-talented man's masterpieces in my little home. He came to the UN knowing nothing of how the UN worked. But within a few short years, he secured the first-ever resolution on the human rights situation in Bougainville, which eventually led to ever-deepening UN involvement, peace negotiations, a peace agreement, and the end of the war. Getting there was far from easy, of course, but we had some serious fun amidst the drudgery of working day in and day out in the halls of the UN, trying to get justice for a land far, far from the peaceful shores of Lake Geneva. We used the offices of Banana Circle Travel, just across the street from the UN, as our office away from home years before that office became my office. When the travel agency went broke, it became the office for my organization, COHRE. There, Mike and his team, often with me tagging along, wrote speeches and made plans, while I drafted resolutions in the type of language the UN was used to, continuously pushing for more attention to the horrendous human rights situation in Bougainville.

One of the Bougainvillians with Mike was the larger-than-life, jovial Joseph Kabui, a tall and gentle man with immense dignity despite all he had endured. His character traits later earned him the Presidency of Bougainville, not long after they signed the eventual peace agreement. But now the future President of Bougainville hung out with all of us in the tiny travel agency office that used old airplane seats as the waiting area sitting arrangements, as we toiled to get Bougainville on the agenda.

I can't recall now if it was the second or third year that Mike and his crew were in Geneva, but when that draft resolution on the *Human Rights Situation in Bougainville* was finally tabled and scheduled for a vote, emotions were running very high. After having scored a growing number of resolution victories at the UN, I would often retreat to a glassed in, and thus quiet, visitor gallery one floor above the massive chamber. There, I could more easily scan the room to see who was where, who was voting which way, and let out a scream of joy upon approval of our resolutions.

I called this place the Victory Box. When I found out the estimated time that the Bougainville resolution was going to be up for the vote, I gathered Mike, Joseph, Ruby, Martin, Moses, and the rest of the Bougi Gang and led the way to the Victory Box along with a few other human rights NGO representatives who had lent a hand to the Bougainvillian struggle. There were probably 10-12 of us up there when the Chairperson announced "The next text is a draft resolution on The Situation of Human Rights in Bougainville. Are there any comments? As I see there are none, does any member of the Sub-Commission wish to ask for a vote? I see none, and therefore adopt the resolution by consensus and declare the resolution approved."

In what will always be one of the most cherished memories ever during all those years at the UN, this stoic man, Mike Forster, the surfer, artist, stoner, cacao farmer from Bougainville who looked so sun-battered that he might have never cried before, burst into uncontrollable tears of joy, hope, sadness, relief all at once, with most of us joining in with our own tears, everyone hugging Mike and the Bougi Crew with one of the most rewarding group hugs I've ever been lucky enough to have been a part of. The whole room looked up at us, hundreds of diplomats, Sub-Commission members, fellow NGOs, and UN officials, all smiling, and all at least a little bit jealous because we truly knew how to celebrate. What a moment. And to think that that very resolution unleashed a whole series of diplomatic, UN and media forces that in the end led to the end of a war. Amazing.

Once the Sub-Commission had approved a resolution it was time to head higher up the UN human rights chain of command and try to get the State-based Commission on Human Rights to approve a similar resolution. With the Commission meeting about six months after the Sub-Commission, this gave the Bougi Crew half a year to lobby more governments, raise awareness about the UN's approved resolution on Bougainville, and prepare for the intensity of the six-week-long Commission session, which can be arduous even in the best of times.

It is, by no means, an easy task to convince the UN to adopt a resolution. It is actually a mentally and physically brutal and exhausting process with some sessions lasting until midnight with nothing but crackers and cheese from the one functioning vending machine that would otherwise never have been used, the only dinner available to the tired diplomats, including us. The bar at the Serpentine Lounge, one of the last places to close around the chamber where the Commission meets (now called the Council), kept drinks on the menu outnumbering food items by a 6:1 ratio. Most of the food sold out by lunchtime, and no one replenished it until the following morning. But without the Bougi Crew's tireless efforts and refusal to take no for an answer—without this bar and its free-flowing, barely acceptable Swiss beer on tap—there might never have been peace on Bougainville.

For it was in a quiet and dark corner of this bar, behind it and out of the peering eyes of the hundreds of spies and diplomats carousing the many low tables that adjoin this famous lounge, that Mike and his new diplomat mates from Guinea Bissau and Nigeria made the plans that led to the Commission approving the Bougainville resolution, which was all well and good in so many totally unique and unpredictable ways. Then alcohol entered the picture and things became particularly interesting. I urged Mike to wait with the libations until after the resolution went through, but nooooo, he had to ply the Nigerian Ambassador with beer after beer after beer as the vote on the resolution kept getting delayed due to more lengthy debates on earlier resolutions. Both Guinea Bissau and Nigeria had already expressed support for the people of Bougainville, but the resolution still needed to be officially presented with a professional speech explaining its contents and why all 53 member states of the Commission should support it. Let's just say that it was beyond unusual for either Guinea Bissau or Nigeria to *ever* lead a move for a resolution, but thanks to Mike they did, and they did it well.

Life Lesson No. 93: Delayed gratification triples the joy in the end.

If it wasn't so funny, I would have been furious that getting the main guy responsible for ensuring that the resolution would be approved wasted off his ass, as was Mike, while the teetotaling, devout Christian remainder of the Bougainville Crew watched in shy and anguished horror what would happen when Nigeria was offered the floor to introduce this historic resolution. By this time, I couldn't handle the tension anymore so I headed up to the Victory Box watching Mike stumble through the Chamber, his Ambassador mate by his side as they strolled audibly laughing and smiling around the back of the room, and then around the curving, amazingly wave-like wooden walls, and then up towards the front where the Nigerian team sat. Whiter than white Mike sitting there with the Blacker than Black Bougainvillian and Nigerian Crews, seen from upstairs in the Victory Box was quite a sight to see. What happened next alarmed me. Mike pulled a family-sized pack of chewing gum from his bag and handed it to the ambassador, in a desperate attempt by these inebriated diplomats to cover up the strong smell of stale alcohol.

I look down at the schedule of speakers and Nigeria is next. As I look up I see the Ambassador put a gigantic wad of gum in his mouth and start chewing as fast as he can, mere seconds before speaking to the world, in a speech that will be recorded forever, on audio, digitally and on paper, and the Chair of the Commission says "I now give the floor to the Honorable Delegate of the Federal Republic of Nigeria to introduce the draft resolution on the situation of human rights in Bougainville." The Ambassador appears not to hear the invitation and then I see Mike nudge him that he's on, and he then fumbled very ineloquently with the microphone and began his nearly indecipherable speech chomping and chewing his massive wad of gum at the same time he's speaking in one of the strongest Nigerian accents I've ever heard. Now, I have many Nigerian friends and can always understand their wonderfully unique way of speaking English, which I just love, especially listening to Fela Kuti singing his incredible songs and who taught me much about Nigerian English. But when combined with 15 pieces of gum and an intoxicated mind from hours of heavy drinking, this lovely tone became a garbled mess. Luckily, I knew that the whole thing would be OK because no country was actively opposing the resolution, even Australia that was not at this stage on the right side of history. The resolution passed late that night, I stood up in the Victory Box looking down at all my friends and fellow pro-Bougainville pals and let out a yelp of glee that turned a lot of heads in my direction.

Eventually, peace talks were brokered by New Zealand and UN peacekeepers deployed. After some time, Australian leadership dispatched a peace-monitoring group, leading to the end of the war and a peace agreement in 2001 that included the right of the people of Bougainville to vote on an independence referendum within 20 years. Somewhat remarkably given the lack of enthusiasm for such a referendum from the side of the government of PNG, the referendum was held in November and December 2019, with a final vote of a staggering 98.31% in favor of full independence! That is clearly what the people want, but more than six years later the people of Bougainville are still not fully free. The night they announced the referendum result, for dinner I made my own version of what Mike called his famous Bougi Stew, replete as it is with coconut milk, sweet potatoes, pea pods, vegetable stock and whatever chilies and fish you might have around. Masterpiece food from a masterpiece dude.

After all of our UN antics trying to end the war in Bougainville in the late 1990s, Spike and Bougainville again entered my life in a major way shortly after I started working almost full-time on the issue of climate displacement and what to do about it. In the early 2000s, climate change was very much on the international agenda, but little attention had been given to the human displacement dimensions caused by global warming. Virtually no conversations took place about preventing and resolving climate displacement, which is expected to—yes, you're reading it right—displace *hundreds of millions of people* from their homes—including, almost certainly, someone you know. For the past 15 years, I've worked to address this void, writing books, helping develop new international norms, teaching the world's first law school course on these issues, and visiting over a dozen climate hotspots around the world. Climate displacement has been and continues to be one of my main obsessions for if we collectively fail to address it urgently and properly, our already ill-housed world will be much worse off with slums growing at unbelievable speed, leaving no country untouched with ever growing armies of landless and homeless people, made poor by losing everything, with nowhere else left to go. There's no safe haven on a planet where everyone, everywhere will be impacted.

Back in the early 2000s, when I started working on this issue, one of the few places where human-caused and accelerated climate displacement was already underway was the Carteret Islands, just north of Bougainville. All 3,000 souls will need to leave before long. Unlike most climate-threatened communities, the Carteret people were well organized, thanks to the tireless efforts of Ursula Rakova. She founded a group called Tulele Peisa to provide an organizational vehicle for finding solutions to their unenviable plight. With some difficulty, I contacted Ursula and began discussing with her how Displacement Solutions could assist, at which point she mentioned Bougainville as a possible destination for the islanders. Around the same time, I was back in touch with Spike, both he and I now living in Australia. After years of delay, he now needed to sadly sell his Raua plantation to get some much-needed cash for the much more expensive life in the Lucky Country. This was a body blow to Spike and something he hoped he would never have to do but given the ongoing instability in Bougainville, the *persona non grata* status accorded him by the PNG authorities because of his stellar work at the UN, and his need for cash, he surrendered and put his 7,000-acre unused and despoiled plantation (now heavily overgrown because of the war) on the market, for which there could only ever be very few bidders. Raua was so big it took over a day to walk across it. It actually had rivers running through it, beaches and seafront galore. I have seen pictures of this magical place and though conditions in Bougainville were surely bad, the physical beauty and lushness of the place carried on as always nature will, with or without us, especially without us.

With our creative minds melding together down the phone lines we then came up with the ultimate win-win-win plan whereby Mike would agree to sell Raua to the local provincial government in Bougainville at market value, not more, not less, but on the strict condition that the land be used to relocate the Carteret Islanders *en masse*. In doing so, Mike would get the money he needed, the government would solve a thus far unresolved problem, and the island community could establish a safe place to relocate. They would also have the opportunity to re-establish the cacao plantation, giving them access to incomes—a new thing for them, coming from a largely cashless, subsistence economy. This would be the world's first attempt to sustainably relocate an entire community because of the effects of climate change, and it would be coordinated by my then new NGO, Displacement Solutions.

After a lot of planning, talking, phone calls and emails—hundreds of them—we rustled up some funding and planned a meeting to sort out the details of the deal. After holding a public day-long conference on climate displacement with UNHCR, the next day we hosted and held a private day-long meeting at the Australian National University in Canberra focused solely on our problem-solving plan. Ursula represented her islanders, Mike came to sell his 7,000 acres, and the local Bougainvillian government official in charge of relocating the Carteret Islanders attended as well. Also present were officials from the Australian development agency, staff from UNHCR, and another potential buyer of Raua—a wealthy beverage magnate from somewhere in Queensland, accompanied by his lawyer—just in case. This was a truly historic meeting where, had it gone as planned, could have made everyone in the circle of concern happy—the islanders, the government and Spike—everyone's problems solved in a single go.

Anyway, you can probably guess the outcome by now; it didn't work. Funds we had hoped to get from AusAID didn't eventuate. The local official flaked out on every task he agreed to do, and not long after leaving, left us to pay for his more than one-thousand-dollar phone bill for a bunch of international calls he made from his hotel room. Despite Ursula's amazing presentation of how everything could work, and all of the nodding heads in the room, without the cash from somewhere there was no way the plan could work, obviously. So, in the end, what happened?

Well, no one was willing to buy Raua from Spike except for that beverage magnate. In the end, as the only buyer of a huge slice of pristine and productive land, he put down an offer of around AUD 400,000 (USD +/- 250,000 at the time) which Spike had no way of rejecting, this being less than half of the median value of one suburban house on a quarter acre block in any major Australian city. We urged the buyer to consider the relocation plan. Though he could have won a Nobel Prize if he'd implemented it, nothing came of it, and I think the 7,000 acres of land making up Raua is still there unused, awaiting a development offer that will give the investor a big profit but providing nothing to the Carteret Islanders as we had hoped. We were so close to setting an extraordinary precedent on how to get the best deal for climate displaced people, but alas, we came up short. Now, more than 15 years later, the islanders have found some small parcels of land on Bougainville, but not nearly enough to relocate them all. Bougainville, which is the closest safe place they could move to, could still provide the solution to their plight, so their struggle continues.

Since then, we have been pushing for the idea of governments everywhere setting up Climate Land Banks to have land held in reserve for precisely cases like this when needed, but few have seriously considered these yet. Some great documentary film makers made an excellent film called *Sun Come Up*, which was nominated for an Academy Award. It chronicles Tulele Peisa and Ursula's stellar efforts to find land on Bougainville and the countless challenges associated with doing that, particularly given the fact that the islanders are Polynesian and the Bougainvillians Melanesian, two beautiful but often quite distinct cultures which do not always see eye to eye. Bring in some oneness, though, focus on their shared humanity, and it all may just work out in the end, or at least we can always hope.

263

Chapter 9

Islands

For as long as I can remember, I've had a slight obsession with islands of all types and sizes. It wasn't the tropical palm vistas or white sand beaches that got me, nor the sense of difference I felt during my early years in places like Hawaii, Nantucket, or Catalina—but the people and how they survive and thrive in such incredibly finite places. The isolation of the 11,000 islands dotted across the globe with permanent populations (and hundreds of thousands if not millions more without people) and the often-arduous task of reaching them always intrigued me and still does, as do their universal challenges in fighting rising sea levels.

But if something stands out these days that still draws me in is how small islands, particularly small island nation-states, do everything that all other States do, but in a miniature format. Yes, they will have a national library, but it's in a single small room, as the one I visited in Funafuti, Tuvalu, and to which I sent and donated three huge boxes of books upon my arrival home. Yes, they will have a national Olympic Committee, but the building will be the size of a small home, as it is in St. Vincent and the Grenadines. They will have a foreign ministry and maybe even an international law section within it comprised of one staff member in a tiny, steamy, non-air-conditioned room as was the case when I visited this room in Honiara in the Solomon Islands. They have to do everything institutionally that everywhere else must, but with far fewer people, resources and experience than much of the rest of the world. That they do it at all, and usually with great humor is always a marvel to behold. Islanders are cool. Working in, living on and visiting islands has surely made my life so much better—Grenada, Dominican Republic, Maldives, Sri Lanka, Tuvalu, Vanua Levu, Yasawa, Guadalcanal, Malaita, Malta, Cyprus, St. Vincent and the Grenadines, Puerto Rico, Ios, Crete, Santorini, Naxos, Vancouver Island, Terschelling, Nantucket, Martha's Vineyard, Catalina, Furuskar, Koh Samui, Bali, Tasmania, New Zealand, Australia and countless others, thank you!

Kiribati - Should They Stay or Should They Go?

Alongside my still-capable, sometimes photographic memory—for which my parents and those before them can take full credit—my other effortless predilection is the ability to see gaps in any system or structure, especially in the world of human rights. I like doing new things, adding on, augmenting and improving where this is possible and needed, and as you can perhaps see from the pages behind us, this is where I have concentrated my human rights energies around the world. The same applies to my work globally on the links between human rights and climate change, in particular what to do about those displaced by the effects of global warming. As I noted earlier, I designed the world's first ever law school course on these issues, which I first gave at the Australian National University back in 2008 or so, well before these issues were mainstreamed as they are now at long last. I've had the good fortune of working with people in Bangladesh, Panama, Papua New Guinea, Solomon Islands, Australia, the United States and many others as they struggle against the worst effects of a changing climate and travelled far and wide to climate change hot spots the world over, everywhere from Tuvalu to Bangladesh, Myanmar to the Maldives and Fiji to Kiribati and others.

Beyond this, I guided the process and raised the big money needed to draft and then adopt the *Peninsula Principles on Climate*

Displacement Within States in 2013. An all-star team of global experts worked to create a model law and policy to protect climate-displaced communities wherever they are. We nestled in an out of the way place in the middle of a pristine temperate forest, with mountain parrots, rainbow lorikeets, and kookaburras singing away all day long and closed ourselves off from the world until the work was done. The *Peninsula Principles* ended up being a rallying point around which people from all corners of the Earth gathered to demand a better future when facing climate displacement. They continue to act as an influence in the development of national climate displacement policies in frontline countries already grappling with climate change like Bangladesh, Vanuatu, and Fiji.

I started what was a very fun program called *Coastal Kids* at my daughter's primary school that lasted for a few years before she went off to high school. Of the hundreds of projects I've been involved with, *Coastal Kids* was surely one of the most rewarding. Besides giving children aged 6-12 basic lessons on climate change, at a time when it was not part of the school curriculum, we arranged for kids from semi-rural coastal Australia to speak directly via Skype with hardcore urban kids from a school in Chittagong, Bangladesh, on a huge classroom screen projected onto the wall for all to see. I get tears in my eyes even now when I think of it. Watching these kids, none of whom had ever met anyone from the other country, almost immediately strike up conversations with each other and then become pen pals, amazed me.

About 40 kids participated from each school every year we ran the course. After a couple of sessions and a few pen pal letters exchanged, the third session was magical. It was beautiful to watch the little Aussie kids—most of whom had never left Australia, let alone met someone from Bangladesh—and the Bangladeshi kids in a similar situation, all yelling out to discover who their pen pal was so they could greet them face-to-face. Little Aussie bruiser boys yelling out "Mohammed, Mohammed, where are you?" "Mustafa where are you?" Khaled where are you?", and slightly less bruiser Aussie girls shouting, "Fatima where are you"? "Shirin, where are you"? "Bashira where are you? All of them, equally desperate to see their new friends, waved with as much energy as they could muster. It was a powerful moment and yet another a reminder of the oneness that connects us all if we just let it.

The Bangladeshi kids then started yelling "Ashton, where are you?", "Daisy where are you?" and "Shane, where are you?" barely able to contain their excitement. One thing that really stood out during the *Coastal Kids* sessions was how markedly better behaved, broadly knowledgeable, and more concerned about climate change the Bangladeshi children were compared to the Aussie kids. This was notable, especially considering that some of the participating Australian students lived on a narrow strip of land on a tiny peninsula between two large bodies of water—far from the safest place to live during an era of global warming and rising sea levels. But all in all, the kids, the coastal kids from two very different places, were awesome and I might just reactivate *Coastal Kids* again now that my lovely daughter has graduated from University.

Climate change, climate displacement and ultimately, climate justice, have been on my radar for a good long time. I approached this challenge, as always, from the perspective of solutions, not just crisis, but how to resolve them in a rights-consistent and sustainable way. This process took me deep into the mid-Pacific Ocean back in 2010 on my first trip to Kiribati which I made together with UN official, Dan Lewis, about 10 years after he implemented my design of the HPD in Kosovo. That the Dalai Lama and dutiful Dan share than same initials only made things even just that bit cooler, though the comparisons between these two great men, except for the compassion, end just about there at the letter 'L'. Far from a religious man, Dan is a spiritual delight, but similar to Tom Robbins, more a Zorba the Greek—let's do it all!—sort of character than the calm presence of a Bodhisattva, and to think I didn't even know him in his wilder years.

Dan and I have done some very fine and adventurous human rights work together in all sorts of places over the years and I would jump at the chance of doing it again somewhere strange anytime, the sooner the better. We had a blast at the same time as kicking some serious human rights ass. That's the best way for me to roll living the human rights life, and so we did so in the atoll nation of Kiribati, home to just 100,000 souls, almost half of whom live in one of the most crowded places on planet Earth, the main town of Betio. Overcrowding, disease, lack of clean water, social tensions and all the rest are all part of life that emerge from too many people living in too small a place, though these are rarely the first things that cross one's mind when thinking about islands. Palm trees, white sand beaches and piña coladas, pink ladies, or margaritas, yes, but two square meters of awfulness per person, not so much. This unusual feature of the main island in Kiribati surprised us, of course, but it was in the contemplation of the query—cue The Clash and their most famous song in the background, please—*should they stay or should they go?* that really stumped us. Such questions are not the human rights inquiries one usually needs to make, for those are normally things like who are the victims, who are the bad guys and how do we stop the bad guys from doing horrible things to the victims again?

Rather, the task we set for ourselves, along with our growing group of amazing friends from Kiribati (pronounced Kir-ee-bas), the i-Kiribati, was simple: Should the government pursue policies allowing people to stay on the islands for as long as physically possible, even as sea level rise severity increases each year—much faster than scientists had predicted—or should we push for what the i-Kiribati call dignified migration? They don't want to be seen as refugees, nor treated as such, particularly given Australia's heavily condemned policy of holding asylum seekers in dismal conditions for years on end in detention far from Australian shores in Nauru, Papua New Guinea and elsewhere.

Now it should be obvious to anyone reading this book where my clear biases lie and that is, of course, with the option involving the least possible disruption, least coercion and certainly least displacement, particularly regarding any movement that was not entirely voluntary in nature. But when you are standing on tiny strips of land with sometimes just 10 meters separating the wild ocean on one side and the calmer, but still very wet, lagoon on the other, the question of "staying bias" begins to look weak, clumsy and downright stupid at times. When you know the highest spot in all of the islands that make up Kiribati is a mere three meters and that the vast majority of the land is far lower than that, options seem to evaporate much faster than any excess water ever could. When you start seeing the rather depressing economic and infrastructure situation in the country and the growing lack of prospects for the islanders of a country with a GDP of only 200 million US dollars, relocation starts looking like a better option than staying.

Life Lesson No. 94: Be a cycle breaker and circle maker.

Then you stay for a few more days, get into the local scene ever deeper, with nightly jaunts to the famous (or was that infamous?) Captain's Bar, which is just so different than whatever images may have just popped up in your mind's eye, you sense that maybe staying is the better option. If only the right amount and types of investments could be made to shore up the coastal defenses, build up the land in certain strategic spots artificially higher and get friendly nations to assist, maybe the lovely i-Kiribati could hold out for centuries more. Get a few more beers into you, play a few more rounds of pool with some totally gang member-like locals who are actually as soft and kind and gentle as you could ever imagine, brothers within seconds, and you think: Really? There's no way they can stay here for much longer. There's no way they are going to solve the very serious underlying economic, social and other problems if all cards are thrown into the "stay" camp, so let's go with planned relocation. And on and on it goes; always grounding everything in the best interests of the populace, the prevailing nature of international legal rules on these matters and the brutal *realpolitik* of island life in the central Pacific. It can do your head in. In fact, and totally unpredictably, I thought doing climate change and human rights work in the Pacific would be relatively easy and pretty clear in terms of what laws and policies to recommend, but it didn't turn out that way at all. In Bangladesh, the options are known and the remedies, while far more abundant than people realize, are nonetheless relatively clear. Not so in Kiribati, Tuvalu, Solomon Islands, Tokelau, Marshall Islands and so many other atoll nations where local options are always going to be limited, but where relocation anywhere, let alone to another country as *dignified migrants*, is fraught with countless dangers.

Underlying all of this is the utterly devastating fact, beyond any dispute, even by the still existent climate change deniers who hold sway in too many governments, political parties, and companies, that the people of Kiribati are 100% innocent. Regardless of political views —left or right—they pay the price of a global economic system driven by ravenous materialism, which has pumped so much CO2, methane, and particulate matter into the air. Collectively, with China, the US, the EU, and the world's billionaire class leading the charge—Australia shamefully topping the per capita list—we have completely altered global weather patterns, causing hotter temperatures, worse storms, and above all else, rising sea levels.

In fact, in some statistical data sets, places like Kiribati are ranked as having contributed literally 0.00% of the world's CO2 emissions, now imagine that. The Palestinians pay the price for what the German's did, and now the islanders and coastal dwellers everywhere are paying the price for what the CO2 emitters did. Will there ever be a Nuremburg Trial for climate destroyers I often wonder? Every year now more than 7 million people die of air pollution caused illnesses and who is held accountable? Who will be arrested and go behind bars for these crimes? Who should pay compensation to the people of Kiribati and everywhere else for this?

Life Lesson No. 95: Climate justice without addressing loss and damage is like a bicycle without wheels.

All of these questions swirl in your head when you're in a place like Kiribati. During the various trips we made there, luckily for us a jolly, white spiky-haired and energetic man named Anote Tong was president of the country. He, more than almost any other world leader, put climate justice onto the global political map, particularly for small island nations. We saw Anote everywhere—at singing events, at church gatherings, at bake sales, and at construction sites. He constantly moved across the islands, trying to help, trying to lend a hand, and trying to instill hope in a population slowly coming to terms with its existential crisis.

To give a sense of the types of challenges Tong was up against, one day when Dan and I were waiting in his office to see his Chief of Staff, we noticed some Japanese guys in full business suits sweating profusely, sitting on the other side of the room that we found a bit odd. We went up to them, asked them if they spoke English and then asked them what they were up to. Believe it or not, they were travelling salesmen of the most classic, formal Japanese type, selling their amazing wares way in the middle of the loneliest part of what is by far the world's biggest ocean. Boats? Nope. Seeds? They must be selling seeds or some agricultural product, fertilizer maybe? Nope. I know, it must be medicines or medical supplies. Those? Wrong again. No, these shy gentlemen, so unused to the particular type of tropical heat that is part and parcel of island life, and shirts and coats soaked to the bone as they said it, were selling *the* solution to all of Kiribati's woes. "We're listening. Let's have it. What's the solution?" And I kid you not, out they pull from their immaculate bags, in a country where nothing stays immaculate for very long, these incredibly professional glossy multi-paged brochures selling....drum roll please....artificial islands! The solution at last? The Holy Grail had come to them, praise be. The only problem is that these lovely looking fake floating islands were going to cost a cool one billion USD *each*! If your country's entire GDP is less than USD 200m and you're being asked to fork out five times that much for a fake new island, chances are you'd have to forego that option. But that's how it is in Kiribati and so many other atoll nations whose options are running out by the day.

But while this option was clearly off the table before the music even started, moving to Fiji was most certainly not. I believe it was our team at Displacement Solutions that first brought this story to the attention of the international media. The government of Kiribati had, or so it seemed at the time, cleverly purchased a large tract of land— several thousand acres—on Fiji's second most important island, Vanua Levu, in an area known as Naviavia, as a fallback option for relocating some of the luckier citizens of Kiribati, should conditions require it. A couple of years after we learned of this USD 10m purchase, we sent our incredibly talented Dutch photojournalist friend Kadir van Lohuizen to Naviavia and what he discovered there was troubling. Allegedly, not only did the Anglican Church, which sold the land, have no right to do so, but most of the land was too mountainous to be habitable. At any rate, descendants of former slaves from the Solomon Islands already occupied much of the flatter land on the site. Well, it was a good idea at the time and may prove to be one later on, but what seemed a rather eloquent way to move forward constructively was full of pitfalls as so many things are in these places.

Beyond the climate change-related pitfalls confronting Kiribati, formerly the Gilbert Islands in colonial times, the current government under Taneti Maamau, dubbed the "Trump of the Pacific," abruptly shifted allegiances from Taiwan to China—a shock decision that still reverberates. Beyond the geopolitical ramifications of this decision in the Pacific and elsewhere, China's proven ability to turn submerged islands into populated, habitable land—big enough for runways that accommodate fighter planes and larger jets, as they have done illegally in the South China Sea—much to the chagrin of among neighbors and the international community, especially the Philippines, puts them in a unique position to help. It is not unreasonable to presume that Maamau and his Chinese allies have considered a similar approach in Kiribati in exchange for ... well, who knows what they might have discussed as an appropriate trade—but I'm sure your mind reels. China will undoubtedly tout its now infamous Belt and Road Initiative to the exceedingly poor i-Kiribati, dangling both the prospect of island fortification *and* millions of dollars in much needed loans, putting Kiribati precisely where China wants them, owing them millions and unable to do much until they've paid back the money. High risk strategies now thus seem the norm in little ole Kiribati, but the land in Fiji is still there just in case.

When we were in Kiribati once, coincidentally the UN Secretary-General Ban Ki Moon was going to visit in a very rare instance of a high-level international personality coming to the country. The people were in a frenzy trying to make the islands look as good as possible for the big guest. Islanders were everywhere sweeping roads, pruning trees, making flower necklaces, picking up litter from the lagoon and all the rest. Somewhat hilariously, yet perhaps intelligently, a UN security official told us he had placed a life jacket into Ban's hotel room in case of a tsunami during his visit. Now if that's not symbolic of the very real challenges facing Kiribati, I don't know what is.

Everyone knew when his Australian military plane would land at the lonely airport, which receives just one or two arrivals a day, so our team and what seemed to be half of South Tarawa's population streamed there to glimpse this historic moment. As pretty much the only foreigners amongst a sea of smiling and giddy i-Kiribati, it was exhilarating but also tragic to see the hope in the eyes of these people that the UN Secretary-General was coming and that that would mean everything might just be OK in the end. How I wish.

After we watched the plane land, standing literally right on the edge of the runway in a way you could never do anywhere else, and seeing him depart the plane waving to the flower-decked throngs, we ran back behind the tiny terminal to see if we could catch a glimpse of Ban getting in his car and maybe have a word with him. Twenty seconds before he got in the car, a staffer took out a huge can of Raid insect repellent and unleashed a massive cloud inside, aiming to eliminate any offending mosquitoes. He sprayed so much for so long that Ban likely felt the poison more than any threat from a dengue-bearing mozzie. We went to Ban's first destination, and with Dan as a UN official, he made it into the line-up to shake his hand, likely neglecting to mention that just days before, while filming at the end of the very runway Ban had just landed on, we had all piled into an old, rickety rental car, driven straight onto the runway, embarrassingly doing doughnuts until the rubber started to burn, then hightailed it to the next village threatened by permanent seawater inundation. I wonder if those tire marks are still visible on Google Earth. Gotta love the islands.

Life may seem idyllic to those who have never visited tropical islands, but life for most is very hard and often debilitating. Health problems run rampant outside the shiny resorts people associate with tropical islands, and Kiribati has precisely zero of those. Diabetes and other preventable diseases are at worryingly high levels without enough doctors or medicines for adequate treatment. I, too—surprise, surprise—once again became severely sick in Kiribati with a long-lasting and fierce case of amoebic dysentery, feeling no joy while stuck in a cinder block room without electricity or running water, shaking uncontrollably, with a high fever, and needing the commode over 40 times a day. Not fun and, I hate to say it, probably the illness that began my slow withdrawal from travelling to such places, which now thanks to COVID feels almost complete. I will go again, but the days spent alone in that unbearably hot 35°C cinder block room will never be far from my memory banks, both cranial and intestinal.

The doctors do what they can in Kiribati. I found a Bulgarian doctor working with the merchant seamen and navy who tried his best but ended up giving me ineffective medicine. For good measure, I also visited a couple of local clinics run by Cuba's incredible international doctors program, which provides free doctors to thousands of patients in the world's poorest countries. In these clinics, pretty much the only available medicine was an antibiotic stored in large glass jars on the reception counter, where people would come and take a handful as needed. I refrained. In a country without a fully functioning sewage system, which is totally understandable, people are forced by circumstance to do their number ones and twos in the shallow lagoon. Let's just say that not all of these ablutions get washed out to sea with the changing tides, so this and generally poor infrastructure means not only that you can't eat a lot of the fish or shellfish that live in the lagoon, but also that at any given time a huge proportion of the population is sick with dysentery and other water-borne diseases.

Kiribati has been dealt a bad hand at the global card table and imagining a rosy future for these incredibly bright and jovial people is increasingly hard to do. Meeting with their foreign minister at the time, Tessie Lambourne (now the leader of the opposition and possibly the next prime minister), who wore beautiful hibiscus flowers in her hair and her classic tropical flowered dress, captured the essence of life in Kiribati—such beauty, with a forlorn look of concern, at a sunset that under normal conditions would look so beautiful, but there seemed a harbinger of dark days to come. I love you and your people Kiribati and pray that the future is kinder to you than anticipated.

Malta - The Hypogeum with the President

Little did I know that one of the world's oldest human structures, the *Hypogeum*, was built on the small and beautiful island nation of Malta in the central Mediterranean at some point around 4000 BC, more than 6,000 years ago. This extraordinary pre-historic structure contains the bodies of more than 7,000 of our *sapien* ancestors. One day, my new friend Ugo Mifsud-Bonnici—none other than the President of Malta at the time—showed me around the empty *Hypogeum*. The authorities had cleared this wild underground structure of everyone for security purposes, so Ugo and a few of us went through this amazing place with his words of insight sprinkled between countless visions of what the world might have been like six millennia ago.

Life Lesson No. 96: The Hypogeum, who knew?

We'd arrived there with jolly Ugo at the wheel of his Presidential car, no driver that day, me riding shotgun next to him in the passenger seat. The cars in front of us parted like the Red Sea when they saw his mean machine with its small bonnet flags fluttering in their rear-view mirrors. Every time we'd reach a crossroads where there were police guiding traffic, Ugo would jokingly say "Watch this", and he'd roll down the window and wave at the cop, who in turn would immediately salute him at which point Ugo would say "That's not necessary my friend, awwright." The Maltese use this *awwright* phrase constantly, so if you're ever wondering if someone's accent is Maltese, if you say *awwright* they will either give a smile of recognition or a look of total confusion depending on whether or not you get their unique accent just right.

I was in Malta to give a lecture at the University of Malta law school thanks to an invitation from Ugo's son Anton who had worked with many different friends of mine and Kirsten's at UNHCR. Anton and I worked together on developing the world's first policy on involuntary resettlement by a large corporation after he left the UN, as I outlined above. His kind invitation to Malta became a memorable trip, as it was our first time in the island nation, and we had the unique experience of staying in the extraordinary presidential palace for a few days, which definitely beat any hotel. The president's truly skilled chefs prepared an incredible array of fine foods for us. Every night, before retiring to our chambers—full of ancient suits of armor from the famous Knights of Malta—staff reminded us to leave our shoes or clothes outside in designated spots for shining or ironing. Yep, we did so every night.

Ugo then took us to the famous Gantija Temples, another Stonehenge-like creation that reminds us that human history, though extremely old to us, is just the tiniest blip on a timescale spanning billions of years. After Ugo showed us around these historical sites of his fine island home, he and I discussed some of the big issues of the day. At one point I mentioned that—as with everything—Earth has a finite lifespan. As it is with humans and animals and plants and concepts and ideas, one day it, too, our very home, will be devoid of life, crumbled into the dust from whence it came. Ole Ugo had thought of many things in his life, but this one was not a dominant theme in his thought processes and he was startled by its implications. Understanding non-attachment and impermanence can come in very handy at times.

As we prepared to depart Malta after playing a round of golf with the head of the local European Union office at one of the very few golf courses in the country, perhaps the only one in fact, we met up again with Ugo. I asked him if he would be prepared to write a chapter for one of my upcoming books which was eventually to have the enthralling title of *National Perspectives on Housing Rights*. Once I mentioned that President Nelson Mandela wrote the foreword, Ugo quickly agreed and wrote a great chapter for the book, which was published in 2003.

Half in jest, I think, Ugo gave me a present as we left for the airport, as far from his political beliefs as possible: *The Little Green Book* by Muhammar Gaddafi, the dictatorial leader of Malta's nearest African neighbor, Libya. Given Libya's proximity to Malta, Gaddafi's diplomats (and spies) were plentiful in Valletta, the Maltese capital. Ugo mentioned they were always distributing copies of the famous *Little Green Book*, and he was more than happy to part with his copy, which reminded me of other books by unusual leaders, such as Mao's *Little Red Book*, Hitler's *Mein Kampf,* or even Newt Gingrich's absurd right-wing harbinger of the doom now permeating every aspect of the cruelty that is modern America, *The Contract with America. The Little Green Book* offered unique insights into the mind of a man who died in agony in a forgotten corner of this oil-rich nation, a fate that brings shivers of fear to dictators worldwide, leading to a tendency toward greater repression.

Chapter 10

And So What Now?

"This is what you shall do; Love the Earth and sun and the animals, despise riches, give alms to everyone that asks, stand up for the stupid and crazy, devote your income and labor to others, hate tyrants, argue not concerning God, have patience and indulgence toward the people, take off your hat to nothing known or unknown or to any man or number of men, go freely with powerful uneducated persons and with the young and with the mothers of families, read these leaves in the open air every season of every year of your life, re-examine all you have been told at school or church or in any book, dismiss whatever insults your own soul, and your very flesh shall be a great poem and have the richest fluency not only in its words but in the silent lines of its lips and face and between the lashes of your eyes and in every motion and joint of your body."

—Walt Whitman

The tragic events in Burma since February 2021 exemplify the perils and pitfalls of a human rights life, the fragility of democracy, and just how far we still have to go as the human race to build the better planet we all deserve. But as a human rights activist, with every drawback you keep chipping away, probing weak spots in the armor of truly heinous governments, and you keep, against all odds, a spirit of hope—that reason, love, respect, and kindness will prevail over the tools of oppression that human rights violators use to maintain power. If there is one thing I hope you noticed in the stories I've shared, it is this: it's not the people, the masses, or the ordinary citizens responsible for the sagas of sadness, but the State, governments, and the companies that support them at the core of the madness lurking just about everywhere today. Yes, we need to trust the State to govern effectively and fairly, enforce the rule of law, create policies and institutions to protect and expand people's rights, and build a secure, stable place for business and living, especially in more democracy-oriented countries. When they work, States are extraordinary things that no one would ever want to live without. Presumably, few of even the most fundamentalist of dogmatists would disagree with that.

But what we fail to often grasp is that it is in the very system of nation-states itself that lies the eternal possibility for the emergence of despots, tyrants, dictators, authoritarians and totalitarians. In a way, for those so inclined—in particular those from family-based dynasties and those aspiring to their creation, whether named Bush, Clinton or Trump, let alone Kim, Putin or Xi—no system could be better designed to facilitate the emergence of one party or one person rule, the very antithesis of one person, one vote democratic systems based on the true will of the people. And at the moment, despite the efforts of millions upon millions of fair-minded believers in democracy, authoritarians seem to be winning in too many places. With each conquest, they unite to thwart—step-by-step—the continued emergence of democracy and its attributes: human rights, equality, and justice—and shamelessly block collective action that would hold them accountable.

Life Lesson No. 97: Let everyone vote.

Of the countless lessons I've learned from working on human rights issues in so many places, knowing thousands upon thousands of people across the world, working within dozens of international organizations, reading what I've read, and living how I've lived—the most important lesson is that now, more than ever, we must evolve together into a single, unified, equal humanity.

Life Lesson No. 98: We are all one people.

We need to collectively take our next evolutionary steps together and begin to really think big again. Our survival depends on it.

We need to do this not only to improve the conditions of our species, but to ensure our continued ability to live on Earth. It is that important. It is a matter of life or death and it is something we all need to think about and do something about much more than we do at present. Passively accepting the nature of our politics, widespread and grotesque inequality, the demise of our once-pristine natural environment, and the many problems confronting us is no longer an option for anyone—including *you*.

We need a new start and a whole new way of envisioning what it means to be human. We need to go far beyond where we have ever gone before. But—and this is crucial—we need to do all of this with as little coercion as possible, as little imposition and as little drama as can be, for ideally it should come from within all of us. It should be part and parcel of our collective tomorrow, all 8.2 billion of us.

We don't need to change or lose our religions. We don't need to change our language or culture. But we do need to change, slowly over time, our obsessions with our nationalities, our worldviews and, in the end, the heights we strive to reach on the proverbial ladder of human consciousness.

Life Lesson No. 99: By becoming world citizens we become our fullest selves.

We don't need to lose our identities; we need to gain new ones. New perspectives, new levels of awareness, new solutions to age-old problems, new ways of doing things that allow all of us to reach the better world all of us know is possible and even more of us deserve. We need—each and every one of us, everywhere—to become our fullest selves; we need to embrace and squeeze with all of our might that dormant kernel of the world citizen that sleeps within all of us. As more and more of us do this and begin to live as world citizens, deepening our care and concern for everyone, everywhere, the true potential of our planet and our species can finally be unleashed, giving birth to a brighter tomorrow for eons and eons to come.

Just imagine the parties.....

So, at this stage in life, after moving dozens of times to all corners of the globe and—in many respects—ready to do it again, I now live on a small, lightly populated peninsula in Australia, far, far away from many of the world's ills. After watching the film, *The Unbearable Lightness of Being* in 1988 and seeing where Sabina ended up on a bohemian coastline, I knew one day I, too, would want to move far, far away from the center of action to a small, quiet and lovely place, and this dream came true far more beautifully than I could have ever imagined. It's a bit isolated sometimes, but I like the peace and quiet these days, especially during the COVID times of the past years. There are many days when I spend not a single dollar, when I shed ever more of the very few material possessions I still have and where to *not* consume, to *not* drive, to *not* use oil or gas, to use nothing for the first time, to tend my vegetables and bring us as close as I can to organic food self-sufficiency, to marvel at the solar panels on my roof and the solar battery on my wall, to be glad beyond belief that I don't need to head to the airport tomorrow for the next trip and to simply be content with *being* and not *having* or *doing*, quiet, light, gentle and easy brings me to the highest points of joy and freedom.

I still teach my climate change and human rights course at law schools for a week or two a year, run my two tiny NGOs, write books, make films and videos, run a podcast and implement various other projects. Instead of UN meetings, and field missions to distant rural areas just overrun by marauding soldiers and wanders through slums I tried so hard to protect but which presently wait for the bulldozers to come and demolish their homes and community forever, now I look after my small family, stroll to our local pristine beach and take a dip in the soothing waters always with a sense of awe and wonder at the translucent water and sea life that swim beneath me and my mask and snorkel, paddle my kayak, fly my kite, ride my bike, run intervals at a local track, throw my Frisbee, work the soil, tend to my two compost heaps and grow an ever-expanding bounty of vegetables and herbs, mentor students, raise money to build homes for the poorest people in the world in Bangladesh, cook organic meals and make never-ending pleas for world citizenship for all of us.

I get to watch games of the best sport anywhere—Australian Rules Football, the AFL—get to eat organic everything, watch my daughter grow and evolve into the wonderful adult she is today, and play golf on empty and amazing courses, often virtually the only guy playing, which is lucky given my tendency to hook too many of those tee shots. When I do hit the road, it's more likely now to be what I call "bro trips" with great friends in a car for a few days on lonesome roads exploring the countryside and enjoying the incredible pristine solitude that Australia is still able to offer.

One of the best bro trips I took in recent years wasn't in Australia, however, but all across Europe with my friend Sid at the wheel for his first big drive across the Old World, winding through Switzerland, France, Germany, Austria, and Liechtenstein, meeting donors, seeing old friends, and introducing him to many of Europe's finest delights. Observing his eyes when he saw a cheese trolley with more than one hundred types of the finest cheese on display in a great restaurant in France for the first time, in and of itself, made the journey worth it. I did this trip with Sid on the condition that he would drive, I would pay for everything and that he would keep one lifelong promise: 30 or so years down the road, sometime around the year 2050, he would do the same for a cool guy in his 20s just starting his career, making the very same deal with him, and hopefully for the mystery man next in line 100 years hence. Better keep your promise, dude!

Back at home sometimes we have a laugh at the rather too insular nature of our little peninsula like the time Kirsten told a waiter at a rather nice restaurant that she was going up to Melbourne the next day to a Bach concert to which in all seriousness, he replied "Awesome, I was not aware that Mr. Bach was still performing live these days," thinking, of course, that Bach was still alive and ready to rock. There are too many cars now, too many paved roads, the house prices are too high, the global perspective too small, but it's still one of the most wonderful parts of this amazing planet that belongs to all of us.

But as it does just about everywhere, inexplicable magic exists here too on this little sliver of Earth. I'd been planning for years to one day, all alone, take the Driver from my golf bag (to the non-golfers out there, the Driver is the biggest club in any golf bag and the club you grab when you want to hit the ball as far as you possibly can), hike through the coastal dunes, tee up my golf ball on the edge of the Great Southern Ocean and film myself hitting a perfect 300-meter drive straight into the ocean. As ecologically horrible as this plan may have been even with the new bio-degradable golf balls out there, I still really wanted to do it but never got around to it. I did, however, tell this story to a friend visiting from Geneva, to which he kept replying, "*Titlist 1*, best ball in golf" over and over again, in reference to some *Titlist* ad he must have seen.

This reminded me of the precise spot on the cliff where I had planned to hit that drive into the sea, and of a nearby secret rock pool accessible only at the lowest of low tides, an extraordinary place to swim and snorkel, freezing cold but totally protected from the rough ocean seas just beyond its rocky edges. I thought this would be a great spot to take my friend who was only used to the crowded and over-used beaches of Europe, so I checked the next day's low tide and off we went, parking in a desolate dirt lot for four cars—ours the only one there, as it is on most days I visit. We hop out, get our gear and hike for a few minutes to the ocean and the rock pools which are still so clean, so pristine and still so full of marine life, especially abalone and lobsters which are everywhere. With no other human in site, I handed him a wetsuit, mask, snorkel and some fins and I got mine, and we carefully tip toed across the very sharp rocks to reach the rock pool, which is about the size of an Olympic-sized swimming pool.

We carefully put on our gear and jumped into the very cold water and began to swim around looking at the fish, kelp and various odd underwater rock formations. Then I remembered a mysterious cave about three meters down that I had always wanted to explore, but because of those ear troubles I picked up on that flight back from Bangladesh, I couldn't go more than a meter underwater without my ear suffering another disaster. I beckoned my friend to come over and showed him the underwater cave entrance, which looks huge from above, and asked him if he wanted to go in and check it out. He said yes, and then after warning him about what he might see in there, I watched him slowly stop at the entrance of the cave, look in and then swim into its mouth totally out of sight. He was gone for about a minute and when he reappeared, I could tell he was smiling through his mask and snorkel. He reached the surface and with great enthusiasm ripped his mask off and excitedly screams: "Dude, you will never guess what I found in the back of that cave." I had no idea but knew it wasn't a shark. I was thinking some exotic shell or a bunch of lobsters or other sea life. But no, he reaches into his pocket and what does he pull out, but a scuffed, cracked and quite old golf ball which had the following written on the side: *Titlist 1*. Yep, best ball in golf. How in the world?

I still probably work too many hours a day, but how fortunate I have been to have been able to work from home throughout the entire childhood of our daughter, to have been able to make lunch for her, to take her to and from school and just to be around to make her life as good as I can. I am able to commune with my countless brothers and sisters on this small planet we all share, especially enjoying time with younger friends at the start of their careers—inevitably encouraging Sid, Jordan, Nathan, Amber, Nanda, Shaun, Timmy, and many others to be courageous in their work. Confiding in them, I find hope that we just might make it, thanks to amazing people like them. I'll keep on reading Ken Wilber's words, wish for posthumous offerings from Tom Robbins, maybe attend a few more concerts right up front, and watch the ever-growing number of cool oneness-minded folks on the net who are surfing more and more on the growing oneness world wave of which all of us are an integral part.

I know our oneness world dream won't happen tomorrow, but I believe our sacred universal mind lattice emerges more and more. As Alex Grey noted, "When beings come together in oneness you have a sacred space," which forms the foundation of a visionary culture. Every changed mind, every person who lets go of nationalist urges to embrace the incomparable beauty of our shared humanity, and every moment of mutual recognition, brings us ever closer to the better, kinder, more equal and fair world we all deserve.

And while it must be truly painful for the caterpillar to transform into a butterfly, isn't it worth it in the end?

I'll never stop dreaming and fighting for true human solidarity—not based on materialism, nationalities or citizenship, but on our shared status as humans, as parts of the broader realm of life itself, integral to the World Soul, the same Spirit within us all, and the same ecosystem on which we all depend. I imagine a world of truly enlightened beings, where the concept of "stranger" or "the other" dissolves, where our shared attributes shape our worldcentric views, and where we all share not only the same planet but the same status as world citizens—one and all.

Life Lesson No. 100: Make some good trouble.

Epilogue

As this book goes to press in mid-2026, the world is in a very different place than it was at the beginning of my human rights life. Had you asked me in the mid-1980s— well before the unexpected fall of the Iron Curtain in 1989—what the world would be like in the mid-2020s, my answer would have described a planet infinitely better than we are witnessing today. As much disquiet as I have always felt about the country of my birth, not in my wildest dreams would I have imagined that actual fascism would begin taking root in the United States. Similarly, as bad as life has been for the Palestinian people since 1948, I was almost certain that a just peace would have been agreed and some way of living in harmony as good neighbours would have been found, and yet, alas we all know where things stand today. I certainly would have not predicted the terrifying scale and impact of climate change, the alarming prevalence of degraded land across the globe (more than 25% of all land is considered as such!), the re-emergence of a nuclear arms race, the brutal illegal invasion of Ukraine, the carnage in the DR Congo and the outrageous civil war in Sudan.

Rather, I would have predicted the continued strengthening and seriousness accorded to the entire system of international law in all of its facets rather than the systematic undermining of it and the United Nations that we see today, again, led by the greatest rogue nation of them all, the United States. I would not have thought that there would have been such an immense growth in the number of billionaires across the world (now numbering close to 3000) or that the majority of the human race would continue to live in situations of impoverishment. I could not have imagined the speed with which AI has developed and, of course, could have never foreseen the terrifying rise of autocracy and dictatorship in far too many corners of our shared world. I could list hundreds of additional points but suffice it to say that the world I and everyone in the human rights movement had envisaged in the mid-1980s, worked, and hoped for, alas has yet to come to fruition. We made extraordinary progress but the path remains long and increasingly narrow and precarious.

In the end, the world we get is really nothing more than the result of the totality of decisions made by human beings that have an impact on other human beings. The quality of those decisions and the foundations on which they are made can be tied directly back to the worldviews, states of mind, levels of consciousness (or whatever you would like to call it) of those making the decisions that build the future we all experience. If you care about humans simply because they are humans, as I do, the types of decisions you will make or wish to have made by your elected government officials, will be based on these and other important considerations.

Conversely, were you to view the world through a prism of us vs. them, built upon the façade of nationalistic delusions of grandeur or some other manifestation of a pathological belief that one's own skin color is superior to all others, that your faith-based religion or insular political movement is the only true one, or even that however you may define yourself in ethnic, class or any other terms, that you are the best there is, the greatest, the finest, the tip of the highest pyramid ever built, the world that will arise will look strikingly different. This self-centered, me-first and me-only attitude is as shocking as it is unjustifiable.

Sadly, far too many of us fall into the latter category of disunity, and not the way that hundreds of millions, likely billions, of others view the world through eyes that see all humans as members of the very same human family with the same rights, the same needs, and the same wishes as everyone, everywhere else.

Say what you will about me but I happen to know that the poor single mother in the favela of Sao Paulo matters as much as I do, as you do, or as anyone else does. And so, too, that disabled former soldier in Krasnodar, Russia has as much value as anyone else, just as the farmer in North Korea, the Olympic champion from Australia or the award-winning chef in Bilbao must be treated as equal to us all. My embrace of all of us 8.2 billion people as true equals has never been stronger and now is the time to use this horrible historical epoch in which we are all living as a kick starter to something far, far better. As much as autocracy may seem to be growing, the democratic, rights-respecting resistance is strengthening even more rapidly and will surely win in the end. But in the meantime, we will all need to deal with some seriously unsavoury characters running too many countries and deploying too much terror to bring humanity to where we could so otherwise easily be.

Change may seem impossible, but to quote my friend Luke Kemp in the final pages of his excellent 2025 book *Goliath's Curse: The History and Future of Societal Collapse*, in a section called "Don't be a dick", the easiest thing all of us can do would simply be to make a simple pledge "not to be a dick." This may sound too rude or explicit to the puritanically-inclined out there, but he makes an incredibly valuable point: at the very least we should *do no harm*. Similarly, as the fantastic duo that made the excellent series *Flight of the Conchords* sang during one of their hilarious episodes, there are "too many dicks on the dancefloor." They had it all too right, as well. No dispassionate glance around the world could possibly deny that there are too many dicks on the world's political dancefloor right now, and the sooner we all commit to not be a dick and then call out the dicks still out there, the better off all of us will be.

Beyond actively choosing to be part of the solution, now is the time for all of us to make a conscious choice. We essentially have three choices that face us all: (1) We can choose, as many seem to have already, to support ghoulish and corrupt dictators and broader aims they have to build an authoritarian hellscape of a world where human rights no longer exist and where empire and power alone determine outcomes; (2) We can place our bets and hopes on preserving the status quo of the international rules-based order, the UN

Charter and the basic tenets of the post-WWII era, flaws, and all; (3) Or we can take advantage of this toxic political era in which we now live where the worst of our nature as humans continues to bubble to the surface. We can embrace a vision of a world that has been around for thousands of years but yet to ever fully take hold. That, of course, is a world built on the idea of world citizenship governed by a democratically elected global government grounded deeper than ever in human rights and an international constitutional framework built not on the basis of our nationalities or nation states but on our shared humanity universally residing on an incredibly fragile and finite planet.

I refuse to support anything other than this. It's Option (3) for me. I know and love people from everywhere and I wish the same reality for you. I have met and befriended people from all corners of the Earth from every country, every religion, every political view, every level of wealth, every possible thing that people use to distinguish themselves from one another. I know as deeply as I ever have known anything, and perhaps even deeper, that the idea of humanity, the notion of cosmopolitanism, our shared good fortune (and, indeed, miracle) of having been born at all are easily more than enough to convince any reasonable person that we need to pursue a future based on the attributes that we share rather than the small differences that too many of us still rely on to divide us.

And, thus, it is to this vision that I will dedicate my remaining days of life. I reject any argument that such a vision cannot come into being. I know with absolute certainty that all of us, even the most heinous among us, have at the very least, a tiny kernel of humanity within them that knows a world in which all of us shared the same citizenship, the same passports, the same responsibility for ourselves and our planet, would be preferable to the world we all inhabit today. I will never give up on this vision. I will never accept that humans as a whole are at their core evil, abusive, disgusting, hateful creatures (eg. dicks) like so many political leaders, their cronies and hangers on show us today. No matter where you find yourself in the world, just quickly think of the first ten politicians that come to mind and calculate what percentage do not fall into the d-word category! Yes, a few of us clearly carry out despicable deeds designed to make other humans suffer, but I refuse to hate them, though I do hate their deeds.

We need a fearless future where more of us know and more of us love more of us. We need a future where pollution-free travel is facilitated by governments everywhere to give more and more people exposure to other cultures and people in a world where—in 2026—some 80% of humanity has never set foot in an airplane, where the median net worth of the human race is less than USD 10,000, an over-heating world of melting ice and rising seas where more than 70% of us are essentially poor and where brutal exploitation of the planet's resources are the norm.

I am fortunate enough to have travelled far and wide and surely more than most. I say this not to aggrandize but simply to say that this was my choice, my wish of how to spend my finite life, and at least in that regard, my dreams did come true. I worked in war zones, in slums, in places affected by horrible natural disasters. I worked within the halls of the UN, wrote international standards designed to build a better world and, most importantly, was able to know people from every corner of the planet. There is no shortage of horribly behaved humans out there, but the overwhelming majority of humans I have met are kind, generous and willing to have a chat and a laugh.

We are a beautiful species and yet we can be so much better. If we all dedicate ourselves to this quest, this will be the better future we will get. If we do not, well, you can't say I didn't warn you....

The overwhelming majority of human beings alive today do not choose to live under the authoritarian regimes backed by billionaires that they are forced by circumstances to endure today. Most people, in most places, almost all of the time, simply want democracy, freedom, respect and dignity. They want human rights. People want to choose who leads them and the types of governance that manage the places where they live. We are a species that seeks both equality and a degree of agency over the circumstances in which we live. This is the human way.

I have tried in my own way throughout my human rights life to help build a legal and political framework that would ensure that every single human alive would have access to a safe, secure, and adequate home every day of their lives from start to finish. I sought to create legal institutions and mechanisms that would protect people against eviction and to ensure that those forced to flee from their homes due to the decisions of people intent on harming them, would be able to get their homes back once it was safe to do so. I don't care where you come from or what you may believe but I will fight for your right to adequate housing and all other rights you should enjoy as your birthright for as long as I am physically able to do so.

There were some wins and some losses but as much as it devastates me to admit it, overall, the world I thought would be in place today—four decades after commencing my global pursuit of housing rights—remains distant, and in some respects, further away than ever. There really are too many dicks on the geopolitical dancefloor. Just think about it for a minute. What if we all truly got the leaders we deserve? What if politicians, just like doctors, lawyers, engineers and so many other professions who are required to pass exams, meet criteria and be subject to professional tests and scrutiny, were also subject to such rules instead of merely being restricted by age and other minor requirements? Just imagine how much better the world could be.

Although this book and the stories it contains are just a tiny snapshot of all the stories I could tell (the *really good* stories will appear in a future book, I promise!), I do hope this book spoke to you at least in some way, and above all else, that you enjoyed it and discovered a few things that you didn't know before. I hope whatever human rights insider tales I included here helped you to begin to understand the day-to-day realities facing those who have dedicated their lives to human rights for everyone, everywhere. It's a world of ups and downs, wins and losses and a degree of intensity rarely found in other fields. It's often dangerous, stressful, and extremely difficult. But, as I hope was obvious, it's also worth it and if you manage it in the right way, it can lead to a wonderful way to spend our short lives.

I will always be engaged with various human rights initiatives, and even now I am working on more than a dozen ongoing human rights projects. As I complete each of these, I find myself filling the gaps by increasingly turning to writing fiction and developing complex and sometimes phantasmagoric visions of the world I want to see come into reality, but which have yet to come into being in the real world. My first two novels *Killionaire*™ and *Psychotic, Despotic* will be published in the coming months. Hopefully these books will soon be made into films, as well, and become accessible to as many people as possible in theatres and online. More novels are already well underway.

Part of the reason I now favor writing novels over the legal books or biographies I have spent time on in the past is that it is within these fictional worlds that I create, usually from 4am to 8am in the early pre-dawn hours when I am in the writing zone listening to the magpies and kookaburras sing their opening notes to another day, where I hope readers can look to as a source of inspiration for turning the real world into a utopian place, the likes of which the world has yet to see.

If we can imagine it, we can then create it.

Unity will get us there, divisions and intentional disunity based on distractions most certainly will not.

So, let's imagine the better unified future that awaits us, my friends.

Let's begin doing so today.

In the Spirit of John Lewis, yet again, go out and make some good trouble....

Acknowledgements

First and foremost, I am incredibly thankful to my parents for not only giving me the gift of life but also—perhaps unbeknownst to them—offering me my first glimpse into the real world, a world of humans just like ourselves, not just Americans but people with different accents, stemming from different lands, with unique foods, music, religions, and cultures. As children, we have no idea which influences will eventually determine our worldviews. I know now that my interactions with exchange students from Brazil and Portugal, discussions with my Norwegian house cleaner (not many of those left in California these days, I'd guess!), Mexican gardeners, and Greek family friends, combined with stories of Africa from my beloved Uncle Bill, and tales of Army life in post-war West Germany from my dad, all played a part. My first trips overseas—first to Mexico a few times as a kid and then to Europe by age 14—kick-started a lifelong journey. This wild voyage has only strengthened with time, first becoming, then fully embracing, a world citizen's perspective. I now see, deeply and profoundly, that there is no difference between people. I will keep dreaming of a world where everyone merges into a single, 8-billion-strong polity, building a cosmopolitan world of world citizens—equals—bound by a shared humanity, working as one for a sustainable future for the ages. So, to my parents and family, thank you so much for igniting a spark in me which has only grown ever brighter with the passage of time.

Special thanks, too, to the thousands of people, maybe tens of thousands and probably more with whom I have shared moments of mutual recognition, respect, and joy. Who knows really how many of the people across the globe with whom I have shared life and discussion, but with each additional interaction, each new conversation, every first glance, my conviction of our need for world citizenship gets just that much stronger. Somehow, I feel as if I remember all of you but some pop into my mind more readily than others, so special thanks to one and all. To Chichi in Santo Domingo who led me through your slum of 70,000 dwellers and who showed me just how universal compassion and care could be, thank you. To Katsuyuki in Japan, who against all odds fights for the weakest and against the strongest, with whom I have shared countless laughs and tears—we, together, from such different backgrounds, are soul brothers of the closest sort, thank you. To Taoaripi in Tuvalu, the world's smallest nation, who wanted unity but chose independence in the interests of his people, which he knew to be part of humanity's family, thank you. To Beja, the Kosovar in the dirty streets of Pristina with a peace sign on your arm, talking just weeks after you endured a brutal beating by Serb militias as they ransacked your home and stole your beloved guitar on which you played Beatles songs, but who was more convinced than ever of the need for a world without borders, thank you. To Khaled, HLP maestro extraordinaire, thank you. To Arif bhai and Shahjahan bhai in Bangladesh, your lifelong commitment to justice is incredible to behold. To Vangelis in Greece - Adonis jester who led me to walk on fire and bow to the Sun, thank you. To Ho in Hong Kong, Rajindar in India and so many other human rights heroes the world over who are no longer with us, may you all rest in peace. Dorelle in South Africa, Nelson in Brazil, Felix in Nigeria, Win in Myanmar, Iene in Holland, soul brother Michael and the entire Stonehenge crew in the US, Dan on your island and truly thousands upon thousands of others, for your grace, your wisdom, your self-actualized world citizen statuses, thank you.

To every nurse and doctor who has looked after me and healed me in too many countries to recall, I bow in humility and thanks to each and every one of you; you are all amazing. To every acupuncturist I have ever received a life enhancing treatment from, thank you for making the world a better place with each and every needle. To every Board member, Advisory Board member and donor who made all of my NGOs possible, thank you so much. To every friend, every lover, every soul sister and soul brother, thanks to all of you! And to everyone who has ever showed kindness towards me and others, thank you, too!

Special thanks to my friend and fellow human rights and justice fighter, Kevin Bell for his kind foreword. His storied career spans years of work on tenants' rights in Australia, a long career as a Supreme Court Judge, as an original member of the Yoorrook Commission, Victoria's and Australia's first formal truth-telling inquiry led by First Peoples into historic and ongoing systemic injustices perpetuated against First peoples through colonization, and many other accomplishments.

A massive thank you to all of those who reviewed portions of earlier drafts of this book, including Sid Vadasseri, Jaap Schut, Mike Forster, Dan Lewis, Reed Brody, Jordan Bakker, Khaled Hassine, Margaret McDuffie, Richard Horsey, Craig Brown, Matthias von Hein, Christa Meindersma, Horst Burghardt, Michael Morehead and others. I am truly grateful to my wonderful agent Liz Trupin-Pulli for all of her work in support of my books and films, as I am to my editor Jen Z. Marshall who makes my scribbles so much more readable and to my good buddy Ron Schultz who has been so helpful in guiding me in so many vital ways.

Special thanks to everyone who was kind enough to write the testimonials that appear at the beginning of this book and those online.

And most of all, the biggest thanks of all to my Harling, my Lidski and my Wudie for such incredible love, such incredible fun, such incredible joy.

About the Author

Scott Leckie (BA, LLM – www.scottleckie.com.au) is an international human rights legal expert. He hosts the popular podcast and YouTube channel @DemocracyTomorrow. He also founded Oneness World Foundation (http://www.onenessworld.org)
a research think tank exploring questions of world-centric political evolution and new forms of global governance and world citizenship. He is also the Director and Founder of Displacement Solutions a global not-for-profit NGO dedicated to resolving displacement generated by global warming and climate change. (http://www.displacementsolutions.org)

He hosted the podcast *Jointly Venturing - Let's Talk World Citizenship* from 2018-2020 and manages the *One House, One Family* initiative, a project in Bangladesh building homes for climate displaced families.

His interventions have: helped to protect thousands of people against planned forced evictions in popular communities in the Dominican Republic, Panama, Philippines, South Africa, Thailand, Zambia and elsewhere; restored the HLP restitution rights to tens of thousands of refugees and IDPs in Kosovo, Georgia, Timor Leste, Burma, Albania and beyond; led to the recognition of the HLP rights of communities threatened with displacement due to climate change; generated the creation of numerous new UN institutions, standards and Special Rapporteurs; and assisted in the fundamentally reshaping and strengthening of HLP rights under international human rights law.

He has established several international human rights organizations and institutions and worked in more than 80 countries. He has advised a number of United Nations agencies on housing, land and property rights issues, including the Asian Development Bank (ADB), the Norwegian Refugee Council (NRC), the Overseas Development Institute (ODI), International Finance Corporation (IFC), the International Federation of Red Cross Red Crescent Societies (IFRC), the Office of the UN High Commissioner for Refugees (UNHCR), the UN Office of the High Commissioner for Human Rights (OHCHR),

UN Habitat, the UN Development Programme (UNDP), the UN Office for the Coordination of Humanitarian Affairs (OCHA), the UN Economic and Social Commission for Asia and the Pacific (ESCAP), the UN Transitional Authority in East Timor (UNTAET), the UN Mission in Kosovo (UNMIK), the World Bank, and the Organization for Security and Cooperation in Europe (OSCE).

He conceived of and was the driving force behind more than 100 international human rights legal and other normative standards, including UN resolutions, guiding principles, general comments, judicial decisions and others - most recently the *Peninsula Principles on Climate Displacement Within States*.

Scott has written 31 books and over 300 academic articles and reports on issues including land solutions for climate displacement, housing rights, economic, social, and cultural rights, forced evictions, the right to housing and property restitution for refugees and internally displaced persons and other human rights themes.

He has taught and designed several human rights courses in various top-100 universities and law schools around the world, including the world's first law school course on climate change and displacement which he has taught at the College of Law of the Australian National University, University of Melbourne Law School, Monash Law, and Mahidol University.

He is a world citizen, grows 50+ varietals of vegetables and herbs and plants at least ten trees a year. He bikes at least 10,000kms a year and tries to swim every day, even in the midst of winter. He loves, lives on and is entirely dependent upon planet Earth - just like you.